Making It Count:

From A to Z,
The Life and Times
of Art Zimmer

LOG CABIN BOOKS

Hamilton, NY

Log Cabin Books
Hamilton, NY 13346
www.logcabinbooks.us

Second Edition: September 2016
10 9 8 7 6 5 4 3 2 1

ISBN 9780997325126

As Told To Lois Gridley

Edited by Shirley Sherburne Zimmer and Brian McDowell

Illustrations by Dennis Calkins

Dedication

I dedicate this book to all the girls in my life.

FIRST and foremost, my wonderful mother, Edna. We all think our mother is the best person in the world. However, when all your friends, young and old, tell you that your mother is the nicest person they have ever met, it is extra special.

My mother not only raised five kids and kept a quality home, she also worked down in the barn and out in the fields, doing more than her share, and also worked outside the home: for several years at the American Management Association, the high school cafeteria, and a meat-processing plant. Mom also was an active member of the Grange, Methodist church, and Eastern Star, and found the time to have another baby, my little sister Ruth, the week I graduated from high school.

She was always supportive to me, and my off-the-wall ideas. When I told her I was going to buy a junk boat and sail to Florida, even though she knew that I had no knowledge of boats, she never tried to discourage me.

When I told her I wanted to quit the farm and join the Army, I was only 17. She and my equally great dad signed the papers.

At age 13 I told her I wanted to hitchhike to Utica to see a girl, and she said OK. She then would frequently drive me to Utica to see Mary Lou Willard. Years later, she took an instant liking to Shirley and always introduced her as her third daughter. She loved Shirley almost as much as I do.

SECOND is Bonnie Pierson Wilcox. Without her as a helping classmate I would never have gotten out of high school.

THIRD is Mary Lou Willard, my first love, the only girl except for Shirley that I loved and trusted completely. I did not like school or the farm; Mary Lou made it possible for all those years for me to get up every morning at 4 a.m. and smile, knowing I would see her soon.

FOURTH are all the many wonderful women I dated after Mary Lou and before Shirley. I had the pleasure of dating a lot of wonderful women, some for as long as three or four years.

AND MOST OF ALL, Shirley Sherburne Zimmer. Since January 23, 1987, the day we met, my life has never been the same and never so wonderful. I did not know until I met Shirley that I could love and trust someone so completely. I could fill an entire book on how fabulous she is. As I write this, we have been together over 28 years and will remain together the rest of our lives. And beyond, as you'll learn when you read about the Smith Valley Cemetery Association.

-Art Zimmer

Let's Go Back to the Beginning

The first day of my life was probably one of the most exciting and harrowing days ever in New London, Connecticut, but I don't remember it well.

It was the day that the worst hurricane in the history of New England hit the little shipbuilding town. It was considered by most to be the fifth most destructive hurricane ever to hit the U.S., and its eye was focused on New London. The U.S. Weather Service didn't name hurricanes at the time, so it became known in the Zimmer household as Hurricane Art.

My father, Carl, worked at a shipyard in New London, the eventual birthplace for World War II submarines. When he dropped his wife—my mother, Edna—off at the beach-side hospital in New London mid-morning on September 21, 1938, he expected to return home to take care of the farm and family and drive back to the hospital that evening.

He *did* return... five days and a hurricane later. The roads and bridges were washed out, and without power or phone service, he could only guess how his wife and new baby were doing on the storm-ravaged beach.

A special pictorial edition at the time chronicled the disastrous hurricane and flood that devastated Eastern Connecticut on the day of Art Zimmer's birth, Sept. 21, 1938.

Printed by the Norwich Bulletin

	FROM		TO		TIME		RATE	AMOUNT	
ITEM	Month	Day	Month	Day	Weeks	Days	Per Week	Dollars	Cents
Semi Private Room	Sept	21	Oct	2	1	4	28 00	44	00
Delivery room								5	00
Laboratory Fee								2	00
Drugs									75
								51	75

New London, Conn., Oct 2 19 38

Mrs. Edna Zimmer

To THE HOME MEMORIAL HOSPITAL, Dr.
(INCORPORATED)

Make Checks Payable to the Order of the Home Memorial Hospital

PAID OCT 1 1938 HOME MEMORIAL HOSPITAL Per M. V. Robenson THANK YOU

This hospital bill to my mother for my birth was the first financial transaction of my life. As in all things, I tried to keep costs down.

Until I came along, "The Zimmers" were Mom and Dad plus two boys, Carl Jr. and Richard. My two sisters, Arlene and Ruth, were born after me; Ruth didn't come along until the summer I graduated from high school.

The five of us, before Arlene, lived in a small house on a narrow road, 15 miles outside of town. Over the years we referred to our home as the "little house." The "little house" was near Oxoboxo Lake, a palindromic little body of water.

I don't remember much about the first three or four years I lived there, except that in front of the house was a cement retaining wall. I was scared to go near it. It was about 15 feet tall, and I knew if I fell over it, I would die for sure. Years later, driving by the house, I realized that the wall was about four feet tall. It is interesting how your perspective on life changes as you mature. Or get old.

My dad always wanted to be a farmer, but in that part of Connecticut, farming was very difficult. The soil was not good; all of the land was covered with rocks and more rocks, many the size of a VW car or larger.

The "little house" was earning its name, with five of us now. (My younger sister, Arlene, never lived there.) So my parents purchased a place about a mile away, up a dirt road. It included a large old farmhouse, a small barn, and about 10 acres of rocks. If pet rocks had been popular then, we'd have had a bumper crop.

My dad, a skilled carpenter, remodeled the entire house over two or three years, and even added indoor plumbing. After a couple of years of hard work, a small field was cleared of enough rocks to raise some hay and corn. There was even room for a large vegetable garden. We had two cows, a couple of pigs, and many chickens. My mother took care of the big garden and did lots of canning. My mother and two brothers did most of the farm work during World War II, as my dad worked double shifts at the Electric Boat Company near New London, where building submarines for the war effort had shifted into high gear.

My parents had a plan and a dream. Dad continued to work double shifts even after the war ended. We produced almost all of our own food, and my parents saved every penny they could so that someday they could buy a real farm, a large piece of land somewhere. It would be nice if more people today thought like that: work hard, save your money, and buy things only when you can afford to pay for them. It was something I observed carefully and later adopted as much as possible in my own outlook on life.

My boyhood home (right) and barns (left) in Randallsville, outside of Hamilton, NY.

Finally, in 1948, they purchased their "real" farm. It was in Randallsville, on the edge of a scenic upstate New York college town called Hamilton, home to Colgate University. Now it was home to the Zimmer family, too.

I don't remember a lot about the years on the Connecticut farm, but a few things do stick in my mind. I attended a two-room school house about four miles from our house. I walked to school each day, regardless of the weather. The school had no indoor plumbing. There were four grades and one teacher in each room. I had to walk past a commercial mink farm to get there. The farm had fenced-in guard dogs. One day one of the dogs got out and attacked me. I got some bites, but no serious damage. For the next year I always made a half-mile detour through some fields to avoid the dogs.

Near our "farm" were some wild blueberries. In the summer I would pick several quarts and take them down to the main road, where six to eight cars would go by each day. Our dirt road would get about one car per week. That was my first experience with figuring out how to get more customers. I sold the blueberries, two quarts for five cents; that was big money for me. About every six weeks we would go to the big city of Norwich. My special treat was to buy a hot dog and an ice cream. I felt like I was really living the good life. In the winter there were no blueberries, so no hot dogs.

I had a job at school, too: I hauled in wood and kept the fire going in our classroom. I liked this because I did not have to do much school work. I would bring in one log at a time to make the job—and my time away from class—last longer.

When I was in third or fourth grade, they were building a big new central school, Fair Oaks, only two and a half miles from our house. There would be no mink farm to walk by. The new school was behind schedule when they closed the two-room schoolhouse, so I had to walk only a mile to where a bus would pick us up and take us to a large school in Montville.

I was now in a big class—nine kids—but unfortunately there was no fire to keep going. The other kids did not accept this new kid from out in the sticks, and the teacher did not like me. The school asked my mother if I had a medical problem as I went to the bathroom about eight times a day and stayed there a long time. I was fine; it was just my way to escape.

The only good thing about that experience was that my grandmother lived about a half mile from the school. I would walk over there every day for

Me, at age 12 (left). I wouldn't need to listen to my school guidance counselor who said, "Your only dismal future is to stay on the farm or join the Army." I'd be a cowboy. I'd be the next Gene Autry or Roy Rogers. I'd be rich and famous. The only problem was I never learned to play the guitar, I couldn't sing—to this day, I can't carry a tune—and I sold my horse to buy a car so I could visit my girlfriend more often in Utica. Oh, well. The Army might not be too bad. These are the actual holsters (right) I got for Christmas in 1945. My cousin, Carol Allen from Connecticut, sent them to me in August 2015. I don't know where they have been for the last 50 years.

lunch. My grandmother was a wonderful person, and I would get hot dogs once a week.

Fortunately, except for those lunches with Grandma, I was at the Montville school for only a few months. Then the new school opened. The following year we moved to Randallsville, just outside Hamilton, NY.

NEW YORK, NEW YORK

I was about 10 when we moved from Connecticut to New York and bought the Randallsville farm. I started working on the farm almost immediately; since this was actually a working farm—not one my father had to create—there was a lot of work that had to be done, and no extra money to hire help.

I attended school on a sporadic basis, being something of a part-time student. I didn't

Goldie was my horse. I'm still planning on being a famous cowboy.

like farming—or the farm—but I disliked school even more. I figured that someday I would be a cowboy. This may have been because the one good thing about the farm, in my opinion, was that I could have a horse. This was Goldie, a beautiful palomino I bought with money I earned doing odd jobs in the village, since there was no allowance or salary on the farm.

Buying Goldie was possible because at about age 12, I started to branch out. When I got a little time off from the farm, instead of playing, I got other jobs. I had three or four houses in the village where I did yard work and lawn mowing. My parents did not pay me or give me an allowance, but they were very good to me. They fed me, and I had a roof over my head. How could a kid ask for more? I did the non-farm work to earn money. I saved the money because I wanted to buy a horse.

ODD JOBS

My father had a good friend who owned the first farm out of the village, on Hamilton Street. He was a state officer in the Grange. Most of you probably don't know what the Grange was; back then, it was a very popular national social organization for farmers. There are still a few Grange chapters around today. Three or four times a year, my father's friend had to go to the statewide meetings for two or three days. He needed someone to take care of his farm while he was away, so I got the job. Big money: I earned $15 each time for two or three days of work.

There was one big problem. He had several cows that were "kickers," and several times I got kicked pretty badly. On my dad's farm, when we discovered that a cow was a kicker, it quickly became hamburger. But this farmer kept them on. I put up with the kicking because of the money.

Murder most foul

As painful as being cow-kicked could be, it was nothing compared to the fact that I almost got murdered because of one job I had. Next door, about a quarter-mile down the road from our farm, a very elderly lady lived alone. I look back on it now and I thought she was very old, because I was 12. She was 81, not much older than I am now. Her name was Mrs. Neff. A wonderful lady.

To make money rather than accept public assistance, or perhaps there wasn't all that much "public assistance" to be had, Mrs. Neff made fudge and cookies that she sold. To make fudge, she needed milk. So three nights a week, when I had finished my work in the barn, I would fill up a four-quart tin bucket and take it down to her. She gave me ten cents each time. If I was late, I would just leave it on the porch. She was hard of hearing and usually was working in the kitchen in the back of the house, so I just walked in. I liked to go in because she would give me a piece of fudge or a cookie.

One night I wanted to go to a movie. I very seldom went to a movie, as it was very expensive: fifteen cents. I was in a hurry to get to the movie, so I just left the milk on the porch. Being young and in a hurry, I did not give it a second thought that there were lights on in several rooms. Usually Mrs. Neff never had a light on except in the kitchen.

After the movie, it was cold, windy, and dark. I was in a hurry to get home. Once again, I did not give it a second thought as I walked by Mrs. Neff's house, but I noticed that there still were lights on, and she almost always went to bed by 9 p.m.

The next morning, the State Police were at our house, asking us if we had seen anything unusual the night before. Mrs. Neff had been murdered, bludgeoned to death with a hammer. Within a couple of days, they caught the murderer. It was a 16-year-old who lived in Kirkland. The police said that when I delivered the milk, the murder was in progress. If I had gone in and surprised the perpetrator, he would have realized that I would be able to identify him. The police said it was likely that I, too, would have been murdered.

BEAM ME UP, SCOTTIE

I managed to escape possible violent death, but there were incidents that still raise the hair on the back of my neck. In 1953, when I was 15, I observed an object in the sky that to this day I have not heard explained as anything from this earth. It was a warm summer evening and I met Bill Steene at the movie theater in Hamilton. After the movie, I walked with Bill to his house. I liked to walk. Bill lived out Madison Street, about a mile north of the theater, on the Hitchcock farm. I lived a mile south of the theater, out Lebanon Street.

As I left Bill's and headed back into the village, I saw a bright light high up in the sky on the edge of the horizon to the west. At first I thought it was a bright full moon, but it did not move. Then I remember thinking that the moon came up in the east, and looking at the light longer, it did not look like the moon. It was round and thick like a stack of dinner plates, and it glowed as if from a bright light from within, unlike reflected light that bounces off the moon.

I had recently done a little study of the heavens for my Boy Scout astronomy merit badge as I was getting close to earning my Eagle Scout badge. The object looked about the size of a football field. I thought it was about 20,000 to 30,000 feet up.

I'd had some training in identifying objects in the sky, as I was a volunteer in the Hamilton defense project. This sounds stupid today, but the Hamilton village officials were very concerned about Russian planes coming to bomb Hamilton and Colgate. On the building that is the current village office, at the corner of Payne and East Broad streets, there is a cupola on the top and on all four sides are windows. In the cupola were photos of Russian bombers, powerful binoculars, and a special phone. Many people—mostly adults and a few scouts—were trained to identify the Russian bombers, to estimate how high in the sky they were and their approaching speed. When we spotted Russian bombers, we were to pick up the special phone connected to the Air Force at Griffiss Air Force Base in Rome. They would send up fighter jets to shoot down the bombers before they could destroy Hamilton. Yes, today it sounds like the government officials were a bunch of idiots (like some government officials are today). Why would Russians send planes to bomb Hamilton???

Back to my original story. After watching this bright object for about 10 minutes, it started to move across the sky, a very smooth, steady movement to the other horizon in the east. Then it stopped. It took only about six seconds for the journey that was probably 60-70 miles. There it hovered for about 10 minutes, then moved back across the sky to the edge of the western horizon again. I observed this phenomenon back and forth across the sky four times. The fifth time it did not stop; it just kept going and disappeared.

My math is not very good. The last math course I took was in 8th grade, and I failed it, in part because the teacher, Mr. Moore, was also the boys' sports coach and did not like any boys who would not go out for his sports team. Mr. Moore made it patently clear to me: no sports, and you were in big trouble with him.

Anyway, that big bright object traveled across the sky a distance of probably 70-80 miles in six seconds. That equals a speed of about 36,000 miles per hour (I asked my editor to calculate that figure).

Even in today's space program, there is nothing that big that could move in that manner at that speed. And remember, this was before Sputnik or Star Trek.

HAMILTON TROOP 15

When we moved to the farm, it would be two years before I began to work almost full-time, so I joined the Cub Scouts and then the Boy Scouts, Hamilton Troop 15. I worked my way up through the ranks to Eagle Scout in

1954. When I left town for the Army in January 1957, I was junior assistant scoutmaster.

The Hamilton Club was the scout troop sponsor in those days. When I earned my Eagle badge, they had an event to honor me. They presented me with an Eagle Scout Trophy that I still keep on my desk. Almost 60 years later the Hamilton Club presented a program titled "From the Randallsville Farm: The Life and Times of Art Zimmer." That evening I displayed the trophy.

Being a Boy Scout was an enjoyable outlet for me throughout high school. I didn't like the farm. I didn't like school. For four years, my main interests were Mary Lou in Utica and the Boy Scouts. I did quite well with both.

Wiith my parents (above) when I received the rank of Eagle Scout in 1954. I still have the trophy (below) and all of my merit badges and Scout awards. I am holding the Eagle Scout trophy presented to me by the Hamilton Club in 1954. The horse cut-out is a shop woodworking project, one of my major accomplishments in 4 years of high school.

MARY LOU

I met Mary Lou Willard when we were both junior counselors at Camp Aldersgate, a Methodist church camp in the Adirondacks. We were a serious couple for four years. We even became secretly engaged in 1956, the year we both graduated from high school. Mary Lou went to Utica Free Academy in Utica.

How did a skinny little farm boy from Randallsville end up with the beautiful honor student from the big city (Utica)? It all started with my mother and Stan Brown. Even though my mother worked the farm, raised five kids and held a job outside the farm, she was very active in the Hamilton Methodist Church. For over 50 years Mom was one of the "pillars" of the church.

In the early 1950s a new minister came to Hamilton. The Rev. Stan Brown was extremely well liked by everyone and quickly became a fixture in the village, active in many events and organizations. Stan was especially popular with young people, and Methodists know that their children are the future of their congregations.

My mother talked me into attending a Methodist Youth Fellowship (MYF) meeting. Actually, it did not take much talk, as I would have done most anything to get off the farm for a couple of hours. I went on to become president of the MYF. Later, Stan asked me to go to the Methodist camp, Camp Aldersgate, in the Adirondack Mountains as a junior counselor with him. I said no; my dad would never let me off the farm in the summer for a week. But under pressure from my mother, Dad said okay.

The first day at Aldersgate, I met another junior counselor. We went on a date that evening. Actually, it was just a walk down to the lake front. Love at first sight?? From that day, on we became a steady couple for four years. During the next three years I would hitchhike back and forth from Hamilton to Utica two or three times a week to see Mary Lou, until I sold my horse, Goldie, and used the money to buy a 1949 Hudson. That car got me to Utica much better than Goldie could have.

How do I explain it? It must be that opposites *do* attract. That still rings true today! After all, look at Shirley, then look at me.

The next year, my dad had a farm accident and was in the hospital for over a week. The morning after his accident, we were all up at 4 a.m. to get started on chores. At 4:10, in drove Stan. "I heard about your dad; I'm here to help," he said.

Mary Lou and me with the 1949 Hudson I bought after selling my horse, Goldie (left); and the two of us all dressed up for junior prom (below). Both pictures were taken in 1955.

Stan stayed all day and came back every day until my dad was back on his feet.

Stan passed away several years ago. His wife Retha still lives in Gouverneur (the church where Stan was assigned when he left Hamilton), and she still sends me a Christmas card every year.

My mother stayed active in the church for years. When she got to the point that she could not walk very well, it became a problem for her to find a parking spot and walk to the church. Today, like back then, the lack of adequate parking in the village is a continuing problem. Mom asked that the village put one handicapped parking spot in front of the church. In typical fashion, our elected officials put up a sign the next week. The sign read: "No parking Sunday, 7 a.m. to 1 p.m." After 20 years, the sign is still there.

That ended my mother's attendance at church.

The 1949 Hudson not only allowed me to stop hitchhiking to Utica to see Mary Lou; I also got a new farm assignment, since I had a driver's license. I delivered the farm's milk to the processing plant in Eaton.

I'm not sure if I ever noticed the plant manager's little daughter waiting for the school bus outside her dad's place of business, but the subject came up on my first date—years later—with Shirley Sherburne, who used to stand outside her dad's workplace weekday mornings, waiting for the bus that would take her to Eaton Elementary School.

Shirley remembers her early years in Eaton:

"As I was one year old when we moved to Eaton from my grandparents' farm near Mt. Upton, NY, the house on the other side of the tracks (literally) from the milk processing plant was the only home I recall. Sheffield Farms (later Sealtest Foods) owned the house as part of the property purchased from the railroad (O&W) when they opened the milk processing plant.

Shirley, age 10.

"Dad had worked at a similar facility in Rockdale, NY, and we moved to Eaton so he could accept a management position.

"I have very dear memories of homemade ice cream, real whipped cream and more made from the milk Dad would bring home. This was also the time I first heard the name 'Zimmer'. When Art's dad, Carl, was going to butcher one of their "kickers," he would call and ask Dad if he needed or wanted any beef."

I also started to work off and on with my very good friend and high school classmate, Bill Steene. Bill's dad was a house painter. I liked painting houses better than milking cows that would kick me, and the Steenes overpaid me: forty-five cents an hour for painting. I worked with them part-time, as I was still working my dad's farm and mowing lawns.

In 1956, I was anticipating graduating from high school. I ranked 43rd in a class of 43. That spring, I sat down with my guidance counselor, Rod Pierce, for what turned out to be about a four-minute session. It was our first meeting in four years. The man said, "You took shop, typing, and driver ed. No math, science, or language, and your attendance record is very sporadic. We can't give you a diploma. Your future is simple: stay on the farm or join the Army (the Army required no diploma in 1956)."

I said, "Okay, I'll just come back to school next year."

A few days later I was called in for another meeting. The counselor said, "Here's the deal. The principal (Mr. Andy Lane) and I have decided that if you promise not to come back next year, we'll give you a diploma."

I had a great time at graduation. Mr. Pierce had told me that one of my three accomplishments in high school was to learn to type. It would become important—along with my shop skills and driver's license—in my immediate future.

My mother, however, was a nervous wreck at my graduation ceremony. She didn't really believe the school would actually award me a diploma. And since graduates are called to the stage alphabetically, she had to wait until the very end of the list. Since I ranked last in my class of 43, that would have been the same if we were called by rank.

That summer I enlisted in the Army for a six-year commitment (three active/three reserve) and signed up for a specific school to attend after Boot Camp: Troop Information and Education. It's fair to say it was PR school.

Mary Lou, who was an honor student, planned to attend college to become a teacher. A week before my reporting date for Boot Camp, the Army said that the school I wanted was full for the first available session after my basic training, but they would assign me to that school at a later date. Some instinct told me to refuse to sign the final papers until I also had a specific order to attend the school I wanted. This turned out to be a good move on my part. With today's all-volunteer military, I would recommend it to all recruits.

I was unexpectedly at loose ends for the summer. I worked as a camp counselor again in the Adirondacks. Mary Lou worked at a resort nearby. In the fall she left for college in Potsdam.

I returned home from my summer job, still waiting to hear from the Army, still without specific orders. So I went to work at Hengst Meat Market on Lebanon Street in Hamilton, located about where Oliveri's Pizza Shop is now. It was owned by Adolph Hengst, Andrew (Jock) Hengst's grandfather. Jock later became the owner/director of the Bouckville Antiques show, which he ran for 43 years. He and his dad, Andy, were the original developers of the Landmark Restaurant in Bouckville, one of the best restaurants in the area.

I also worked with Bill Steene again, painting more houses. Bill's dad was very ill, and Bill had to quit school and go to work full-time to support the family. Bill went on to become very successful in life.

Much later, Bill and I figured out that we had painted at least one house on every street in Hamilton. One of our proudest accomplishments was painting the entire Colgate Inn. It took us three weeks. Great pay for the time. I'm sure Bill and his dad overpaid me at 45 cents an hour. A couple of years ago, when Ben Eberhardt remodeled the Colgate Inn, I told him I would paint it for him, but it would cost him more than 45 cents per hour. Ben had a professional paint crew there with many people and lots of equipment. We had nothing but ladders and brushes. It took us three weeks. It took them two months.

In the fall of 1956, Mary Lou and I started to drift apart. It was a natural progression, I suppose. She had left for college and I was waiting to be inducted into the Army. The last time I saw her, we parted as good friends who knew we were going in different directions in life. Proof of this might be that now I remember only that at some point during the next year, I got a brief message from her that she was engaged to be married.

~ 2 ~

In the Army Now
1957-59

In December 1956 I finally got my orders to report for boot camp, with PR school to follow right after that. Even though I was anxious to "get started" on my Army commitment, I'm still glad I refused to sign the enlistment papers until I had a set date for my public relations training.

Off I went to defend our country. The Army's mission in that decade was the Cold War with the U.S.S.R. It seemed like every day the Russians were going to drop an atomic bomb on us. Once I joined the Army they apparently had second thoughts, because they never did drop that bomb.

My first assignment was at Fort Chaffee, Arkansas. I got there on a little 1949 Vespa motor scooter, which went 26 miles per hour downhill. I got about 100 miles per gallon for gas that cost 24 cents per gallon. In 1957 all roads were back roads; there were no problems with big trucks. From hamilton to Arkansas, I rode from sun-up to sunset. It was summer, so I rode 13 to 14 hours per day.

My first Army transport was a 1949 Vespa scooter. Can you believe I rode this little put put at 26 miles an hour over 2,000 miles? Well, I did.

When it got dark, I just stopped and slept by the side of the road. I didn't even have a sleeping bag. I didn't talk to many people; just drove and slept, with quick stops at roadside diners and gas stations. The trip took about nine days. Now, Google maps says you can drive the trip comfortably in two and a half days.

Since I slept by the side of the road as needed and had a travel allowance, I doubled my $72-per-month Army salary with the money I saved by travelling on that scooter and camping out. Fort Chaffee was near where Bill Clinton was probably in grade school, age 12 or so, and another new recruit was named Elvis Presley. I never met him.

The Army had just decided that all recruits should have high school diplomas, so they started to recruit dozens of teachers for the people who had already enlisted but didn't have their diploma. When I arrived at Ft. Chaffee, they thought I was their new teacher. Disappointed, they transferred me after two months to Fort Hood, Texas; then to White Sands Missile Range in New Mexico; Sandia Base in Albuquerque; and then back to White Sands. The Vespa got me to every destination; I finally sold it to buy a car in White Sands. But much to their disappointment, I still wasn't a teacher for any of them.

At White Sands they discovered that I had taken typing at Hamilton High School, a class most males never took in the 50s (guidance counselors told them it would lead to secretarial jobs). It turned out to be the most valuable thing I learned in school; when everyone else had to go on a 20-mile hike with full packs, usually in the snow, I would be sent to the office to type up the daily reports. Between being in shape from being raised a farm boy and the typing, I thought boot camp was a breeze!

While I was at White Sands, I became the scoutmaster for the base's Scout Troop. And I continued to earn badges: I attained my wood badge there. The knowledge I gained earning that badge became vital later on when I started fixing up my rental properties.

After a few months of desk duty, boredom overcame my sense that I had landed in a cushy assignment. I applied for another school: radio repair, at Fort Monmouth, New Jersey. I did not do well in that school. I discovered that radio repair required good math skills. My last math course was in 8th grade,

White Sands Missile Range, New Mexico in November 1958.

and I had flunked it. Somehow I got through the school (I hope I have never repaired a radio for you) and went back to White Sands and a desk job. Still boring. But I jumped at the opportunity to become scoutmaster of the base's Boy Scout troop. Unfortunately, that led to my losing a stripe when I refused to promote a major's son because he hadn't done required work for a badge.

I returned to Hamilton in December of 1959. This was my first opportunity to get acquainted with a new member of the family, Little Ruth. I still refer to her as Little Ruth sometimes. She's my baby sister, and she was born in 1956, during the year I graduated from high school and waited to leave for the Army. Now she's a college vice president in Virginia.

I spent three years in Hamilton before hitchhiking to Syracuse in 1963. College seemed like a good idea, except for the problem of my high school record. But, as an Army veteran, I got a conditional acceptance at the school now called Mohawk Valley Community College (MVCC) in Utica. Every academic quarter was touch-and-go, as my grades were so low.

At least one of my high school classmates was not surprised that my major at MVCC involved advertising and public relations, apparently because some of my high school shenanigans, which probably stemmed from my low academic skills, were considered creative by my fellow students. Bonnie Pierson Wilcox remembers:

> "Mr. Kelly, our English teacher, asked us to write an essay. Art titled his "Day Dreaming." He left the middle of the page blank. At the bottom of the page he concluded with: 'Oh, I must have been daydreaming.' I thought it was funny. Mr. Kelly did not."

To pay for school, I started the Zimmer Maple Sugar Candy Manufacturing, Sales, and Distribution Company. It did very well until I closed it down to prepare to depart on my two-year boat trip to Florida. I also kept painting houses and working at the TV repair shop.

Bill Steene welcomed me back to the house painting business. I worked some painting projects with Bill and some on my own. And I worked part-time for Bob Woodruff, a high school classmate who owned a radio/TV repair shop in a space near the former Wayne's Market on Eaton Street. "Woodie" had multiple sclerosis and had difficulty walking. He was an electronics wizard, but house calls were impossible for him. Back in those days, repair shops (and doctors) made house calls. Televisions were huge pieces of furniture with 14-inch screens, and it was not easy for owners to bring them in to be repaired.

I did not know how to repair a TV. But I would go on Bob's house calls. I would take the back off the TV and do a little poking at the innards of the "big screen" 14-inch television sets. My standard line was, "It's a serious problem." Then I'd take the set to the shop and Bob would fix it. The next day, I would deliver the repaired set. No extra charge for house calls, and the sets worked perfectly, so everyone was happy.

My income was now up to 70 cents an hour.

I also worked for the Mid-York Weekly newspaper. Back in those days, the Mid-York had its own presses and production department located where the Colgate University Bookstore is now. Around 1960, the Mid-York moved into a new building across from Russ Ray's Wayside Store. Actually I had worked for the Mid-York off and on since the ninth grade so I had an insider's peek at a mystery the paper never solved.

One evening shortly before I moved to Syracuse, my friend Keith Benedict and I were cruising around Hamilton. Keith is a very unusual person. He has dedicated his life to better understanding between nations and world peace, a very enviable position for a native Hamiltonian to take. After more than 50 years, Keith and I still keep in touch.

Just how did Keith go about reaching this wonderful goal of promoting better understanding among nations? He did it by marrying a woman from Sweden, then marrying one from Spain, then England, then Russia, and finally, Japan. Yes, he did get divorced in between.

But that was later. Back to the main topic. As Keith and I drove past William Colgate Hall one evening, we noticed that the front door was wide open. Back then, that building was the university's administration building, near the shore of Taylor Lake. Being civic-minded youth, we were curious as to why, on a Sunday evening, the building would be wide open. So we went to investigate.

We wandered around and found no one in the building. Pretty soon we found ourselves up four-and-one-half stories, in the attic. There we were surprised to see several larger-than-life-size statues. Keith, the cultured one, said, "Look: that's a statue of Minerva, the Greek goddess of education and knowledge." After some discussion, we decided that Minerva deserved to be standing tall and proud—in an exceptional place of honor. The statue was very heavy, weighing hundreds of pounds.

I'm not sure how two skinny kids got this big heavy statue down four-and-one-half flights of stairs (no elevator) and out to the car. But we did. We laid her down across the back seat of the car, but she was so tall that she stuck out both sides. So there we were, driving with the doors open and a statue hanging out each side. Good thing that Ozzie Hess was not on patrol. Ozzie was Hamilton's one and only part-time police officer.

We had decided that the goddess of education should stand in front of the new Hamilton High School. The school that Keith and I had attended had been torn down a couple of years before. This would be a wonderful addition to the new school, we thought. I still don't understand why, but the board of education did not agree.

This is where the Mid-York Weekly newspaper got in on the story. They took photos and ran an article. Where had Minerva come from, and who had put her there? It was a big mystery; the entire town was abuzz. After a while, Colgate realized where Minerva had come from. They sent five strong men and a truck from the maintenance department to reclaim her. Unfortunately, Colgate did not have the vision that Keith and I did. They trucked her back to campus and up to the attic, where she died a terrible death a couple of years later when the building burned down. (NO, Keith and I did not torch the building.)

A couple of years later, Nick Verro, with whom I kept in touch until he died in 2014, told me that his dad, Fred, head of Colgate security at that time, kept after him to find out who had stolen Minerva. Colgate felt that a gang of at least 10 kids must have done it. Nick knew all along that Keith and I had, by ourselves, done it, but he would not tell.

A few months ago, I saw a photo of the old Colgate Library. I don't know the date it was taken, but it looked to be 75 or more years old. There in the photo of the library's main reading room were, around the edges, ten or so large statues. One of them looked like Minerva.

Probably, at some point, they remodeled the library, took all the wonderful statues and stuck them up in the attic of the administration building...and forgot about them. Until Keith and I came along.

AN ARMY VETERAN TAKES TO A BOAT

Passing through Munnsville one day, I saw what I called at the time a "big old boat" for sale. It was a 32-foot cabin cruiser, and I couldn't get the sight of it out of my mind. I started thinking about taking a two-year sailing adventure to Florida. I had no experience with boats at all, by the way. But I have never tended to let inexperience get in the way of what I want to do. Nor did I have any idea of what to do in Florida. I had been there only once before when Bill Steene and I drove his parents to Florida. His dad was quite ill.

"The boat" at the beginning of my brief nautical journey. After I thought I had made it 'seaworthy', it sank in Oneida Lake.

About two hours after we got there, we turned around and drove back to Hamilton without stopping except for gas and food. No sightseeing. I did not even know what the intercoastal canal system was... or that it even existed.

I bought the boat for $35, hauled it to Bill Steene's backyard with my father's tractor and 18-foot hay wagon, and enlisted Bill's help, with his excellent carpentry skills, to help me "fix it up" in our spare time.

The "plan," if you'd like to call it that, was to launch the boat in Oneida Lake, continue into the New York State barge canal, sail along for a few days until I ran out of money, then stop and work for a week or two washing dishes, waiting tables, digging ditches, whatever work I could find. I finished my two years at MVCC, continued my jobs to save money over the summer of 1962, and worked on the boat with Bill.

In the fall, we overloaded the tractor and little hay wagon with the now-restored boat again, and I launched it in Oneida Lake at Marion's Manor Marina, now owned by the Oneida Indian Nation. I had saved $600. Enough, I thought, for a month or two of sailing. I was ready to start the adventure.

On the eve of departure, I went to a restaurant and was talking with the diners there about the trip. A man asked if my "charts" were up to date. What charts? That was when I learned that, to sail to Florida, you needed to take the inland water route by following up-to-date charts. And the man had a complete set—over 100—that would get me all the way to Florida. The set was worth about $250; the man offered to sell them to me for $150. I figured I'd learn to read the charts en route to Florida.

The first morning, I set sail—for about a mile. The motor quit. It was not, apparently, in the same good shape as the boat's woodwork. Since it was fall, not many boats were on Oneida Lake. Eventually one came along, and the occupants towed me and my boat back to the marina. I found a boat mechanic, who looked up the parts for the motor, a 1932 Scripper; he could order the parts.

So, a week and $125 later, I set sail again. At almost the same point on the lake as the week before, the motor quit again. In a now-familiar scenario, I waited for rescue, got towed back to the marina, and found the mechanic, who decreed that the motor really needed a complete overhaul if it were going to make it to Florida.

This time it cost $150 to order parts, which came in a week. I went to a restaurant to celebrate my third eve of departure. And again I told the patrons there about my trip. A man said, "Do you know what tomorrow is?" Except for my own agendas, I had no idea. "Tomorrow," the man said, "they close the canal for the winter. You might get a couple of miles down the canal, but then you'll be there for the winter."

Back to the marina. They agreed to store the boat for the winter: $100 up front. After securing the boat, I had $18 left. I decided to hitchhike to Syracuse, where I didn't know anyone. I planned to spend the winter in Syracuse waiting to launch my two-year trip to Florida in the spring....

Almost 50 years later I returned to Hamilton. That sounds dramatic, but it's true only in an existential sense. I DID go back in the spring to launch the boat. By then I had taken a boating course in Syracuse and discovered just how much I did NOT know about boating and charts. Sometimes a little knowledge is a dangerous thing.

This time, I didn't need to be rescued. That's because the boat sank in the entrance channel to the marina. I sold its submerged hull for $1 with the understanding that it was the new proud owner's responsibility to  remove it quickly from where it was blocking entrance to the lake.

Three jobs, school, and the boat had kept me busy for two years. In my free time I became the scoutmaster of Hamilton's troop for two years, along with Bob Holcomb. I still drive to Utica frequently as a member of the Scout Council Eagle Scout Review board, working with Eagle Scout candidates. In the fall of 1963, when I made that hitchhiking trip to Syracuse, I thought I'd be back. And as it turned out, I did return—50 years later.

My Early Years in Syracuse

The boating course wasn't the only thing that occupied my time in Syracuse while I awaited the start of my Florida adventure. I rented an apartment in a two-family house, got a job with the National Biscuit Company, joined Onondaga Ski Club, met a nice girl, and by spring I had decided I really preferred to stay around Syracuse for a while.

The Syracuse I moved to in late 1963 was very different from the city today. Worden Avenue is still lined with neat houses, but at that time they were just beginning to switch over from one-family to duplexes. Just a mile or two south, Salina Street boasted big department stores, small specialty shops, and services catering to shoppers. There were strip shopping centers, complete with grocery stores, but no malls.

Route 81 was just being finished, and President Lyndon B. Johnson's visit to the SU campus to dedicate "Newhouse I" was still in the future. During his speech for that event, he announced the Tet Offensive in Vietnam, where the Army was performing very different service in a much more dangerous arena than I had experienced in the 1950s, a few short years before.

Richard (Dick) Flaherty met me in November 1963, when the family of his future wife, Dona, lived in my neighborhood and he and I both had joined the Onondaga Ski Club (OSC). As he recalls:

"I had just gotten out of the Army and returned to Syracuse to work at Chrysler as an engineer. We both were learning how to ski at Drumlins. Oh, and we were also learning how to party. We had other things in common. We were both raised on a farm. I lived in the village of Adams, but I was from a farming family, so we had similar life views from a farming standpoint."

Onondaga Ski Club (OSC) was a 50-year career in itself for me. When I joined for the 1963-64 ski season, the club was a very active, excellent group of 700 members. I quickly started to take a leadership role for the organization. The first year I went on several bus trips, traveling to Canada and New England. By the third year I was running bus trips for OSC members and traveling all over the eastern U.S. and Canada.

A picture from an Onondaga Ski Club gathering in the early 1960s. I still wear that same sweater.

Next I went on a ski charter to Europe; later I would run ski club charter flights to Europe and the western U.S. and Canada. I became president of the club, was chairperson of every committee at one time or another, created several new programs, and conducted membership drives and marketing initiatives.

Dick Flaherty thinks a lot of my so-called executive abilities stemmed from my experiences with OSC, "Ski Club" as he refers to it:

"I saw him develop very, very well as president of the group. I was treasurer; we both became very involved in Ski Club and then eventually in real estate. Where he was a guru, I was more of a supporter of his ideas. I learned a lot by watching what Art was doing with his real estate. We also became business partners for some of his acquisitions, including the Vermont ski lodge that the Ski Club bought. I helped build a financial structure for the bonds we used to purchase it. At first Art wanted to sell no-interest bonds for the financing, figuring the club members would be happy just to be getting their own lodge. I convinced him to offer six percent interest. That helped a lot with bond sales. And they were all paid off when they matured!

"Art was key on that lodge. It also caused him a lot of grief. I told him he ought to be spending his time on his own business—real estate—rather than on this volunteer project. He started diversifying; he bought two ski lodges of his own. And then he bought the New Times."

Thinking out of the box

One of my favorite Onondaga Ski Club projects was the "trophy case committee." The club had won a lot of trophies, and they were scattered around town in the homes of various members. I suggested to the board of directors (I was 2nd vice president at the time) that we buy a glass display case and place it in a prominent place in the city to display our awards. They laughed at me and voted it down unanimously, except for my vote.

I kept bringing up the idea, and it became the butt of jokes around the club. The next year I became 1st vice president and brought up the trophy case idea again. So they made me chairman of the trophy case committee, but with no budget. They thought that would be the end of it.

A Ski Club photo from 1969. We were visiting a tennis club; I had organized a tennis program. It is still in operation today. Note that I had replaced the old Vespa from Army days with another one.

I found a jewelry store that was going out of business and got the owner to donate a nice glass display case. Before Syracuse University took it over, Drumlins was the social center of Syracuse. The ballroom hosted wedding receptions and parties almost every day. The various meeting rooms were used by almost every community organization in town. They had bowling alleys going full blast all the time, an actual ski hill with a lift and lights for night skiing, a large skating rink, and of course the current public and private golf courses.

To everyone's surprise, I got Drumlins to let me place the display case right in the lobby, by the main entrance. I collected trophies from members and included promotional information on the club. For several years, about 50 new members each year reported having first found out about OSC from the trophy case.

THE SKI SHOW AND SALE

In 1970, when I purchased the Vermont Ski Lodge for the Onondaga Ski Club, I was president of the club. I knew it could not sustain itself financially just from room rentals, as we wanted to keep the price of going to Vermont to ski as low as possible for club members.

My plan right from the beginning was that the Vermont Lodge committee would conduct fundraising events to supplement the lodge income and allow the room rental price to stay low. Today, after more than 40 years, you can still stay at the lodge for under $30 per night.

The fundraising project that I decided to try was a used ski equipment sale. Back then, no one had ever even heard of such an event. Today, due to our success, there are lots of used equipment sales.

The plan was that the lodge committee would take in used ski equipment and sell it, taking a small commission. It was hoped that this would become popular, especially with families, as kids outgrow expensive ski equipment so fast. Hopefully, we planned that it would be a money maker for the lodge as well as a valuable service for the skiing public.

The next question was where to hold it. I knew about a show at the State Fairgrounds called the Winter Leisure Sports Show. It was primarily a snowmobile show and sale. I went to talk to Colonel Hartman; I don't know if he was a real colonel or not. He was the executive director of the Center of Progress building and also owner of the show, which was held in the Center of Progress building. Today, that would probably be considered a serious conflict of interest. When I proposed to Colonel Hartman that he donate space to the lodge committee for a used ski equipment sale, he was very happy to do so. He said that for years he had been trying to get ski areas and ski shops to partner in his show, but to no avail.

Back in those days, there was a lot of animosity between skiers and snowmobilers. Over the past 20 years, that has pretty much disappeared. Colonel Hartman thought that, with the ski sale as part of his show, it would encourage other ski businesses to come in. Also, he had lots of extra unused space in the building during the show. So he donated a ten-foot-square booth to us.

The first ski sale was a big success. The lodge made a few hundred dollars and provided a very positive service for the public as well, as the club picked up quite a few new members from it. After the show, I talked to Colonel Hartman about the next year. He said yes. We needed a lot more space, and he said OK. Year two was a huge success, even better than my own optimistic projections. However, no other ski businesses had come into the "snowmobile show."

After the show, I had a meeting with the colonel to put together a plan for the next year. The colonel would hang a big curtain across the middle of the Center of Progress building. One side would be for the snowmobile show and the other side for the ski show. Admission would be $2 for each show, or both shows for $3.

Ski Show Highlights: The ski sale (left) and ballet skier Alan Schoenberger (right).

World-renowned skier Alan Schoenberger was the celebrated guest at the 1986 Ski Show and Sale. This picture hyped his visit in the Syracuse New Times Ski Guide that year.

I was to go out and promote the show to all the ski areas, ski shops, and other ski-related businesses. That was okay with me. A week later, Colonel Hartman called me in for a meeting and presented me with a show contract. I would rent half of the building from him and resell the space to ski businesses. If I did not sell out the space, the ski club or I would be responsible to pay him the difference.

Hmmm. I reminded him that I was a 100-percent volunteer and was not interested in going into business with him. I would do all I could as a volunteer to get ski businesses to sign up with him. He said no. I had to either rent the space or the ski sale was out. So I started to look around town for a new location for the ski sale.

Remember what I said about Drumlins being a major center of community activities. The ski club had its monthly general meetings in the ballroom. Every week there were ski club committee meetings in the smaller rooms, and the club operated its own ski school classes on the ski hill, for which I was a volunteer ski instructor. And the trophy case was there. Years later, when Syracuse University purchased the property, they took out the bowling alleys, closed the skating rink, and closed the ski hill. The banquet food went way downhill and the prices way up. It ceased to be an important social center for Central New York.

Back to the ski show. I asked the owner of Drumlins to donate the use of the ballroom for one day for the ski sale. That would also help to promote Drumlins' ski hill. He said yes. We filled the big ballroom. We gave some ski shops a table to set up promotional displays. The lodge committee made several thousand dollars profit. The next year, we took over the entire building at Drumlins and started to turn it into a ski show and sale. The building was jam-packed. The next year, we turned it into a two-day show, paid Drumlins some rent, and sold space to ski shops and ski areas.

Now this was getting to be a big, big project, and I was still the volunteer ski show/sale director. I resigned as chairman of the Vermont lodge committee to spend more time on the show. Even at two days, the building was always so packed that I did not feel people could really enjoy the show as much as I had hoped. I wanted this to be a major fun event for the entire ski community. We needed more space.

I looked all over the Syracuse area and could not find an acceptable space. One day I went out to the Center of Progress building for a craft/antique show. As I left, I saw a sign advertising more exhibits next door at the Arts and Home Center in the Women's Building. So over I went. As I walked around I said, "WOW–this would be a great place for the ski show/sale." Monday morning I was in the building director's office. It turned out that the director was Elizabeth Crowley, an avid skier. She had a ski cabin at the Labrador Mountain ski area and was a big fan of the ski show, having attended it several times. Now with more space and a new location, I developed it into a real ski show with a used ski equipment sale as a big part of it.

We quickly grew so big that the next year I rented the entire building, including the theater that was in the building. We put on a full-fledged big-production ski fashion show in the theater. Many years later, that theater became the Syracuse New Times Newspaper Theater, and I presented musical theater shows there for many years.

To keep up with the show's growth, I expanded it into a three-day weekend event. It was becoming a full-time year-round job for me, but I was a volunteer who worked a couple of paying jobs and ran some businesses. I began to feel people were not able to enjoy the show as much because it was always so crowded. I was afraid our success would lead to failure. As Yogi Berra said, "No one goes there anymore. It's too crowded...." Or was that Yogi Bear?

I started the hunt for space again—to no avail. I went and talked to Tom Young, the State Fair director and later Syracuse mayor. The Center of Progress building was much too big and too expensive. Also, Colonel Hartman was unhappy with me, as his winter sports show had gone out of business as he watched my ski show/sale grow and prosper.

The Vermont ski lodge committee was now making tens of thousands of dollars in profit each year on the show. Because of the show, OCS paid the entire Vermont lodge mortgage off early. We also paid back all the lodge bonds early. We had sold lodge bonds to raise the money for the lodge down payment and made lots of major improvements on the lodge. One of the original lodge bonds is on display on the dining room wall at the lodge. It

The cover of the Ski Show program that Art published in the New Times beginning in 1984. The publication grew to a 32-page separate newspaper supplement that Art published annually for 18 years.

had been sold to, guess who, Richard Flaherty, when he was club treasurer. He was always an avid supporter of the lodge and show.

There was one problem I had with Richard, and I still chide him about it today as we still, after 40 years, have lunch often. I remind him that he was club treasurer and drove a brand new expensive car. I was club president and drove an old beat-up pickup truck. I always thought that there was something wrong with that picture. Dick just smiled and disagreed.

I explained to Tom Young that the club was a nonprofit, and some of the show/sale profits were donated to the U.S. Olympic ski team, to local junior ski racing programs, and other nonprofits, including major financial support of a local program for blind skiers.

I asked Tom if we could get a discount on the fee. Tom said yes. But there was another major problem. Over the years, I had donated the show's concession stands to all the other ski clubs in the area so they could raise money for their clubs, including several junior ski programs. I had given the Ski Hawks ski club the beer concession and other clubs various food concessions.

The problem was that the Center of Progress building had a restaurant and bar in the building, and the person who had the contract had the exclusive rights to all food and drink concessions in the entire building, at all times for all shows.

I talked to Ed Hewitt, the owner of the concessions contract. I explained our nonprofit status and all the good work we did in the community with the ski show profits. He said, if we kept it quiet, we could have all the concessions for the show. I even asked him if we could use his restaurant coolers, and reluctantly he agreed.

My next big problem was the ski show committee. I did run the ski show/ sale with an iron hand, but the show had gotten so big that I needed lots of help. I had a ten-member committee that met monthly year-round. On show weekend, over 300 volunteers were needed to run the show. At committee meetings, the subject of moving the show was discussed, and the majority was very opposed to it. I needed to keep the committee members happy to keep them working, but I felt that for the long-term success of the show we must move. The committee meetings were held in the Women's Building. When our friend Liz Crowley left work, she just left the door unlocked, and we would lock up after the meeting.

The next meeting after my talks with Tom Young and Ed Hewitt, I told Liz not to leave the door unlocked. I arranged with Tom to leave the side door of the Center of Progress building unlocked. That evening was a cold rainy night. As we huddled under the canopy, I said, Liz must have forgotten to leave the door unlocked. It was suggested we go to a nearby bar for the meeting. I asked Stu Sturman to go across the driveway and check that side door. Surprise, surprise--it was unlocked. So in we went and sat down at the picnic tables that I had arranged to be placed just inside the door. I said, "Folks, look around. This is the new home of the ski show/sale. I signed a contract today."

The committee members went crazy. They made a motion to vote me out as director. I told them that they did not have the authority to do so. To make a long story short, the entire committee came around. And they all worked hard. We filled the building and made more money than ever. The show/sale continued to grow and prosper for many years, becoming the largest event of its kind in the U.S., and I remained the volunteer director for over 18 years.

One thing that concerned me was that, as the show/sale had grown so big, the ski club board of directors voted to take the show away from the lodge committee and make it an all-club event. The problem was that the board started to use some of the show profits to supplement other club committees. When I was president, I instituted a policy that each committee had to be financially self-supporting and actually return a small profit to the club's general fund to help pay the club's operating expenses. That way we could keep membership dues low. For many years, the dues were only $10 per year. All the committees operated financially by my rules for many years. Now they started to be financially irresponsible, as they had all the money from the ski show/sale, and didn't have to worry about returning a small profit.

For the next several years, more and more of the show money went to support club activities and less and less to the lodge and ski charities. I felt the club was starting to kill the goose that laid a golden egg every year. So, after 18 years as show director and about 25 years actively involved in running many other club activities, I decided to retire as show/sale director. I still remain a club member today after 50 years.

I informed the board that, in 14 months, I would retire from the show. This meant I would still run the next two shows. I started to keep a daily log, a diary on every detail of the show. Every contact was listed, what to do, and when to do it. It ended up being a 200-page notebook. Anyone could have taken that notebook and run the show effectively. The board appointed Glenn White as the new director. I gave him the notebook. Mysteriously, a few weeks later, the notebook disappeared. After a couple of years, the ski show was going downhill (pun intended) and was soon out of business. A few years ago a Rochester ski company that had opened a shop in Syracuse started to run a ski sale at the Fairgrounds. They still do today, calling it a ski show/sale, but it has never achieved the success we had.

Over the years, many things happened at the shows that were a real challenge. One I remember well. There was a sports shop called Joe Charles. They ran a very successful and profitable golf show and sale at the Fairgrounds each year. They wanted to run their own ski show and sale and did not think that the ski club should be doing one on its own. One year as we were getting the show all set up, an hour before opening, several hundred people were already lined up at the door. In walked a fire department inspector. I later found out that he was a personal friend of Joe Charles. Charles put him up to it. The fire inspector walked around and then told me the way the show booths were set up was a public hazard, and we could not open. I asked him exactly what was wrong, and he gave me a list that he knew would take a full day to reset. I knew that we could not open and probably were out of business. Actually, the way we were set up was the same as every show had been set up for years. He called the town police chief to enforce his order.

I got on the loudspeaker and asked everyone to drop what they were doing and come to the front. There were about 300 people working in the building, volunteers and exhibitors. I quickly explained what had happened and said, "Let's get to work and do what the fire inspector wants." I assigned about 20 people to each item on his list. We ripped the show apart and rebuilt it as the inspector wanted—and had assumed we could not do. We opened the show two minutes after the advertised time. The public never knew what had happened. I told the police chief he should put the fire inspector in jail. He agreed with me, but did not do it. Several years later, Joe Charles went out of business.

A REALLY DOWN-HILL SKI SHOW

Another ski show and sale venture that was not a big success for me, but which may explain why Syracuse's current ski show/sale is run by a Rochester company, was the Rochester Ski Show. During the time I was running the Syracuse ski show and sale at the Fairgrounds, I got a call from a man named Warren. He was an avid skier from Rochester who had attended several of my Syracuse Ski Shows. He said that Rochester needed a ski show and asked if I'd meet with him about starting one in Rochester.

We had several meetings, and decided he would co-produce a Rochester show with me. Unlike having the backing of a group like the Onondaga Ski Club as I did here, the Rochester event was to be a private for-profit venture. The Syracuse show made up to $20,000 in profit per year, but it all went to the U.S. Olympic Ski Team, the OSC, and other nonprofit ski groups.

To start the ball rolling so to speak, I rented the Dome at the Monroe County Fairgrounds. The contract had the standard clause: the Fairgrounds could not rent any space out for 30 days before and after our event that had to do with skiing.

Admission was $5. We expected about 5,000 people; that was where we would make our money. The day we opened a two-day show, at the entrance of the Fairgrounds was a huge sign with an official-looking uniformed guard next to it. The sign read "Free Ski Show" and had an arrow pointing to the building next door, on the Fairgrounds. When I complained they said, "Hey, you're an out-of-towner from Syracuse; we don't like you coming into our town."

Needless to say, I lost a bunch of money. I probably could have sued them, but why bother? To this day there has not been another Rochester ski show, free or paid.

After my presidency and more than 20 years and a series of marketing events and initiatives such as the trophy box and the ski show and sale to promote and support the group, the OSC had grown to more than 1,700 members, about the population of Hamilton.

The ski club had become a year-round sporting and social club and even owned its own ski lodge in Vermont (that I had purchased for the club... which they still own and operate today after more than 40 years since I purchased it).

JEAN CLAUDE WHO?

One of the ski-related programs that I conducted did not turn out to be a success like most of the things that I did (I didn't take the Rochester Ski Show personally). But it was an interesting experience. In approximately 1969, one person became just about the most famous skier in the entire world. He was a Frenchman who had won more Olympic ski gold medals than anyone in history, up to that time—Jean Claude Killy.

Through the ski show, I had worked with one of the major airlines. They were exhibitors at the show to promote ski trips. They had signed up Jean Claude to do promotion and commercials. So I was able to arrange a personal visit to Syracuse by Jean Claude Killy.

It would be a major event, especially in the ski world. The club could use it as a fundraiser for the U.S. Olympic team and attract a lot of new members.

I rented the big field house at Le Moyne College that could seat about 2,000, a huge crowd back then, and spent money on advertising and promotion. The admissions happily would cover all the expenses, and our profits would come from the concessions that Le Moyne had agreed to let us operate.

The program was to show two new super ski films obtained by the airlines. I had to rent a special movie projector and projectionist. Jean Claude Killy would talk about his life and experiences at the Olympics, and then conduct a Q & A with the audience.

I was flying high. Wow, Jean Claude Killy here in Syracuse. The day before the event, I was on the phone with the airline rep going over details when she said, "You have the French interpreter all set." I said, "What?" She said, "Yes, you need an interpreter. Jean Claude does not speak English." I scurried around and hired an interpreter from SU's foreign language department.

Then I got a call from Le Moyne. My contact there said a truck was there to deliver 20 kegs of beer. I said, "Yes, skiers are big beer drinkers, so that is where we will make our money in the concession stand." He said, "No, Le Moyne, a Jesuit college, allows no alcohol on campus." The beer company took the kegs back, but I had to pay them two hundred dollars, plus I had arranged co-sponsorship from the beer company. Their logo was in the advertisements.

The day of the show, I had arranged a noon press conference at the Hotel Syracuse, the "in" place for big events, approved by the airline rep. I got all the radio, TV, and newspaper reporters there. About 11:50, I asked the airline rep where Jean Claude was. She kind of blushed and said that he was up in his room with an airline stewardess that he had picked up on his way over and did not want to be disturbed for an hour or two.

At about 12:45, after two thirds of the press had left, Jean Claude came down. He stayed about five minutes, mumbled a few words in French that the interpreter had a problem understanding, and went back upstairs.

We did have a large crowd at the show—we almost filled Le Moyne's field house—but there were a lot of unhappy people with no beer. Then... the next disaster...the advertised super ski films turned out to be lousy airline promotional films with a couple of bad ski scenes. People were really mad. The final disaster was the famous Jean Claude Killy in person. He mumbled, acted hung over, and the interpreter could get only about every third word he said.

At the end of the evening people booed and asked for their money back. The next day, the press had a field day reporting on what a disaster the entire show was. My only consolation was I kept valiantly telling people that the only people who don't get criticized are those who do nothing to start with.

Another experience with an Olympic skier turned out much better. Stein Eriksen won Olympic gold in the early 1950s. Sometime around the mid- to late-1960s, I arranged for the ski club to rent a house from Fred Gruner for the entire season. Fred was co-owner of the DeWitt Ski and Sports Shop. I had worked for Fred part-time in one of his ski shops at Trainer Hill, a nice little ski area on the Colgate University campus across the street from the hospital—a convenient location. The house we rented was located on the back side of Mad River Glen ski area, Vermont, considered by many as the most difficult ski area in Vermont. It is where all the expert skiers liked to visit. But it was located near the Sugarbush and Glen Ellen ski areas. I had been at Glen Ellen (now part of Sugarbush) several years earlier on the weekend they first opened. I had also been at Gore Mountain in New York and met Governor Harriman the day Gore first opened. So after I made the deal with Fred, I went to Vermont for a few days in early October to get the house ready for the ski season. We had had an early season snowfall that dumped about four feet of snow. I heard they were skiing at Sugarbush.

Stein had just become ski school director at Sugarbush. There was no one in the base lodge except Stein, a dozen skiers he was training to be on his ski school staff, and me. I got to sit and talk with Stein for about an hour. He said, "We are going to go out and take a couple of runs. Would you like to join us?" WOW – me, skiing with Olympic gold medal winner Stein Eriksen? Of course I said yes. It was a fabulous experience.

A couple of years later, I was at Aspen Highlands, Colorado. Stein was now ski school director at Aspen Highlands. I had lunch with him. He said he remembered me from Sugarbush, but I'm not really sure that he did. I did visit with him several years later at his new hotel in Park City, Utah. The Stein Eriksen Lodge is one of the most elegant luxury ski lodges in the United States.

And of course I was fortunate to meet and know Vicki Fleckenstein. Vicki was probably the best skier to ever come out of Central New York. I was a gatekeeper one day at Song Mountain in Tully for a junior ski race. Suddenly a girl with long red hair streaming out behind her came flying down the mountain, twice as fast as any other racer. It was Vicki. Over the years, I got to know her very well and was even invited to her wedding.

Vicki became a member of the U.S. National Ski Team and then a member of the Olympic team for the 1980 Olympics at Lake Placid. I was at the 1980 Olympics and had some very interesting experiences there.

When I first joined the OSC, many of its parties were at my rented apartment. I also started to manage a band, whose members practiced at my apartment. Perhaps it shouldn't have come as a surprise that I was evicted from three apartments before I bought a two-family house of my own at 152 Worden Avenue on Syracuse's North Side.

My landlady, who owned that house, on one of her trips to my door to complain about the noise, mentioned that she was tired of having tenants and managing a house on her own. I offered to buy the house from her if she would sell it to me for no down payment. She agreed and I bought it with a G.I. loan. I lived in one apartment and three girls rented the other one from me. I soon realized that their rent paid the house expenses and I was living for free.

For a while I lived in the little apartment upstairs at 152 Worden. Once I owned the house, I moved into the large apartment downstairs, and turned it into party headquarters.

Dick Flaherty was nearby.

"I was happy at Chrysler, but I knew that eventually I wanted to get into business for myself. Art discovered real estate first, and then I got involved. His Worden Street property was an interesting place. And it was where I first met him. Dona, then my future wife, lived in her family's house on the next street, backyard neighbors to Art's place, and her father warned us to 'stay away from that guy,' as Art was considered that 'one neighbor' everyone felt they had to keep an eye on.

"No wonder. In addition to presiding over Ski Club, Art managed several bands—or rather one band with several names for different audiences. In addition to setting up venues and assignments, Art let the band practice in his apartment. He had the place totally blacked out, with cork-boarded windows.

"There was always a lot of action around Art. He's a gatherer, a collector of people, a lot of different kinds of people. And there's always something happening around Art; it's never boring when he's around.

"Girls liked Art. One in particular, who lived down the street from the infamous AZ, wanted to go out to dinner with him. The catch was that her parents wanted to meet her date, and they would have immediately realized he was the 'untouchable' from down the street. So Art asked me to pick her up, and I did."

Dick is being kind about my life on Worden Avenue. I was still never sure exactly where my next meal would come from. Just a block down the street was the Schnitzelbank Restaurant, which became The Change of Pace in the mid-80s. The Schnitzelbank had a banquet room and frequently hosted wedding receptions. When I would see a lot of cars parked along the street, I knew that they had a party going on. I would put on my one suit, go down and mingle in, and get a good meal. Frequently that turned out to be my only good meal of the week.

Since I always was a polite "guest" and did my best to entertain the invited guests, at the time I didn't feel that I was an intruder. Belatedly, I apologize to any reader whose wedding I crashed.

Liz Anderson was one of my first tenants. She moved into the upstairs apartment on Worden when I bought the house and moved downstairs. Unlike most landlords of the time, I allowed pets. Liz remembers:

"When I was in my late 20s, I lived in an upstairs apartment on the north side of Syracuse owned by Art. He lived in the downstairs apartment. Art was very generous in helping to make the space comfy. My cat, Gus, was a 'Morris'-looking kitty and weighed around 20 pounds. I was concerned that he would run away, so Art offered to 'build a cat line' for Gussie. He hooked up a line between the garage and the house, and then hooked up a leash line that slid across and came down to hook onto the cat's collar. Gussie had this great space in the back'yard to be outdoors.

"Art left, and I went upstairs. Soon I looked out to see Gussie running across the space the line reached and then UP INTO THE AIR. When the line did not break, he did it again! And again! And again! Shortly after, I heard meowing outside my door. There was Gussie, still hooked up, dragging the whole line behind him. Followed by Art, saying, 'Guess we don't have to worry about the cat running away.' Eventually, I relaxed about the cat and let him out on the back roof. It was just outside my kitchen window and he enjoyed sitting there and watching the world spin. Once in a while Gus would sit over Art's back door and track anyone coming or going. When someone spotted him you would hear, 'Oh my god, there's a cat up there!' Gussie sort of fit in with Art's Atmosphere!"

Liz also remembers more details about that house than I do. And Gus wasn't the only pet in the place:

"While living in my upstairs unit, I did things to make it comfortable. The apartment had originally been a bathroom and three bedrooms. It had a stairway on the side where you entered. At the top of the stairs to the right was the bathroom, nice and big with a claw-footed tub. Across the hall from the bathroom, you went into the kitchen. Going left from the kitchen through barroom-type swinging doors was the bedroom. Turning left again you went into the living room. Turn left again and you were back at the top of the stairs. It must have been a huge difference in 'decor' for the guys who lived there before me. Art asked if they could see what it looked like now. The guys were saying, 'Wow, omg, this looks nice.'

"When I finally did see the inside of Art's apartment, I was surprised with his decorations! On first glance everything looked normal. But then you began to notice the man-cave touches! The coffee table was a coffin with bottles of various liquids appearing when the lid was lifted. The living room was darkish; the curtains were tacked down to keep them in place. But the best feature was a very shy, huge black bunny rabbit who lived in his basement and was free to roam the apartment."

For several years, I would go to the barber school on West Genesee Street, across from the main post office, and get my hair cut for 35 cents. I would let it grow long, then have it cut short, so I could go eight weeks between haircuts.

I drove around town on my little old Vespa motor scooter, similar to the one that got me around in the Army. It got over 150 miles per gallon. More people should try that today for trips around town. Or even an electric version.

Don't fence me in

After I bought the two-apartment house at 152 Worden Avenue and moved downstairs, I threw a lot of parties. When the weather was nice, I used the backyard. That was good because I usually had 100 to 150 people there.

In the backyard, I put up a very large solid-wood fence. At each party, I put out a bucket of paint and some small paint brushes. Everyone attending signed in on the fence, usually writing various comments. Couples would usually sign in together with a heart or sweet saying around their names. Before each party, I would put out brushes with a different color of paint and paint the date. After a couple of years, inevitably some people showed up with a different boyfriend or girlfriend. Their previous sign-ins proved to be interesting.

Of course Dick Flaherty was there, and remembers my "interesting" guest book:

"Art considered himself the guru of spaghetti. He'd host huge spaghetti dinners at the Worden house, inviting the Ski Club and anyone else he encountered. I remember that fence. Thing is, this was a young, dating group, and as partners changed, names on the fence became incriminating, and there was more than one uneasy moment as new partners discovered names of former dates."

After eight years and about 100 parties—probably 50 in the backyard—the fence became a must-see legend. When I sold the house and moved to North Syracuse, everyone said, "Take the fence with you." I really did plan to do so, but just never got around to it. After all, at the time I was working three jobs, running a business, conducting a very active social life, and running the 1,600-member Onondaga Ski /Club.

After a while the new owner took the fence down, and a piece of North Side history was lost.

All my life, I've always respected and liked the police. Many people in law enforcement have been good friends of mine. I'd always been a "good boy" and stayed out of trouble. But I did have one interesting incident soon after I bought the house on Worden. Remember I had basically turned the place into party headquarters for the bands I managed.

A few doors down the street lived a Syracuse police officer. I did not know him, never met him. One neighbor told me that he and several other neighbors were not happy with me because my parties filled the street with cars and the parties sometimes got quite loud. One of my three bands would frequently play at the parties.

One day there was a big wind storm, and a tree came down on my garage in the backyard. I got a chainsaw, cut up the wrecked tree, and put it out on the curb in front of the house, ready for the city DPW to pick up. Three days later, I had just gotten home from work when there was loud banging on my door. On my front porch were about six uniformed police officers. Parked on the street were four patrol cars with lights flashing...and a paddy wagon. Wow, I thought, did someone get murdered in the neighborhood?

One officer said, "Are you Art Zimmer?" Yes. Bang. Two of them grabbed me and slapped handcuffs on me, dragged me to the street, and threw me into the paddy wagon. With sirens blaring, downtown we went.

The charge, violation of city code so-and-so, was for having debris piled up on my front lawn. They actually booked me, fingerprints and all, and put me in a jail cell. That evening, I was scheduled to have a date with a young lady whom I had just met a few days before. It was to be dinner and movies, probably McDonald's and the theater in Mattydale where tickets were 75 cents each. I had her number on a slip of paper in my pocket. They said that I could have one call. I tried a couple of friends and got no answer. No answering machines in those days. So I called her. I said that we didn't really know each other so I wouldn't be surprised if she hung up when I told her that I was in jail. I needed someone to come down with $200 cash to bail me out. I was so surprised when she said "Okay," and she *did*!

The next morning I appeared before a judge. He said that legally the city did not have to pick up tree limbs; they did so as a courtesy sometimes. He dismissed the charge. I went home, rented a truck, and took everything to the dump. That was my only brush with the law, except my one and only speeding ticket in Oklahoma about 20 years ago.

Is that you coffin?

Perhaps my dicey relationship with the neighborhood cop involved his spying my macabre coffee table. Many years ago, a good friend of mine presented me with a gift. I'm not sure if I should have been complimented or not. She said, "When I saw it, I just had to get it for you. It is as unusual as you are." It was an antique wooden coffin. The date etched into the bottom was 1898. It had been a  display model in a funeral home in Palatine Bridge, a village on Route 5 near Albany.

As it had a flat top, it worked perfectly to be a "coffin table" in my living room. There was lots of storage space inside and I put everything on it that you'd usually expect to see on a coffee table. When I had a party, which was frequently, my friend Dennis (a neighbor who was 12 years old) would lie down in the coffin table before the party started. After the party got going, Dennis would start to move and scratch the sides. Then he would push open the top and jump out. Some people would freak out, but most thought it was the funniest thing that they had ever seen.

The Syracuse Ski Hawks ski club, second only to Onondaga Ski Club as the biggest club in the area, for many years had a "bury the winter party" each spring. They would borrow my coffin table each year, stand a pair of skies up in it, then parade it into the party and have a bury-the-winter ceremony.

One year, my friends Murray and Karen Chesebro were active in a community theater group in Manlius. They were doing a play with a funeral scene in it. My coffin table was the "star" of the show, and I was given a credit in the program booklet.

When Shirley and I got married, she asked if the coffin table could leave our living room. So I put it in my home office. I had about five offices in various places that I worked out of for my businesses. Later, we created a home office for Shirley within my office, and the coffin table moved to the barn. I don't remember what finally happened to it. I'd hate to think it got buried.

Several years later, we went to a graduation party for one of Shirley's former students. The student's mother said, "Wow, you're Art Zimmer. I used to go to parties at your house. They were always the greatest. Whatever happened to the kid who would jump out of your coffin table?" I could happily tell her that the "kid" was Dennis Payne. He owns a successful drain cleaning business and is a pilot, perhaps not quite as successfully: he has crashed three airplanes.

Dennis, then 13, worked for me for several years at the apartments. He later worked for Dick Flaherty for a while.

A REAL CAREER BEGINS

I had learned an important lesson about real estate from my experience with buying the house on Worden Avenue. I started to look for other two-to-four family houses that were for sale. Since I still had no capital to invest,

I would buy only houses that required no down-payments. This always meant that they were pretty shabby and the owners wanted to get rid of them. I would buy the houses, and then spend nights and weekends repairing and remodeling them for tenants. Remember all those houses I painted in Hamilton, and the boat I refurbished and *almost* sailed to Florida. I had usable skills for being a property owner/manager.

I would work whatever my current day job was, usually putting in 10-12 hours, and then go home to take care of my rental real estate for two to four hours, then go to work painting apartments for Mike Taddeo until 2 or 3 in the morning.

I eventually owned about 200 rental units. And I was still pretty much broke except for money to pay expenses. How did I manage to maintain my growing empire? A lot of the credit goes to John Biggs, who with his wife, Linda, became a life-long friend after we met during a loan transaction that was to lead to many more, including financing for the New Times building and equipment for Izitart, a typesetting and commercial design business.

John was a young lending officer at Oneonta Savings & Loan when Bob Bolton, president of that bank, introduced us. As John recalls it,

"Bob was friendly with a broker named Cecil Akre from Syracuse Securities, who referred Art to the bank. Art came down to Oneonta to meet with us and we just hit it off!

"Art has an entrepreneurial spirit that wasn't a familiar concept back in the sixties. He figures out ways to do things. If he went 'by the book' sometimes, nothing would get done! He's a gracious and generous man who is quick to share his hard-earned expertise."

Meanwhile, I was enjoying that sales job at National Biscuit. My first job in Syracuse had been selling signs, cold-calling door to door to businesses. I did not do well at that. After a few months, I got perhaps the best job of my life when I became a sales rep for the National Biscuit Company (NBC), where I worked for more than three years.

Having made the move to the big city, I had left all of my Hamilton sources of employment behind; initially I was very poor and had no money. Each morning at NBC started for us sales reps with picking up a box of samples at headquarters. I would go to the office and then start my rounds. I would sell really fast and eat the cookies and crackers for lunch. Frequently, it was my only meal of the day, since all of my money was tied up in houses. For more than a year my main meal each day was Oreos®.

Every few days, I would splurge and get a fifteen-cent Carrols' hamburger. You might remember Carrols' as a local forerunner to McDonalds' and Burger King in Syracuse. Often around Central New York, Carrols' little drive-through restaurants (you could also go inside) were right next to Micky D's or Burger King. The Carrols Corporation is still in Syracuse, with several hundred employees. They are now the largest Burger King Franchise owner in the world.

Even though I was a sales rep, most of the NBC work was stocking shelves in grocery stores with cookies and crackers. After four years I was doing very well. Every month I was the top or number-two "rep" in the company. But I knew that a lifelong career of stocking shelves was not for me.

Next I worked at the American Heart Association of Upstate New York. I was hired as the assistant executive director. Doing marketing, PR, and fundraising sounded great to me. My third day on the job, the secretary asked me, "How long do you think that you can stand this job? The last three people to have it left after four or five months." I soon found out what she meant. The executive director was a very elderly man (now I look back and think that he was probably younger than I am today). To my 20-something mind he seemed to have dementia and was always ordering people around in a very obnoxious way, changing his orders every five minutes.

After a few months I felt that he was a major liability to the association. So I went to a board of directors meeting and reported what was happening. George Wortley, who later became a member of Congress, was president of the board at that time. George took me out in the hall and said, "Art, you don't understand. A member of the board owns a large Syracuse manufacturing company in which the [Heart Association's] executive director was a vice president. He became such a pain in the butt to everyone that they moved him out and into this job. Most board members don't have the time or care about the day-to-day operations. They are just here on an ego trip."

The next morning I was fired. A friend of mine in ski club applied for the job. I pre-warned him. He said that he could take anything. He lasted seven weeks.

Before I left the Heart Association, I had saved up some money so I decided to take a few months before looking for my next job. I owned several apartments and had plenty to keep me busy. During this time, I grew a full beard.

Talking about the Heart Association reminds me that at the time their offices were in Midtown Plaza in downtown Syracuse, in a massive building, the former Smith Corona typewriter factory. It was seven stories high and covered an entire city block. It sat vacant and abandoned for many years and was slated for demolition. Then it was rehabbed into a great facility (early 1960s). The OCC (Onondaga Community College) campus was located there, the entire school, with a large restaurant (Meltzer's Deli), and about 100 professional offices.

By the time I actually had an office there, Midtown Plaza was like a second home for me. My friend Murray Chesebro was working for Larry Appley in Hamilton. Larry was president of AMA (American Management Association), where my mother also worked at one time. AMA had built a big conference facility, Americana Village, all around Lake Moraine, near Hamilton. Next to Colgate, it was the biggest employer in the Hamilton area. Murray created Americana Village for Mr. Appley. Mr. Appley also owned Saddleback Farms, home to many of the top champion Morgan horses in the country.

Through Murray, Mr. Appley hired me to create some booklets and marketing materials for the champion Morgan horses. I had a friend who worked in Midtown Plaza at the largest, state-of-the-art printing and graphic arts design studio in Syracuse. I started to visit Midtown Plaza frequently to use their creative designers and quality printing. I published several booklets and brochures that Mr. Appley was very pleased with. He said that they were as good as his New York City AMA people could do.

Since I was there so much, when I needed a dentist I found one in Midtown Plaza, Dr. Wayne. He was great and was my dentist for 40 years. When Shirley and I got married, Dr. Wayne became her dentist. Lots more visits to Midtown Plaza.

Of course, I was always working two or three jobs at the same time. I got a job working for a travel agency which sold prepaid vacations. It was located in Midtown Plaza and was owned by Bernard Fleckenstein. He was the father of Vicki Fleckenstein, the Olympic skier. I got to know his family well through both the job and skiing. I felt quite honored when I was invited to Vicki's wedding.

Later when I went to work for Brown Newspaper in Baldwinsville, there were several employees at Brown to whom I had sold vacations (small world again). Fortunately, they all had had a great time on their vacations.

But before that, I got the ill-fated job at the Heart Association. So I was in Midtown Plaza every day. One day I went upstairs from my Heart Association office to Dr. Wayne for a cleaning. Then I went downstairs to the cafeteria for lunch. The cafeteria was full of OCC students. I bit into something and broke off a tooth. I carried the tooth up to Dr. Wayne, he cemented it into place, and now, over 45 years later, it remains solidly in place and has never bothered me.

Eventually I applied to Brown Newspapers for a job (Brown became part of Eagle publishing many years later). The owner, Dick Manville, called and told me I had the job–on one condition: "Shave the beard." Many years later, after I had left Brown News, Dick Manville, who lived in Baldwinsville, grew a beard for their centennial celebration. He liked the beard and kept it. For many years, Dick and I would occasionally have lunch. Dick took great delight in telling everyone (he with the full beard) that he would not hire me until I shaved off my beard.

My next job after Brown Newspapers was with Gold Crest Electronics and turned out to be my last stint as an employee. It was a good job, and I did well. After a couple of years, an older gentleman came to work. The owner explained to me that he did not really need another employee, but this was his father-in-law. His wife told him, "Hire my dad or get a divorce." As this nice gentleman was older, he could not really do the job, as it involved a lot of heavy lifting. So I covered for him.

One day, the boss said, "Art, I can't afford you both. It's you or a divorce. So you are fired." I went home, had a beer, and said to myself, "Art, you are never getting fired from another job." In each job I did well, and each time I eventually got fired. After the third time, I promised myself that I would never be fired again. I decided that the only way to keep that promise to myself was to become self-employed.

So at the age of 33, in 1971, I announced my retirement. I threw myself a retirement party, bought a gold watch (a Timex, actually), and asked Dick Flaherty to present it to me at the party. Even though I worked until I was 73 years old, I never did work for anyone else again.

Lucky 13

I'm fond of saying that I have owned and operated 13 businesses before, during, and after my stints as an employee. Here is an annotated list that explains, among other things, why it is actually MORE than 13:

- Zimmer Maple Sugar Manufacturing, Sales and Distribution
- A – Z Music Management Company
- A – Z Estates Apartment Rentals
- Village Edge Apartment Complex
- Syracuse New Times Newspaper Publishing
- Izitart Typesetting and Graphic Arts
- Rapid Graphics Printing
- Austrian Haus Ski Lodge – hotel and restaurant, Vermont
- Family Times Magazine Publishing
- Bavarian Haus @ Killington Mountain – hotel and restaurant, Vermont
- Zimmer Neo-Classic Motor Car Company
- Rochester Ski Show and Sale
- Zimmer Musical Theater Production
- House painting business
- Not a business, but in a way I was a private contractor: Six years in the U.S. Army

Onondaga Ski Club was not a business, but for over 25 years, I spent more time on it than most owners would on a business.

Now that I'm retired, I find myself compiling a new list: projects in Hamilton that are sort of businesses and/or community service:

- Publishing the Map and Visitors Guide
- Chocolate Train Wreck Site
- Musical Theater Productions
- All-Class Hamilton High School Reunion
- Boards of directors for four non-profit community organizations
- Volunteer at many events
- Hamilton International Film Festival committee
- Chairperson, Hamilton Business Association business awards
- Producer of business seminars
- Chairperson of 2nd Chance Thrift Shop marketing committee
  (2nd Chance raises funds for homeless dogs and cats)

Real Estate

In "retirement," I continued to buy and manage real estate. This was perhaps a natural extension of my decision to buy my rented home years earlier when the landlady was ready to evict me and my loud parties and band practices.

Eventually I bought two hotel/restaurant/ski lodges in Vermont: Pico Bavarian Haus and Austrian Haus. I also bought a bankrupt newspaper, a defunct luxury car manufacturing company, a printing company, and a graphic arts and typesetting company. I produced ski shows in Rochester and Syracuse and got into theater production. Stay tuned for details.

For a farm boy from Randallsville whose whole life was the farm, Boy Scouts and Mary Lou in Utica, my prospects of ever seeing the world were pretty slim. I was as innocent and naive, just-off-the-farm as you could get, not to mention being grossly under-educated. And of course on the farm, we never had television or got a newspaper. My parents bought their first TV after I left home. Perhaps they had thought that I would not leave if they had a TV.

[Above] Pico Bavarian Haus near the Killington Ski Resort in Vermont. [Below] Austrian Haus, in West Dover, VT, offered skiers easy access to Mount Snow. [Opposite page] Pico and Austrian Haus deals, circa 1984. Art owned these lodges and ski resorts for years.

I quickly had my eyes opened that there was more to the world than the farm. Where I've been and what I've experienced around the world have truly amazed me. I believe everyone starts adulthood with a set of pluses and minuses. It's what one does with them that determines how life turns out.

So I'll start with how I started my retirement: real estate investor.

A DISAPPOINTMENT—NOT A MAJOR DISASTER— THAT COST ME A LOT OF MONEY

There I was, in the early 1970s and retired from working for anyone else. I had owned 6030 East Taft Road, a North Syracuse 26-unit apartment

complex, that I had named A-Z Estates, for several years. The Estates included two buildings with a lot of open land between them.

I decided to build an additional building on that land. It would be an upscale six-unit townhouse project. I hired an architect, applied for and got the necessary permits from the town, arranged bank financing, and hired a general contractor. This process took about a year.

I had a payloader come out and threw a big ground-breaking party. At the party, we cut the ribbon, took the first scoop of dirt, and entertained about 100 special guests.

A few days later, I got a call from the bank. Several of the bank's officers had been at the ground-breaking party. The person who called said that the economy was slowing down, and they could see a recession coming and were cancelling my financing.

I was never able to arrange other financing. And there was a recession. That land to this day sits vacant.

Several years later, I sold the complex to my friend, Dick Flaherty, who still owns it. I had painted all the exterior doors bright fire-engine red. For years, people identified it as the complex with all those red doors. I think the doors made it easy for people coming to look at an apartment to find the complex. Soon after Dick bought it, he repainted the doors an off-green. I still see Dick often and regularly (after 30 years) chide him about his yucky colored doors.

DICK FLAHERTY LIKES GREEN, AND A TO Z ESTATES

"One of Art's largest pieces of real estate as his portfolio grew was that 26-unit place that I eventually bought from him. I still suspect that he named it A to Z Estates because the alphabet has 26 letters. But it's fun to think he named it for his initials. Art lived in one of the ground-floor apartments. That was where he cut a hole in the floor and built a stairway to a party room in the basement. The floor was sealed off when I bought the building, but the door in the basement retained its sign that says A to Z Party Room. And this time it definitely is named for Art.

"At some of his other properties, the whole buildings were red, not just the doors. It was easy to find Art's apartments!

"I always identify properties by their street number. That one was 6030. At 6030, Art had a scooter again, descendant of the one he rode to all of his Army assignments. When Art had accumulated a lot of properties, he named them Castle One...Two...Three..."

LOWRY REAL ESTATE

Over the years, one thing I have done regularly is go to meetings or trade shows early and stay late. This was something I did—especially at trade shows—over the years for various businesses I owned. Frequently I would do a lot of business early on, when other exhibitors were still setting up. At the end of the day, I would be doing business as others had already left. Some time back in the 1970s, there was an ad in the paper that Dr. Albert Lowry would conduct a seminar in Syracuse. Al Lowry had written two books on rental real estate investing and co-authored another with Bill Nickerson. The books were on the New York Times bestseller list for several years. So I signed up for the seminar.

I arrived at the meeting site, the Hotel Syracuse ballroom, very early. No one was there except a worker setting up the sound system. I offered to help. It turned out that the workman was Al Lowry himself. I got a 45-minute one-on-one meeting with him. As a result, Dr. Lowry appointed me to the board of directors of the national Lowry-Nickerson Real Estate Association. As a member, I received about six all-expenses-paid trips to California for board meetings. I also received permission to organize a local Lowry Real Estate club for people interested in real-estate investing. I was president of the club for several years, with the membership growing to over 100 members. Between the national board and local club, I learned a great deal that helped me create my own real estate business, which grew to be worth several million dollars.

And it was all because I went to a meeting early. Maybe it was from being used to getting up at 4 a.m. when I worked on the farm in Randallsville....

I became the East Coast rep on the National Lowry Real Estate Foundation. I had developed my own real estate holdings into about 200 rental units.

WHERE THERE'S SMOKE...

Long ago—I can't remember just when, but I think around 1970—there was an organization in Syracuse called Concerned Citizens for Better Housing. It was basically a group of landowners (landlords) who got together each month to discuss common problems and to try to improve the rental housing situation in Syracuse. I became a member and then president of the group.

It was our experience that the city government in general, and the housing code office in particular, was very corrupt. Code officers would demand payments in cash to issue required certificates of occupancy. If a landlord refused payment, the code officer would write up lots of code violations that did not exist. When a code officer asked me for a cash payment, I informed him that it was illegal. His answer was, "My boss, Mayor Lee Alexander, takes kickbacks, so we do also." Alexander later went to jail. I feel strongly that, to this day, Syracuse has not recovered from the economic damage he created.

Soon after, I sold all my property in the city and practiced real estate investment only outside the city limits, as I would not pay bribes.

Lee Alexander was, in my opinion, the very worst mayor ever in the history of Syracuse. The gullible people of Syracuse kept electing him. Most city residents were Democrats, and Lee was a demigod. They knew he was a crook, but they kept electing him anyway.

Part of his game was that in those days of the 'Great Society', Washington, D.C. was passing out billions of dollars to the country's cities. Lee would go to D.C. and get photographed receiving a check, then come home and tell the people of Syracuse that theirs was the only city getting all the money—and that they got it solely because of his efforts. And the people swallowed it hook, line and sinker.

Of course, he took a slice of it all.

A lot of the economic damage he did to Central New York stemmed from the fact that national companies that wanted to come to Syracuse and create jobs stayed away because they knew City Hall was corrupt. It was common knowledge.

Later on, I knew people in the DA's office who told me they knew Lee was a crook, and they conducted two major investigations over the years, but could never get court-admissible proof.

The feds finally nailed him and sent him to jail when one of his bag men made a big mistake on his tax return. The man was given a choice: got to jail or wear a wire to a meeting with Lee and his fellow crooks. He chose the latter, and the feds finally had their proof.

In a show of how arrogant he could be, Alexander returned to Syracuse after prison and got a job as a maitre d' at a restaurant next to City Hall—where he had ripped off taxpayers for 16 years.

Looking back, I guess what Lee did was minor stuff compared to the extensive crimes committed by elected officials in Albany and D.C. these days. And guess what? The voters still reelect these crooks to office, knowing they are crooks. I don't understand it.

Back to Concerned Citizens. We decided to invite the head of the housing office to a meeting to discuss our concerns. About a dozen of us, including my friend and fellow landlord John Murphy (yes, the John Murphy who brought down a very popular District Attorney) joined together at Mr. Mike's Restaurant on Wolf Street in Syracuse (remember that terrific, blind organ player, Al Rando, who played for years at Mr. Mike's?). Also at the meeting was Morris Goldfeld, a city landlord.

The next day, the Post-Standard published an article about a fire the previous evening at the city code office. A couple of years later, Morris Goldfeld was indicted for arson. At his trial, a few things came out. When an apartment building that Morris owned got a lot of code violations—most created by the tenants or a code officer—and the kickback payments got expensive, Morris would just burn the building down and collect the insurance. That would end the code problems. It was determined that Morris torched about 200 buildings. Also at the trial it came out that Morris had ordered the fire-bombing of the code office as we were having dinner with the chief code officer.

I LOSE A FAVORITE PROPERTY

Probably the biggest disaster I ever had was the loss of one of my Vermont ski lodges in 1987. The Pico Bavarian Haus was a large, beautiful motel, restaurant, and ski lodge located in central Vermont, right at the base of the Pico/Killington ski area.

It was the kind of place that you would see in a movie about luxury skiing in the Alps. It had a large lobby/lounge with 40-foot cathedral ceilings and a massive stone fireplace, over 30 feet wide; three fire pits, stone soaring all the way up the top of the cathedral ceiling, and a dining room that seated a hundred people, with walls of windows that looked right out on the mountain. One night we hosted the United States Ski Writers' Association and served a sit-down dinner to 134 people. The lodge also had a large bar and cocktail lounge and swimming pool. It was a fabulous place.

And I treasure my memories of the people I met or worked with because of my time there. Maria von Trapp was one such person. She was one of the most interesting, accomplished, and famous people I've ever met and become friends with. She of course was not Julie Andrews. The wonderful things she did in her life happened mostly after the end of the movie, The Sound of Music, which was based on her family's life.

I was operating the Pico Bavarian Haus at the Killington Ski Resort and another at Mt. Snow when I met Maria at a resort trade association meeting. She operated the Trapp Family Lodge near Stowe, Vermont, about two hours north of my Pico/Killington resort. We developed a friendship and I would have dinner with her every month or two for several years.

The stories she told me about the interesting life she had! I always thought another movie should be made called The Sound of Music After Austria. A glimpse of that life can be had by reading her book, The Trapp Family Singers. The first half of the book covers the time the movie covered, although Hollywood took many liberties with the actual story. The second half of the book covers her life and accomplishments after her family left Austria.

Another such person was Adam Kaufman, my friend and great supporter of the Onondaga Ski Club. He was a native of Austria who owned a ski shop in Syracuse and then in Oran. He asked me about helping a friend of his whose daughter and her girlfriend, young college students who were studying Hospitality in order to have careers in that industry, wanted to come to the U.S. to work a semester at a resort. They had had no luck finding a place to work. I said I'd bring them over to work at my Vermont Bavarian Haus Lodge. They added European flair to the place, plus they had a fabulous time and added a lot to the experience for my hotel guests.

But that era of my life ended sadly. I suspected one of my employees at the Bavarian Haus had been stealing, and I was gathering evidence to prove it. While this was going on, the lodge burned to the ground and the employee disappeared. It was definitely arson, but the police said that without court-admissible proof, there was not much they could do to indict anyone.

On the April evening of the fire, Shirley and I were in Syracuse meeting with Father Peter Conroy, discussing plans for our wedding (much to his

RUTLAND HERALD

INSIDE: Body of Ludlow Drowning Victim Recovered

ESTABLISHED IN 1794

VOL. 131 – NO. 84   COPYRIGHT   RUTLAND, VERMONT, WEDNESDAY MORNING, APRIL 8, 1987

Blaze Destroys Pico Bavarian Haus

By STEVE ROSENFELD

Fire engulfs Pico Bavarian Haus in Sherburne Tuesday. The 42-room motel was destroyed. (More photos, Page 17)

(Photo by Vyto Starinskas)

surprise, as we had met just three months earlier). When we got back to Shirley's apartment about 10 p.m., there were a dozen panicked phone messages from John Jablonski, my partner in the Rapid Graphics printing company, alerting me that there had been a fire at Pico.

The insurance company covered the mortgage, and the sale of the land to the Killington ski area covered all the other outstanding expenses. So I came out of it just about even. I had planned to rebuild, but local political opposition stonewalled me for a year. So I sold the land. It turned out to be a good thing, because at the end of the year, just as I would have been opening a new hotel, the country went into a major recession that would last for two years. The Vermont ski industry suffered very badly, and many ski lodges in the Northeast went out of business. Surprisingly, after 27 years, that land is still vacant, even though Killington paid over $250,000 for it. Today, with inflation, that would be close to a million dollars.

MERRILL LYNCH AND I DISAGREE

Going back to the 1980s in my real estate career, I was putting together deals to buy and sell various businesses and properties. I would accumulate money in a savings account and then as needed I would transfer money to a checking account.

About that time Merrill Lynch came out with a new program that is common today, but was unheard of back then. It was a savings account that you could also use to write checks. Back in those days, savings accounts paid interest of around ten percent. Also, remember that to borrow money, interest rates were 15-20 percent and credit card interest could be over 25 percent. Definitely not the good old days.

So I opened a Merrill Lynch account. Sometimes the account would be dormant, with a balance of just $200 for six to eight months. Then when I got ready to close another deal, the account could have several hundred thousand dollars in it. At one point the account had not been used for several months, and I was thinking of completing another deal. I called Merrill Lynch to check on the balance. They said, "You have a balance of $12,000." I said, "There must be a mistake. There should be about $200 in the account. Please check it out and call me back." I was very busy and forgot about it for a few days. Then I remembered that Merrill Lynch had not called. I called and asked for my balance. It was $26,000. Again I said that there was a mistake and requested that they check it out and call me back. Again, no call back.

Let's make a long story short. Week after week I called and started to ask for a supervisor. Each week the balance was larger, and no one called back. The balance got up to $186,000. I was getting upset that no one would ever call back. So I decided to get their attention. I wrote a check for $186,000 and deposited it in a Marine Midland account I had (remember Marine Midland–that bank name is long gone, but not because of this).

I was sure that in a few days I would get a call from Marine Midland that the check bounced or I would get a call from Merrill Lynch. Two weeks passed with no call from anyone. I went into Marine Midland, and they said, "Yes, your check cleared. The money is in your account."

Finally, a couple of weeks later, I got a call: "This is Merrill Lynch. You have a problem with your account." I said I had no problem; perhaps *they* had one, and hung up the phone. Through about five more calls I would just repeat, "*You* have a problem, not me," and hang up. By the fourth and fifth calls, all the obscenities the Merrill Lynch person used would have embarrassed a drunken sailor.

The next day played out like a scene from a cheap gangster movie: two big, burly guys who looked and talked like movie thugs walked into my office at the Syracuse New Times and said, "We are from Merrill Lynch, and if you know what is good for you, you will give us the money." I told them to get out, or I would call the police. They left.

I talked to my friend and attorney, the late John Kenny. John said that I couldn't keep the money and suggested that I give it back right away. He has a gift for understatement.

At this point, Shirley and I had been married only a short time. Shirley had lived "under a rock" (her term) in the sheltered world of education. She was getting very upset over all of this and kept saying to give the money back.

This all happened while we were living in a farmhouse out in the country near Otisco Lake. The next night after the 'thugs' visited my office, a helicopter suddenly approached our home and hovered low, directly over our property, and put a powerful spotlight on the house. It stayed for almost a full hour. Shirley was a nervous wreck. She kept saying that they would kill us if I didn't give the money back.

I could have played the game out longer, but I didn't want to drive Shirley crazy. After all, living with me might do that anyway. So the next day, when a very nasty Merrill Lynch person called, I said, "Okay, I'll put the money back in my Merrill Lynch account, and you will have to illegally take it out." I did, and *they* did.

A couple of weeks later, I got a call from a Merrill Lynch representative, "We want the interest on that money." Politely I suggested that he go to hell and hung up. Remember this was almost 30 years ago, when $186,000 was equal to almost $500,000 today. I never heard another thing. I closed the account.

Several months later, I heard rumors of several Merrill Lynch executives under investigation for fraud and money laundering. Apparently incompetence is not an indictable offense. But if the American people knew just how frequent and serious are the criminal activities by executives in big banks, big insurance companies, and big government, I think they would be glad to pay higher taxes to build more jails and put them all away.

The New Times

First, let me clear up a legend that I may or may not have helped establish. When I decided to buy the paper, I did make a U-turn on Route 81, just before Lafayette, to return to Syracuse and finalize the deal. I DID like the idea of moving my moribund ski column, that had recently been (ski)booted from the Post-Standard, to my newly purchased newspaper. I made that transfer and continued to write the column for another six or seven years.

My ski column, which benefited greatly from the excellent editing of Syracuse newspaper editors, qualified me for membership in the U.S. Ski Writers' Association. This group has the enviable task of visiting and reviewing ski venues all over the country and the world. This involves much free travel, lavish entertainment hosted by eager resort owners, and all the perks such a lofty pulpit might offer.

But my writing skills were what you'd expect from my high school record and adventures since. My first editor, Bob Atkinson, worked magic on my words. But when he moved upstairs at the paper, his replacement took one look at the tortured prose and said, "NO."

I was almost 50 when I bought the Syracuse New Times (SNT), which I published for 26 years. As a marketing tool for all my businesses, I always kept my "brand" in the public eye; when I bought the weekly paper, I was the New Times and the New Times was me. I was at every kind of community event almost every day and night.

Dick Flaherty agrees:

"For the 50+ years I've known him, the over-riding business passion of Art's career has been publishing and public relations—PR. From the Schussboomer newsletter for the Ski Club forward, and starting businesses, those two passions figured heavily in all he did. There was a thread of interest and the ability to start any sort of thing. Then he'd get it running with his added interest in writing and publishing. He always produced flyers to promote everything he did.

"We would have discussions about engineering vs. PR, and we came to an agreement: with the best engineering and no PR, a project fails. Mediocre engineering with good PR can often succeed. A good example of this is Beta tapes. We both agreed that the Beta tapes were a better product, better technology, than VHS tapes. But VHS tapes were marketed better.

"The ability to start a business and get it going is rare. Running a business, in comparison, is easy. But starting out is a real trick. Getting it to be self-sustaining takes a set of unique skills, and Art has them. He has always impressed me; some people have a flurry around them and don't get much done, but Art is quieter and gets more results."

I wanted the New Times to become famous as something different and special, so I had to be, too. At events, I always wore colorful ascots. Actually I wore an ascot every day, at a time when no one else in town wore an ascot cravat. I always wore bright colorful sports jackets so I would stand out in any crowd, and I always wore a large lapel pin that said New Times. It was all part of the success of the New Times.

I took the newspaper from one publication under 2,000 copies a week to about 15 newspapers, magazines, and program books, with up to 88,000 copies for special issues. We became the largest weekly newspaper in New York State outside of New York City.

One of my favorite ascots, presented to me by the staff of the New Times at an anniversary party. Note the lapel pin I always wore. It was just good marketing. An example: I'm in line at the bank, someone sees the pin and says, "I have a business. Should I advertise in the New Times?" Within an hour, an ad representative from SNT was calling on them. Similar things happened many times.

When I acquired the New Times in 1984, it was bankrupt. Except for the IRS, I had no legal responsibility to pay any old debts. I took them on—six months' back rent, the unpaid print bills, the unpaid salaries, miscellaneous debts around town.

In all my business life, I have tried always to make sure everyone got a better deal than I; I do not believe the old win-win scenario. For me it's win-win/win: two wins for you, one for me. I paid every back bill the SNT owed and, for the next 26 years as owner of the New Times, no one could ever say they did not get a good deal from AZ and the SNT. And, at one time or another, and often for years, we sponsored or co-sponsored most every community event in CNY.

Long-time editor Mike Greenstein remembers those days, when he worked at the paper as managing editor under Roland Sweet:

"I read my 2003 quote from a letter I wrote about Art to the Syracuse Chamber of Commerce's Small Business Person of the Year nominating committee in 2003 ('When the newspaper was about to cease publication in 1984, Art's business acumen and entrepreneurial vision resurrected the newspaper and enabled it to become the award-winning journalistic enterprise it is today.'), and I would say the same thing now. The New Times would have died in 1984 if Art had not bought it.

"While Ed Green had been part of a group that once owned The New Times (with Ken Simon), by then the owner was Time-Advocate, part of the Advocate papers based in Springfield, Massachusetts. Geoff Robinson was the Advocate person who was in charge, with Peter Orville as local publisher. He is now an attorney in Vestal, last I knew.

"The mood among the editorial holdovers at that point was optimistic skepticism. Art had saved the paper, but none of us knew him or what to expect. At his first meeting with us he wore a Nehru jacket (to demonstrate, he said, that he never threw anything away). He could have thrown us out, but didn't. He knew Kathy Kane, who worked in the office and became his right-hand person, and then he hired Roland Sweet as editor. I worked there as a writer and an editor, but I really didn't deal with him directly until Roland moved to New Orleans at the end of 1985 and I became editor, and then only because Kathy Kane told him I was OK."

Roland, who died recently, also remembered the New Times' early struggles in an earlier conversation:

"My three stints as editor coincided with the paper's repeatedly being on its last legs: once when Ken Simon owned it (and the offices were downtown), just before Ken moved to Armory Square and named Molly and the late Steve Moss as co-editors; again when Peter Orville was the publisher and the Advocate Group owned it; and after Art bought it. Mike was editor in the early 1970s, managing editor with me and then took over when I left in December 1985.

"Art was a legitimate community and cultural booster who brought financial stability and even a measure of prosperity to the paper. If anyone ever gets around to writing a history of the New Times itself, he'll certainly merit a few chapters."

Jim Mackillop got his first byline in the New Times in 1972. In 1984 he started writing for the Post-Standard as well. He started writing the New Times music and theater reviews in Fall 1987.

"I was with Roland Sweet and Mike Greenstein at the meeting when we met Art. They were professionals; they accepted what having a new owner/publisher could mean to editors, but for some staff members, hearing that the paper had been SOLD was unsettling. As for myself, I was a professor at OCC; I wouldn't be totally out of work if he dumped all of us. But I was very interested in meeting him when he requested a summit at a downtown restaurant near the Hotel Syracuse.

"Now that I know him, I can tell you that he is not frightened at all. Ever. But his demeanor looks tentative, sort of deferential, when he enters a room. Art bought the paper in August 1984, and I remember the date we met: Wednesday, August 8 that year. It was also the night President Reagan, we learned later, signed the Iran Contra deal.

"After introductions, Art got down to business. 'Others see the New Times as a failure,' he said. 'I see an opportunity.' He outlined his resume at Brown Newspapers, Nabisco, Onondaga Ski Club, and the paper's own annual ski supplement. His message: The paper is hurting because of debt. I think I can turn it around into a going concern."

How did I get everything done, now that I owned a newspaper? I would get up at 4 a.m. (just like the old farm days) and drive to the Austrian Haus, my hotel, restaurant, and ski lodge at Mount Snow, Vermont. That's about a four- hour trip. I would arrive about 8 a.m. and work until noon. I'd meet with the manager, staff, as needed with accountant or lawyer, work on planning, marketing campaigns, and inspecting the property.

At noon, I would drive north an hour and a half to the Pico Bavarian Haus, my other hotel, restaurant, ski lodge, and repeat what I had done in the morning. At 4 p.m., I would drive back to Syracuse, arriving at the New Times office about 9 p.m. I'd take care of what was on my desk in about two hours, drive to Camillus and do the same at my Rapid Graphics print shop office, drive to Tully's Village Edge Apartment complex and do the same, then drive home for an hour or two in my home office...and to bed by 3 a.m.

Feb. 25, 2004

As *The New Times* rockets upward and onward, Shirley and I just fasten our seat belts for the wonderful ride. Yes, 2004 marks the 35th year of *The New Times* and the 20th anniversary of my purchase of the paper. Little did I imagine in 1984 the wonderful monster I was creating.

For the past few years I have delegated to the staff the complete control of day-to-day operations of *The New Times*. They have responded by making *The New Times* the most popular newspaper in all of upstate New York. All of Central New York can be proud of the national-level reputation of *The New Times'* quality and excellence. Proof of that is the 500-plus awards for excellence that all departments of *The New Times* have won nationally, locally and at the state level over the years. It is very gratifying when I meet with out-of-state visitors to hear them say, "I wish we had an excellent paper like the *Syracuse New Times* in our city."

What I am most proud of, however, are the 98 community nonprofit and charity groups that the newspaper has assisted in various ways over the past few years (see box, page 14). We are really one of the major "do-good" businesses in Central New York.

So each week I send out 46,000 **thank yous** to our loyal readers and advertisers for making *The New Times* the tremendous success it is and will continue to be.

Thank You,
Art Zimmer

Feb. 24, 1999

As the years fly by and the success and popularity of *The New Times* continues to grow, I am constantly amazed at the huge positive effect the paper has had on the entire Onondaga County community.

More than 136,350 fiercely loyal readers seek out every issue of *The New Times* at more than 650 outlets throughout Central New York. Our biggest problem each week remains getting enough copies of the Syracuse area's most popular newspaper into the hands of everyone who wants it.

It is now hard to imagine that 15 years ago I purchased *The New Times* out of bankruptcy. The paper was going under for the third and final time, and the chances of success were almost zero. When you talk about the phoenix rising from the ashes of disaster to soar to phenomenal heights of success, that is *The New Times'* story.

So what do the next few years hold for *The New Times*? I'm confident that our talented and dedicated staff will find ways to match and exceed our past successes, including winning awards of excellence on the national, state and local levels.

Readers will continue to flock to our pages in even greater numbers, using our advertisements to guide their life's activities and thus continuing to make *The New Times* the best advertising buy for all the businesses in Central New York.

On a personal note, I am putting my money where my mouth is. I keep preaching that Central New York is a wonderful place to live. I'm not taking my success and fleeing South. Instead, I am building a new home at the edge of the city and plan to remain here and do what I can to help make the greater Syracuse area an even better place to live.

In closing, I say thank you to everyone for everything and ask, "Do you want to by a Zimmer Golden Spirit automobile from me?"

And yes, the car company is going well.

Art Zimmer
Publisher

Feb. 2, 1994

When I purchased the *Syracuse New Times* 10 years ago, I was very optimistic about its possibilities for growth and success. I must admit, however, that I was not prepared for what happened. The phenomenal growth and success that the *Syracuse New Times* has achieved in the past several years has exceeded my most optimistic dreams. I can only say it has been phenomenal, exciting and fun.

The New Times' success has come about primarily because of three groups of people, and I sincerely wish to thank each and every one of them. In one group are the business owners and managers of Central New York. Their loyalty in providing consistent paid advertising to the *Syracuse New Times* has made the paper a profitable and stable business.

In another group are the hard-working, dedicated and professional staff that produces the most popular newspaper in Central New York every week. This small group of highly motivated people does a great job of serving the needs of both the reader and advertiser throughout Onondaga County and surrounding areas.

In the last group are you, the readers, the public of the greater Syracuse area. Your loyalty and dedication to finding a copy of the *Syracuse New Times* every week and using it as your personal source for news, entertainment, dining, shopping and recreation is deeply appreciated. You have truly made the *Syracuse New Times* everyone's favorite newspaper.

If you, the readers, keep responding to *New Times* advertising in the future as you have in the past, it will ensure that our staff can continue to bring you a FREE high-quality newspaper every week.

Thank you, one and all, who have contributed to 25 years of publishing excellence.

Sincerely,
Art Zimmer

Some of my publisher's notes were reprinted in the paper's 35th anniversary edition in 2004. **Opposite page**: political leaders were frequent visitors at the paper. Top: Syracuse Mayor Tom Young; bottom: State Sen. Nancy Larraine Hoffmann at the 20th anniversary party of my ownership of the paper. I told the mayor at that event that I was buying the Syracuse New Times building because the corrupt former mayor (Lee Alexander) was gone.

Proclamation

from

Senator Nancy Larraine Hoffmann

In honor of the extraordinary
ART ZIMMER

Whereas, it has been my policy to bestow honor and accolades upon those individuals in the community who have enriched it by their presence and contributions; and

Whereas, we are gathered this evening to celebrate both the presence and the contributions of a most extraordinary individual in our midst; and

Whereas, the stated purpose of this event is to commemorate the twentieth anniversary of the publication of the *Syracuse New Times* under the leadership of Art Zimmer; and

Whereas, such description is rather like celebrating Sir Edmund Hillary's conquest of Mount Everest as "a pleasant hike;" and

Whereas, Art Zimmer is absolutely unique, having excelled in numerous diverse enterprises, ranging from the purchase and steady growth of the *New Times*, to the creation of his Zimmer Motor Car Company, and other commercial and artistic endeavors too numerous to mention; and

Whereas, Art has accomplished all of his successes with style and élan, although any one of these undertakings would daunt most people; and

Whereas, we have learned from experience with Art that the question, "What's new?" is not rhetorical -- he is likely to have at least one new project cooking; and

Whereas, Art absolutely defines the phrase, "Lead, follow or get out of the way," by clearly leading in so many fields he has become the modern Renaissance Man; now therefore be it

Resolved, that we pause in our daily lives to celebrate the extraordinary life of Art Zimmer, and

Resolved, that this document be presented to Art Zimmer on the occasion of the celebration of the Twentieth Anniversary of his publication of the *Syracuse New Times*.

Senator Nancy Larraine Hoffmann
49th Senate District

May 5, 2004
Date

Citation

from

Senator John A. DeFrancisco

SALUTING ART ZIMMER ON THE 25TH ANNIVERSARY OF OWNERSHIP OF THE SYRACUSE NEW TIMES

WHEREAS, Art Zimmer, Owner of The Syracuse New Times, is celebrating his 25th Anniversary of Ownership in 2009; and

WHEREAS, Art Zimmer took ownership of the New Times when it was teetering on the brink of bankruptcy and turned it into a respected and vital publication that serves Central New York; and

WHEREAS, In 1984, the plight of the New Times had come to the attention of Art Zimmer; Zimmer was an area businessman who also wrote a winter ski column that had just been dropped by another local paper; and

WHEREAS, Once he gained ownership of the Syracuse New Times, Art Zimmer increased circulation by investing in a growing professional staff on both the editorial and publishing sides of the business and resumed his wintertime column; and

WHEREAS, As his weekly newspaper grew, so, too did Art Zimmer's investment; in 1986, the Syracuse New Times relocated to its own building located at 1415 West Genesee Street - the former Olum Furniture Store; in the years that followed, additional investments were made to produce the Syracuse New Times in a modern, state of the art computerized facility; and

WHEREAS, Today, the Syracuse New Times looks back to its modest beginnings and the 40 years of growth that have led to sales of more than two million dollars a year and a payroll of more than 30 full-time employees and a dozen freelance contributors; now, therefore, be it

RESOLVED, That I, John A. DeFrancisco, New York State Senator from the 50th District, offer my sincere congratulations to The Syracuse New Times publisher Art Zimmer on the occasion of his 25th Anniversary of ownership, with the hope that this outstanding weekly newspaper enjoys continued success; and be it further

RESOLVED, That a copy of this citation, suitably engrossed, be presented to Art Zimmer and the Syracuse New Times.

John A. DeFrancisco
New York State Senator
50th District
Dated: September 9, 2009

This was a pretty standard routine three days a week until the Pico Bavarian Haus burned down. The other four days per week would involve extended hours at each and every one of my Syracuse area offices.

By then I had met Shirley, and life had changed. After we married in 1987, Shirley and I would always be in the New Times office by 7:30 a.m., as we wanted to set the example for the staff and be first in... but Lesli Mitchell was always there before we were. People would ask why Lesli was the most successful sales rep in the area. Always being in the office by 7 a.m. probably helped a lot.

We had a production manager who was not working out and needed to make a change quickly. There was no one we could promote into the position. At that point, Shirley had been manager of circulation and distribution for a year. The department was running well, and she had trained an assistant. So Shirley moved over to take over production, under protest as she had no technical knowledge or training on how to produce a newspaper. We were also short on staff in that department. For over a year, every Monday and Tuesday (deadline days), Shirley and I would work until midnight; then we would go across the street to Dennys and have supper—or was it breakfast?—and get home by 2 a.m. Other days we worked only until 8 or 9 p.m.

A lot of work, a lot of hours, yes; but that is typical of most business owners. I was fortunate, as Shirley worked those hours along with me for over 20 years.

During the 26 years I owned the New Times—1984 to 2010—we went through three recessions. In those downtimes, most businesses laid off people and cut back on services. I'm very proud of the fact that I never laid off one person. When things got tight, Shirley and I took no pay. In one recession our janitor left. Instead of replacing him, Shirley and I just worked later at night and on weekends. We cleaned the toilets, mopped and vacuumed, and took out the garbage.

I FOUGHT THE LAW...

The upside of working long hours as the owner of a business is that you can also give yourself little breaks. One nice warm day while I was in my New Times office, I decided to go out for a walk. The West Genesee Street office is near Solvay. I was walking down the sidewalk in Solvay, and I noticed a Solvay police car approaching me. The window was open, and the officer was on a cell phone, laughing loudly and sort of rocking back and forth like he had just heard a good joke. As he came alongside me, I smiled and said that if I was driving and talking on a cell phone (actually impossible as I've never had a cell phone or computer), you would give me a ticket.

He sort of veered over the center line and slammed on his brakes. The car behind him almost plowed into him. The officer jumped out of the car. I had kept walking. He ran over to me, leaving the car door open and blocking both lanes of traffic. He told me that the law allowed police to use cell phones and drive. I said yes, but probably only for official business in an emergency. He said, "Well, I think you had better come down to headquarters with me, and I'll show you the law." I said to myself that this could be trouble. So I said nothing and kept walking slowly.

Now his car was blocking a long line of traffic. Already about a dozen cars were backed up in each direction. A couple of drivers started to blow their horns. The police officer looked back and returned to his cruiser. I quickly walked around the corner, ducked into a store, and stayed there for a while. That afternoon, I decided to report what happened to the Solvay police headquarters. I called and told the officer who answered what had happened. He said that the officer was right and that I was lucky he hadn't arrested me for harassment.

Another incident wasn't exactly a brush with the law. I was a volunteer for a nonprofit fundraiser that simulated locking me up in jail. Then I called all my friends to bail me out with a generous donation to the charity. I did a lot of these over the years for various groups. It was a very popular and effective fundraiser for many organizations.

For this particular fundraiser, I called my friend John Murphy (yes, the John Murphy who brought down a sitting DA). John was the chief investigating officer in the district attorney's office. John knew the jail and Public Safety Building very well. When I called, John was not home, but his teenaged niece was there. I asked her to tell John that his friend Art was in jail, needed bail, and to call this number. A little later, John came home, got the message but did not call. He rushed down to the jail to find me. After a couple of hours going through the city jail, the PSB and the county jail in Jamesville, and after calling the State police, he went home and finally called me.

That was probably 30 years ago, and I still kid John about it.

ME FOR LEE

Over the years, the New Times never endorsed candidates running for office. Except once. My philosophy is that news media should share information. And that's what the New Times did, presenting both sides of an issue or candidate, and letting the readers make up their own minds based on the facts. Today, facts are few and far between in politics.

I feel that if a newspaper tells its readers or a union tells its members how to vote by endorsing a candidate, in effect they are saying, "You are too stupid to make a proper decision, so we will make it for you and tell you how to vote by our endorsement."

My friend and colleague Norma Jean Young was an observer of how we ran the New Times:

"He surely figured out how to run a newspaper whose political leanings were well known—and not necessarily his own—for he turned a failing newspaper business into a highly successful publishing firm."

Almost 30 years ago, I was still putting on the Ski Show and Sale. I would take a week off and work putting the big show together at the State Fairgrounds. I would spend all day, all of that week, at the Center of Progress building. Even though I owned the paper, unlike most publishers, I kept hands off the editorial department.

That year, Tom Young was the director of the State Fair and was running for mayor of Syracuse. Monday, several of his campaign people came to see me at the Center of Progress building. They said they had heard rumors that the New Times was going to endorse a candidate for the mayoral race. They were concerned that Tom had not been contacted by the SNT editorial board for consideration. I told them that I would check into it, but that the New Times did not endorse candidates. They were quite surprised that I, the owner of the paper, did not seem to know what they thought was going on.

So I called Roland Sweet, my editor-in-chief. He said, "Yes, we are endorsing a candidate." I asked who. He said, "I can't tell you. It's an editorial secret."

Roland remembers that incident.

"I don't believe I informed Art ahead of time about the paper's write-in 'endorsement' of Lee Alexander. I don't even remember telling Joe Orsak, who drew Alexander's portrait for the cover, what it was for."

For the next couple of days I was visited at the Fairgrounds by Tom Young and various political leaders, all very concerned. The New Times was the most popular newspaper in Central New York, and Walt Shepperd, our political editor, was considered the number-one political media person in the area.

Wednesday morning, publication day, everyone—including me—rushed out to get a copy of the New Times. Sure enough, the entire front page was a Joe Orsak illustration of Lee Alexander and a headline pushing a write-in campaign: Lee for Mayor. By that time, everyone knew Lee was going to jail. I think it was one of the biggest jokes—or maybe it was a hoax—in the political history of Syracuse.

Of course, Tom won, but Lee did get a lot of write-in votes. I heard recently that even now, almost two decades after his death, Lee still gets write-in votes in every Syracuse mayoral contest. And Roland won an award:

"I still have the Syracuse Press Club Award for 'Best Newspaper Editorial' for the Alexander endorsement. The award was made in 1986. Mike submitted the article after I'd left, so he was editor when the award was given."

I kept my nose out of the paper's content in other ways. Roland Sweet said, "I worked for Art from when he bought the paper in summer 1984 until I left in December 1985. He supported my efforts (or at least never interfered with them), but he and I had very little interaction, so I'm sure our recollections of this period differ significantly. I remember writing an editorial in my first or second issue addressing Art's reputation as a political conservative as it pertained to buying a radical-cum-alternative-cum-liberal-cum-bankrupt weekly newspaper. I don't recall what exactly I said, but I endorsed the move. I might even have used the term 'laissez-faire,' although I wouldn't bet on it — 'hands-off,' maybe.

"I do recall that at some point the daily paper [the Post-Standard] dropped the popular comic strip "Bloom County.' I decided to pick it up and approached Art because I needed money that wasn't in my budget. He admitted liking 'Bloom County' and gave me the go-ahead. The deal didn't last long because once we started touting that the strip was running in the New Times, the daily told the syndicate it wanted it back, and the syndicate kowtowed. But I appreciated Art's backing."

Walt Shepperd reminded me about two questions I did raise, even while keeping my hands off the editorial department. I always had my own opinions on things, but I kept them to myself. The world would be better off if others did the same. Over 26 years, I put my foot down only twice with the editorial department. Once I objected when we published a pot brownie recipe. And once I objected to coverage that I considered to be disrespectful of our American soldiers.

"That was when the Gulf War began," Walt remembers. "I thought Art was objecting to our coverage of the war itself, but later I found out he didn't want to create the impression that we were in any way criticizing members of the U.S. military."

Mike Greenstein also remembered my two objections, to a point. "Certainly after the brownie recipe, Art made it clear where lines were drawn, and I remember few controversies beyond that regarding censoring of content. I'm not recalling at all any clash surrounding Gulf War opposition. When Art and I disagreed, it was more likely to be about his promotion of his other endeavors, such as when he and his auto company graced the cover. When we disagreed, he won, and I continued. For the most part, he didn't meddle or influence editorial agenda. Regarding his laissez-faire policy toward editorial content, I would largely agree. Without 'editorials' per se, there wasn't really much of a political agenda to set. We could be everybody's pal."

I can say that I was much more "hands-on" when it came to the nuts and bolts of owning a newspaper. When I bought the New Times, we were still downtown, something of pioneers in Armory Square.

As Jim Mackillop points out,
"The New Times at 406 South Franklin Street was as much of an
Armory Square pioneer as Pastabilities."

Two years after I bought the paper, it was growing and prospering. One
of our growing pains was the need for more space. I decided to buy my own
building to house its offices, rather than continuing to pay rent. I settled on a
24,000-square-foot historic office building on the near west side, on the edge
of downtown Syracuse at 1415 West Genesee Street. We moved in 1986 and
it's still occupied by the SNT today.

And even though Shirley can tell you that I sit down at our computer
only when she insists there is a message or file I need to review, I knew right
away that we needed to keep an eye on the rapidly changing world of print
media and production.

Dick Flaherty remembers that:
"At the New Times, even though he personally isn't a computer person,
Art pushed for converting to computerization, and effected two or three
re-dos on digital media for the paper. Leading-edge 'stuff' has always
interested him. Not all of it works, but he's open to trying."

Leading-edge "stuff" indeed. Before we moved to our new location on
West Genesee Street, I drew up plans for a major renovation of the top floor,
where the New Times would operate, hired an architectural firm to draw up
blueprints and oversee the renovation, and hired a contractor to do the work.
Then I departed for a four-week ski trip (it was August) to South America to
ski the Argentinean Andes Mountains. When people saw me walking through
the Syracuse Airport, it was 92 degrees. I was carrying my skis. I suspect they
were thinking that they now knew for sure, if they hadn't before, that Art
Zimmer was really crazy.

When I returned from my ski trip, it was early on a Monday morning. I
was in my office at the old building when Kathy Kane, my associate publisher,
who really ran the paper, came in and said, "Art, you better go over to the new
building." I said, "Yes, I'll go over this afternoon." Kathy said, "No, go over
now. The scanner just sent police and the fire department to the building."

When I got there, I discovered the meaning of the phrase "all hell broke loose." The workmen had taken down a wall that was not supposed to be removed, causing the ceiling to collapse. Remember, the building is over 100 years old. The ceiling supports were beams larger than railroad ties. When they came down, the workmen were hurt, but by some miracle no one was killed. The main sprinkler pipe split open. In about two minutes several hundred thousand gallons of water came pouring down from the attic, flooding two floors and turning the basement into a swimming pool.

The week before, a new tenant—Hair by Forar—had moved into that basement (I think they are still there, under a new name or new management). The contractor blamed the architect, and the architect blamed the contractor. The case dragged through the courts for over five years.

As an example of how stupid our legal system can be (actually smart lawyers making lots of money), after about three years of discussions, I went to one meeting where the architect and the architect's insurance company, the contractor and the contractor's insurance company, and my insurance company each had several lawyers present. There were 17 lawyers at the table, each probably billing $150 per hour. The meeting lasted three hours and accomplished nothing.

My insurance company promptly settled with me so renovations could continue, but now we were two months behind schedule. So I went to my soon-to-be-former landlord and said that we would need a couple of extra months before we could move. He said, "Sorry, I've already rented your space out and you need to move by the end of the month as per the original schedule." So I went and talked to the new tenants and asked for extra time. They said no, because their previous space had already been rented and they had to be out on schedule. So I talked to THOSE tenants, and they could delay moving, but only for about two weeks. That was a start.

The New Times was occupying two floors of the old location. I made a deal where we would move everything upstairs for two weeks, and the new tenants would get into the first floor. It would be a problem with everything in half the space, but better than being out on the street. But two weeks was still not enough time to get the renovation work done.

The work was further slowed down by the City of Syracuse. Inspectors demanded work be done that everyone agreed was totally unnecessary. But it was required.

We eventually moved into the new location. The SNT staff worked alongside the contractors in a constant cloud of dust and dirt and hammering, with noise all day long. Some of the female employees were entertained by and others were upset with the constant salty language they were exposed to from the workers.

We all got through it, and I actually ended up with a better building than I would have had otherwise.

But my trouble with paper pushers wasn't over. I could write a book about government harassment, but I'll give you just two examples so you'll have an idea of what I had to deal with on a regular basis.

There was a large freight elevator in the New Times building, which I always kept in great shape. An excellent company serviced it every six months. The City of Syracuse inspected it every year, and it always passed. One time the inspector found a minor problem. I said (confident in my years of owning real estate and renovating apartments), "I can easily fix that." But he replied, "No, it must be fixed by a certified technician and we need the paperwork to prove it."

I said, "Okay, I'll have my professional elevator maintenance company fix it." The city said, "No, it must be fixed by a city-approved company, and there is only one we approve of. And the work must be done in 30 days or you will be assessed a daily fine and we will shut the building down."

So I called the city-approved company, and they said they would be able to fix the elevator in three months; they had a huge backlog of work. "No no no," I said, "I have 30 days." They said, "No no no. Three months."

I called the city. "Sorry; 30 days or we close down your entire building and levy a daily fine." I called my friend and long-time lawyer, John Kenny. He got the city not to close the building, but the fine remained. I ended up paying thousands of dollars in fines and was listed by the city as a deadbeat.

A second example. One day I got a letter from the New York State Department of Labor. One of my independent contractors had filed for unemployment; there was just no work available. The State said the person should have been an employee, not an independent contractor, so I was up for a big fine. I went to John Kenny. "I know I'm right," I told him. "Please go to court on this for me."

He replied, "Don't waste your money on me; all the judges that handle these cases are employees of the State Department of Labor. They always rule against the business; makes no difference if you're right."

So I went to court myself. I had a copy of the actual state law that defines what an independent contractor is. I said, "Your Honor, here is the actual New York law that proves I'm right."

I started to read the law. Thirty seconds in, he said, "Mr. Zimmer, I've heard enough of this crap (his word). You are dismissed."

I said, "But your honor—"

He cut me off. "Bailiff, escort this man out or I'll put him in jail."

A week later I got a letter. I lost the case and was fined.

When you are running businesses, there are always unnecessary and expensive hassles with various levels of government. It has been my experience that about the only thing government does well is come up with ways to make running a business more difficult and expensive. There were some unqualified people in city government (Syracuse) and New York State who constantly caused me (and most other small businesses) lots of unnecessary work and expenses. If I had not had an abundance of government-caused unnecessary expense, I could have hired more employees, paid them better, and given them more benefits.

This has led me to believe that most businesses that move operations overseas don't necessarily want to; they are pushed there by our government. Unfortunately, in the past few years things have gotten much worse. I'm so glad to be 77 and able to retire.

I always worked through business problems by myself, with only Shirley's indispensable help after we met and married in 1987. Most of the employees never knew of the many unnecessary and expensive problems the various levels of government caused me, not just with the New Times, but also with most of my other businesses. I have found that this is true for most business owners everywhere.

One aspect of owning a business was always very positive for me. Over almost 50 years in business, with 11 businesses that had about 300 employees, I'm happy to say I had to fire only four people. A pretty good record, I think.

BUT WAS IT ART?

Once the New Times was settled in its new building, another problem arose. We had outgrown our typesetting and graphics machine capabilities. After a lot of research, mostly done by staff members, we decided on a system that I believe was an early Dell Computer product, the Quadex. It was the biggest, most modern system of its kind on the market, with the most bells and whistles. It was also the the most expensive at a quarter of a million dollars. We actually had to send people to Boston for a week to learn how to operate it.

Once the Quadex was installed and running at the New Times, I realized it had great capacity, far beyond our needs. It sat there unused half the time. So I decided to form a separate company and market high-end typesetting services to other businesses. We needed a name for the company. I cannot claim credit here. The staff came up with it. The company product was graphic arts and it was owned by Art. They came up with a play on the words reflecting a popular phrase of that time used in critiquing activist art: "But is it Art?" – Is it Art – and the name stuck. But we spelled it Izitart.

At the end of the first year, we had done a quarter million dollars in work (today probably close to a million), and the second year a half million. Everything was going great. I did the marketing for Izitart. I hired a separate staff to put out the work. Then a problem started.

The New Times newspaper was growing fast, plus we had started to publish other types of publications and a lot of free community work for non-profits. All the growth from the New Times and Izitart required the Quadex to run full-time and even some overtime. Soon conflicts started to arise over which jobs got priority.

I had to decide if I was in the publishing business or the typesetting business. Being the publisher of the most popular weekly newspaper in New York was a lot more fun and prestigious than owning a high-end typesetting company. Izitart had to go. In 1988, I closed it down.

It turned out to be the best decision ever. Within a year, a new system came on the market: desktop publishing. Anyone could buy a cheap computer (cheap compared to the $250,000 Quadex) and do all their own typesetting. Within a year, most typesetting companies were obsolete and out of business.

Technology quickly passed the Quadex by. The machine had served us well and had paid for itself several times over, but up to the attic it went. After a couple of years, I shed a tear and paid a junk man $100 to have it hauled away.

RAPID GRAPHICS

In 1984, I had several businesses and needed quite a lot of printing. My requirements included envelopes, stationery, flyers, promotional booklets, and more. And this was the year I bought the New Times. I started to use a print shop in Camillus called Rapid Graphics. The owner, John Jablonski, did good work, but there was a constant problem meeting deadlines. Finally, I said to John that I was taking my business somewhere else as my printing was so deadline driven.

John explained to me that his was a small one-person operation, working on a shoestring and always short of money. Frequently he could not afford to buy the paper to run my jobs until he collected from a couple of other jobs, and collection was difficult and time consuming.

He also said his partner, who was supposed to help run the business, had become inactive. John was not even sure if he would be able to stay in business much longer. I said, "You need a new partner. How about me?"

John said yes. The deal was that I would invest some money to build a stock of paper and clean up some bills. I would handle the administration, finance, sales, and marketing. John would operate the press room. This arrangement worked out well, and the company grew and prospered.

Within two years, we needed more space and wanted to be closer to downtown Syracuse. In 1986, we moved the entire operation to 6,000 square feet of space in the New Times building. This worked out particularly well for me, as now I had the New Times office upstairs and my Rapid Graphics office downstairs, which saved running out to Camillus all the time.

I was most proud of the fact that, for many years, Rapid Graphics did a lot of printing for free for many area non-profit charity groups. This allowed them to print more items in larger numbers at a higher quality than they could otherwise afford. It helped them to grow, prosper, and serve more people.

One day, Lucy Popkess came to me. Lucy was the president of the Syracuse Symphony Association. Later Shirley served on the Association's board. The Symphony Association sponsored the biggest gala event in Central New York, an annual Symphony ball, raising large amounts of money for the Symphony's operating expenses.

Lucy asked if Rapid Graphics could help with the invitations for the Symphony ball and other printing. So I put together the creative people in the New Times production department and the Rapid Graphics creative person. They designed a really fancy and unique invitation that would be expensive to print. The New Times and Rapid Graphics did the entire job for free. This continued for several years. Each year the team created a bigger and fancier invitation, which became the envy of every organization in town. The Symphony Association said that the ball invitations were so spectacular that they felt it actually helped increase attendance. And as there were no production costs for the Symphony, they were able to send out a lot more invitations than they otherwise could have afforded.

After a few years, I bought out John's share and became sole owner of Rapid Graphics. In two more years, the company had grown to about 10 employees. However, problems were developing. More and more of the printing jobs were four-color process work. It was difficult for us to be competitive because we had just a two-color press. Everything had to go through the press twice to produce four colors, so each job cost twice as much to run. This made it difficult to be competitive with print shops with four-color presses. It reached the point that I would have needed to invest almost half a million dollars to stay successful. And I was now overseeing the print shop. Running the business side was fine, but I really did not want to be a press operator. So in 1992 I closed the business down, sold everything off to other print shops, and rented the space in the New Times building out for more money.

CHAMBER MUSIC

Don't let my descriptions of interactions with and opinions of government agencies make you think I was not involved with anything but the New Times and my other businesses in Syracuse. I joined the Chamber of Commerce as soon as I could, and ended up chairperson of several of its initiatives, including the Buy Local committee. It was through this committee that I met and started to help quite a few people, including Peggy Piontkowski. Peggy had a business, and she had some problems that I helped her solve. The business became quite successful and very famous as "Sassy Scrubs." My part was minor, but I was happy to help where I could. A lot of it was practical advice and hand holding (figuratively).

Peggy had created a line of hospital uniforms she dubbed Sassy Scrubs. The uniforms became famous when they were used on the very popular television show of the era, "ER." Peggy, her husband Al, and adult daughter were invited to Hollywood to the show's production set to watch the filming of an ER episode. Peggy got to meet George Clooney and said that, next to meeting her husband, meeting George Clooney was the biggest thrill of her life. And he was wearing her scrubs!

Peggy then started to have some problems with the business that I tried to help her with, but we were not completely successful in solving them. Peggy retired, her husband retired from the state police, and they moved to Florida. We kept in touch, and one winter Shirley and I travelled over to where they were living, in the Melbourne area, and had lunch with Peggy and Al. We had fun rehashing the old days at the Chamber of Commerce.

I knew Peggy was having some health problems, but I did not realize just how serious they were until I got a call from her husband. He said, "Art, Peggy has only a few hours left to live. One of her requests is to talk to you and thank you for all you did." Then Al gave the phone to Peggy. After an emotional conversation, I began to realize just how big an impact I had made on some people's lives. Later, Al called me back and said that when Peggy finished our conversation, she smiled for the first time in a long time and said, "Okay, I'm ready to go." She passed away an hour later.

Peggy was a true "pay it forward" person before that term entered the popular vernacular. When Linda Pompo joined the Chamber of Commerce, Peggy related to her that she should request my input about her new business. As Linda relates her story,

"My husband had passed away a couple of years before I met Art at a Chamber of Commerce meeting. I had been trying to start a small errand service and this was an opportunity to get involved with other small business owners to announce my new business. I thought that many would need this service with their busy schedules. As I was networking, I noticed a very handsome man also working the room. He kept watching me. Soon the secretary of the Chamber came over to introduce me to Art Zimmer. She explained that he had helped many people start businesses in the Syracuse area.

"A very pleasant man, he invited me to his newspaper office to show me around and help with some of the questions I had about a new business and some of the contacts that I should make. He was so helpful, making me very comfortable. As private as my personal life was, I told him the story of the last two years without my wonderful husband. I was 48, very alone, and very scared, with the attitude that I had nothing to lose trying to start a business. But I knew that I needed help to do this right.

"Art talked me into joining the Chamber's Small Business Group. It met once a month. He introduced me to many people and took me to some of the productive people in and around Syracuse. I met Peggy, the creator of Sassy Scrubs, a wonderful woman who had had a hard life, but told me that meeting Art had helped her successfully start her own business. We became friends and during my working hours I would often get a phone call from Art to meet at Joey's restaurant for lunch with him and Peggy!

"My life was sad, for my husband and children were my whole world and now I felt I was alone and had lost my world, the love of my life. Art took a special interest in helping me, invited me to events with him and Shirley, and introduced me to many people. This may sound like a nice story, but Art changed my life for the better by encouraging me to focus on this project and concentrate on creating a better life for myself.

"I often wondered what would have happened to me, for my depression was overwhelming, if I hadn't met Art. He helped me to become confident, use my personality, have a goal, and stop being afraid of life. He did this very quietly, in his own way.

"I now live in Florida. I had the confidence to sell my Syracuse home, get in the car, and move here knowing that I could make the move alone and still be content. He taught me that any decision I made for the rest of my life I could accomplish on my own. Art was the Angel that I met; he saved my life and I will never in this lifetime find the words to thank him.

"Art has helped many people with business creations, but there is so much more to this man. He helps people daily with their lives and we don't realize that until we stop to take a look at ourselves and say "OH MY GOD" look at me and what I did.

"Remembering some of the stories that Art told me about his early days, one that I remember most was that he used Walt Disney as an example, telling me that Walt Disney failed seven times before he succeeded. I never forgot that bit of information. Art encourages without lecturing."

MY EXPENSIVE FREE HAIRCUTS

The owner of that once-flooded hair salon in the basement of the New Times building on West Genesee Street, Robert Silver, told me that he did men's haircuts as well as women's. I decided to get my hair cut there, but Robert refused to take any money. For several months, I kept trying to pay. He always refused the money.

After about a year, I just stopped trying to pay and got a free haircut for the next 20 years. This continued until Robert retired.

All those free haircuts were really quite expensive, because, since I was getting free haircuts from Robert, I was reluctant to raise the rent as often as I should have. When I did occasionally raise the rent, I never raised it as much as I should have. So all those free haircuts were really quite expensive in the long run. But I liked his work.

We must all hang together...

Soon after I bought the bankrupt New Times in 1984, I found out that there were similar newspapers in Buffalo, Rochester, Ithaca, and Albany. I got in touch with the other publishers and suggested that we get together informally to sit around and discuss common problems and share ideas to help one another.

I hosted the group in the New Times offices several times a year. I would put on a big lunch and feed the entire staff at the same time. Things worked out so well that we started to sell advertising to regional clients, in each other's papers.

As a side note, the Ithaca Times was originally founded by the Syracuse New Times (before my time) and then sold off to an employee, Jim Bilinski, who still publishes it today.

Most businesses qualify to belong to one or perhaps two trade organizations. Surprisingly, most businesses don't take advantage of the networking and learning opportunities that are available to an active member of a trade organization. Because of the unique type of newspaper the New Times was, I qualified to belong to multiple trade associations. I would join, take part and learn, and it helped to make the New Times a very successful newspaper. This would often involve going to a warm place—the Caribbean Island of Barbados in mid-January for example—for conferences. That's how organizers were able to lure some members to attend. But Shirley and I always attended the meetings, and in between we walked the white sand beaches. That was where we heard about a new concept for the back page of the New Times.

For several years, we had a continuing struggle selling ads on the back page of the newspaper. Traditionally, the back page is a prime location and should command a premium price, but for some unknown reason, we never did well with it. One January, we went to Barbados for a newspaper convention and learned about a new concept for the back page. We got all the details, brought the concepts back, and put them in place at the New Times. By the third week, we were consistently filling the back page.

Thanks to those back-page ads, we averaged over $500 in additional income every week for over 15 years. Do the math... that one idea netted SNT an extra $360,000 profit over the years. That certainly paid for a lot of business trips. Almost every trip we went on, we brought back ideas that helped make the paper more successful for years.

Also for many years, the advertising sales reps for the Post-Standard and, until 2001, the Herald-Journal, would tell our clients, "Don't advertise with the New Times. They print those terrible personal ads." Then one day, BANG! They started to run personal ads. They sure had to change that negative sales pitch. They ran the personals for a short time. They were never very successful with them. We continued with them very successfully for many more years. Often when Shirley and I were at events around Syracuse, people would come up to us and say, "Thank you. We met through the SNT personals and ended up married." Then they would show us photos of their kids.

In 1986 I researched a group called New York Press Association (NYPA), a statewide association of weekly newspapers. The New Times met the membership requirements, so I applied for membership. After several months, I had heard nothing so I called their Albany office. They said that memberships needed to be approved at special board meetings, and there would not be another one for several months. I sent in another application...once again no word. This went on for over a year.

I called my friend in Rochester, Bill Towler, who with his wife published Rochester City Paper. Bill was a member of NYPA. Bill said, "To be honest with you, they don't want you and the New Times in their organization. They consider your paper inferior to theirs and look down their noses on the alternative press." So, of course, I pushed the point and threatened to sue them. They finally voted me in.

Each year NYPA presented awards to the top papers in the state in a variety of categories. I submitted entries for awards. Fortunately, the awards judging was done by out-of-state groups that judged entries just by the materials in front of them. The awards banquet came, and they reluctantly called out the New Times as a winner. I was sitting in the back of the room. Very slowly I walked up front to accept the award, waving and smiling at everyone. That was repeated five times that night. Over the years the New Times was always a major winner of quality journalism awards. One year, we took home 14 awards out of 25 for New York State.

Free Community Papers of New York (FCPNY) was another trade organization to which SNT belonged. FCPNY gave out a coveted award each year—"the overall general excellence award"—to the newspaper judged as the best in many areas. The New Times won this award every year for 13 straight years, a record that no paper will probably ever equal.

Another group that I joined was a national organization called the Association of Alternative Newsweeklies (AAN). They had just one meeting each year, in the summer. I suggested that they do a winter meeting, and they said no. I kept pushing the idea, and after a couple of years, they said okay, if I organized it. I said okay, if I'm in complete charge. They said okay. So I started to organize a February meeting as a roundtable discussion. That way, I did not need to prepare programs and obtain speakers. Also, I felt roundtable discussion among peers in the same business was much more worthwhile than were outside speakers. And I was right.

Since I was in charge, I chose locations in February that I wanted to visit, such as Key West, Las Vegas, Palm Springs, and Aruba. And since I was in charge, according to organization policy, Shirley and I usually went for free. We learned a lot, and the entire organization became much better and stronger.

The Syracuse Press Club was another interesting experience for me and the New Times. It was dominated by the Herald-Journal and Post-Standard. I like to claim that the competition from the New Times is what put the Herald-Journal out of business. Perhaps that's a slight stretch, but it always made for interesting conversation around town, especially when Syracuse Newspapers publisher Stephen Rogers, Jr. was within earshot.

Just a side note. Steve Rogers and two of his top executives asked for a meeting. Shirley and I treated them to a lunch of Danzer's big sandwiches at our Sentinel Heights home and had a very interesting three-hour meeting.

They wanted to explore buying the New Times, they said. We were not really interested in selling, but were open and honest with them about our operation. In retrospect, I don't think they really wanted to buy us out. I think that they were just on a fishing trip to find out why we were so successful while they were having problems. Over the next few months, it appeared that some of the things we told them about what we were doing began to creep into their papers. Anyway, I always liked Steve Jr. He is a nice guy.

Back to the Press Club. Even though the daily papers were the big dogs, our own New Times political editor Walt Shepperd was elected president one year. For several years, they came after me to be president, but I declined. The New Times started to win a lot of Syracuse Press Club awards and the daily papers got very embarrassed. Because they dominated the board of directors, they changed some of the awards and rules and created a separate category for weekly papers so they would not have to compete against the New Times.

But we liked competing; competition kept us on our toes. Whenever the governor or lieutenant governor came to town, the Press Club would arrange for a stop at the Post-Standard, but never the New Times. I would complain about it. Before one such visit, the SPC president (not Walt at that time) called me and said that the lieutenant governor would be in town the next week, and they would arrange for her to come to the New Times offices and meet with our editorial department.

It was to be at noon. I arranged a very lavish lunch for her and the entire New Times staff, as well as her entourage of about eight people. We cleaned and spiffed up the office. I asked all the staff to dress up extra nice....They did. Most of her entourage arrived about 11:30...and we waited...and waited.... At about 12:30, her press assistant got a call. There had been a change in plans; she was not coming. We all had a fabulous lunch. Later I found out that at the last minute, the Post-Standard found out she was coming to the New Times and not the Post. The Post quickly called all the members of the press club board and put up such a stink that they changed her schedule.

I didn't take my continuing skirmishes with the Post and Herald personally. As Jim MacKillop told me, The New Times had been more antagonistic toward the Post-Standard before I bought the newspaper. Maybe they thought I was a pushover. And just because I annoyed the daily press, it didn't mean that I didn't have happy relationships with other media in Syracuse.

At one time, Ron Curtis Jr. had a late-night weekend show on Syracuse's CBS affiliate, WTVH Channel 5. It was called Freaky Flicks and Food. Ron would find the absolute worst movies that had ever been produced by Hollywood, and Channel 5 would broadcast them Saturday nights after the 11 o'clock news. The show was their answer to Saturday Night Live on NBC. During the very long commercial breaks, local celebrities would come on and prepare a food dish. Surprisingly—to me anyway—the show was very popular.

I was scheduled to be on the show the week after County Executive Nick Pirro. Nick had prepared his famous meatballs that won several "Men Who Cook" contests. "Men Who Cook" was a major annual community fundraiser that the New Times had helped start and sponsored for years.

Back to the show. I decided to prepare a big salad with lots of ingredients. I arrived at the studio carrying a big box with everything I needed. I even had my "Men Who Cook" apron to promote that event. We were well into the demo, and I had a can of tuna to add to the salad. Unfortunately, I had forgotten to bring a can opener. So I punched some holes in the can and pried it open. Unknown to me, I cut my hand on a jagged edge of the tuna can. A surface cut from the sharp edge of the can spurt a lot of blood with no pain. As I frequently do, I waved my hand around to demonstrate  what I was doing. I didn't notice that blood had started flying around the TV set.

At first Ron Curtis, Jr. thought it was a joke and I was spraying ketchup around. Then he realized it was real blood. The program was being aired live. Now blood was dripping into the salad.

Ron started to get flustered on air. He pointed out to me what was happening. The viewers probably thought that it was part of the show. So I immediately held my hand over the salad, dripping blood into it and saying that it was a recipe for vampire salad and required real human blood.

It was one of the most memorable episodes of the series even though for some reason we never sampled my salad on air, as was customary. A couple of years later when a new host took over, I was asked to be the first celebrity guest. But that time they had a can opener on hand.

Another time I talked my friend Wayne Mahar into doing his TV3 weather report live from the roof of the New Times building. Part of our roof was flat and had a great view across the city. It was fall and on the scheduled day, it was quite cold and very windy—especially on the roof.

Wayne was a good sport, even though he and the equipment almost got blown off the roof. For years, Wayne would gamely comment that it had been one of the best and most exciting weather reports he ever did.

For most of the time that I published the New Times, there were active news departments at the television network outlets and at many radio stations. Their news directors were always interested in our goings on, and one time they inadvertently even helped me avoid a possible sit-in. A staff member rushed into my office (the door was always open). He said, "Big trouble. There is a person on the sidewalk with a sign picketing the New Times. He is upset about something we printed."

I went outside and asked the picketer, "Sugar or cream?" He gave me a dirty look and asked, "What do you mean?" It was a cold day. I said, "I'll bring you a hot cup of coffee, do you use sugar or cream? I want to keep you comfortable until the news departments that I called get here. I don't know what your problem is, but I'll get a million dollars' worth of free publicity out of this."

He threw his sign down, got in his car, and drove away.

Late in my New Times tenure, in 2008, a movie was filmed in Syracuse. The working title was Lonely Joe, and it was eventually released on a very limited basis as Haunted Traxx. Most of it was filmed along the railroad tracks in Camillus. The opening scene was in a newspaper office in New York City. I talked them into using the New Times office as their set. The film crew rolled in with three tractor-trailer loads of equipment, a couple of big RVs, and a cast and crew of about 30 people. For the next two days, our entire operation was in exciting chaos. Several of our employees even got bit parts in the movie...including me.

A year later, as I was preparing my Academy Award acceptance speech, I found out that the script had been redone. My entire scene and character were left on the proverbial cutting room floor. Oh well, Hollywood's loss...but guess what...they sent me a check for over $1,000. Pretty good pay for about five minutes of work.

LET'S EAT!

You may have noticed that FOOD crops up often as I remember life at the New Times. That's because there was a lot of eating, one of my—and, I suspect, most people's—favorite things to do. One morning a staff member, Krista, brought a delicious breakfast pizza to the office. It was a big hit. So, for a long time, Shirley and I would stop at DiBello's every Wednesday morning and pick up five big tasty breakfast pizzas for the staff. We did it on Wednesdays because that was when the drivers were in to get their papers for delivery. The whole staff celebrated Wednesday.

Over the years, Shirley and I hosted the entire staff at lots and lots of lunches, dinners, and parties; every time we published a special section or had a big paper, we would bring in food. For about 10 years when we lived on the farm by Otisco Lake, we had a big, big garden and orchard. Each summer we would bring in baskets of fresh vegetables for all.

LOOKING AHEAD

When I was 68, I attended the 50th high school reunion that I had organized for my classmates from Hamilton High School. I was the only one there who was still working full-time. More than full-time in fact: Shirley and I were each putting in over 70 hours a week. I realized that I had been working full-time since I was 11 years old, and Shirley had worked since she was 16. Perhaps it was time to shift gears a little. I had been owner/publisher of the New Times for 25 years.

I had received a few offers from out-of-town people interested in buying the New Times, and each time, I had decided not to sell. To me, local ownership of a community newspaper was important. I had seen many great local companies bought out by big out-of-town investors and it almost always was a disaster for Central New York. I had a great and loyal staff; many had been with me for over 20 years. I wanted to do what was in their best interests. I could have sold for more money to an out-of-towner, but I wanted to find a person or people closer to home.

One day Shirley and I were at an art exhibition sponsored by Point of Contact. We met Gary Grossman, a well-known Syracuse accountant. Gary told us he had worked at the New Times many years before I had owned it, and how he loved the paper, read it every week, and used it extensively in planning his life...at least for dining, entertainment, and shopping (as thousands of people throughout Central New York still do).

A few days later I called Gary and asked him to lunch. Because of his love for the New Times and his possible connections, I told him very confidentially that I was thinking of selling the New Times, but it had to be to someone local. Gary said that he had a client who was thinking of buying a business. After a few back-and-forth confidential messages, Gary introduced me to Bill Brod, a Cazenovia-based businessman.

In 2010 I sold the New Times to Bill Brod. Now Bill is the publisher of the Syracuse New Times and Family Times and CEO of All Times Events Company. He also serves on the board of directors of his wife Lisette's company, Spinnaker Custom Products, a Certified WBE—100-percent woman-owned and operated business. Spinnaker has a retail outlet on the first floor of the New Times building in addition to its comprehensive online presence and business show displays.

I left the New Times in good and capable hands, and I enjoy following its progress online and in print from my new base of operations in beautiful downtown Hamilton!

CELEBRATING FEBRUARY 4, 1969
DATE OF THE FIRST ISSUE OF THE SYRACUSE NEW TIMES

Every five years after I bought the paper, the New Times would throw some big bash or celebration to celebrate its anniversary. It would often start in February and include various events until September, to celebrate when I brought the paper out of bankruptcy in September 1984.

These events included:

- A widely hailed display of Michael Davis photos at the Everson Museum
- A lavish event at the Landmark Theater with then-Congressman Jim Walsh as emcee

- A gala at the Galleries in downtown Syracuse
- A big party at the Empire Room at the New York State Fairgrounds, where state Senator Nancy Larraine Hoffmann danced with Hot Dog King Bob Barker to the beat of a fabulous band
- Special picnics for current and former staff at venues as disparate as Sylvan Beach and the New Times parking lot
- Dedication of a monument on the corner of Comstock and Euclid on the SU campus, near the site of the building where the New Times was born
- A special evening at the Lost Horizon featuring musicians/singers who were current and former New Times staff members
- Five-year glowing proclamations from the mayor, the county executive, and even a couple from the governor —even though he probably did not know who we were. One year, our state representative, Michael Bragman, commented at a press conference that he thought the government proclamations where a silly waste of taxpayers' money. Two months later, we received a wonderful proclamation (mounted on fancy paper with a gold border) for our anniversary from, yes, Michael Bragman.

Joe Glisson had been a regular cartoonist for the New Times for many years—about 30—when he proposed doing a collection of his best New Times cartoons. He asked if I would publish it for him. So I got to add book publisher to my resumé of titles. I must admit that Shirley did a lot of the collaboration on it with Joe. She should have been listed as co-publisher, but was too modest to do so. We did it as part of an anniversary celebration. We had several book signings at various galleries. It was a very successful book.

As part of the 20th anniversary in 1989, the staff wanted to sponsor a concert at the nightclub Lost Horizon, on Thompson Road. They wanted everyone on staff to have a part in it and selected the Frank Sinatra song "My Way" for me to perform as a song that sort of paralleled a lot of my life.

I said, "Absolutely no way. I can't sing. I won't do it." After they threatened to cancel the entire show, I sort of said yes. I decided to have the band play

Joe Glisson's book, which Shirley helped bring to press, was a big hit. Art was the publisher.

loudly to drown me out. Then I came up with the idea to read the words in a stirring manner to the music. In all modesty, I must say that it came across quite well—certainly better than if I'd attempted to sing—and I have the video to prove it.

For a long time, whenever the song "My Way" played, people who knew about that performance would look at me and say, "Frank Who?"

The Zimmer Motor Car Company
1997-2012

THE OFFICIAL
ZIMMER-ZAR
HOOD ORNAMENT

Zimmer-Zar hood ornament created and rendered by
Dennis Calkins

I did not even start the Zimmer Car Company until I was about 60, at an age when my peers were retiring.

I was never a car guy; cars to me were just basic transportation. That got me in trouble with a lot of my gear-head friends. They would say things like, "My dream is to build cars; it's wonderful that you have achieved your lifelong dream to actually own a luxury car manufacturing company." Then they would get very upset when I'd say, "No I'm not a car guy; I just saw a great car with my name on it and, at my wife's insistence, bought the company. So now I manufacture Zimmer Golden Spirit motor cars. It's just another business."

Shirley remembers her "insistence" as more like her simply "getting out of the way."

"Chat and Gata were the kittens we adopted in 1997. Art got to start Zimmer Motor and I got kittens.... Yup, that was the conversation in the car on the way to Florida in January 1997. Art started by saying,

[Left] 'Made in Syracuse' was very important to me.
[Top] One of the cars ordered by the Kuwaiti prime minister. I would pose with each new model when it was produced.

'I have something I would like to talk with you about.... You've always wanted kittens...how about we get two (so they'll be company for each other while we're away)? And I would like to build cars with my name on them....'

"My reaction was, 'Stop the typewriter; your starting the ZMCC has nothing to do with OUR getting kittens!' As I would pray for direction whenever Art said, 'I have something I would like to talk with you about...' I was praying and felt the response to prayer: 'Just get out of the way.' So I fastened my seatbelt and enjoyed the Zimmer ride... and, yes, delighted in getting two kittens in the spring upon our return from Florida. As they were the next generation of Zimmer cats (Art already had had Cat when we married, our 21-year-old feline who had just died) and I was a Spanish teacher with a French minor, Chat and Gata seemed like the natural names for our babies we got together (rescues from the Fayetteville Animal Hospital)."

I'm flattered that Dick Flaherty took my ownership of a car company more seriously than I did:

"When Art bought the Zimmer Car Company, coming from Chrysler, I could see that he did it exactly right. He manufactured the cars only after they were sold. He had always loved big cars. One of his first that I remember was a Hudson convertible, sort of a performance car of its era. He also loved Cadillacs. He had a convertible that he'd drive to meetings in Skaneateles and offer people rides back to Syracuse. Unfortunately, the top didn't work well. Several times it rained during the meetings and the seats were wet."

Over the nine years I owned the company, I sold about $4 million worth of Zimmer cars that I manufactured. I had some interesting experiences along the way.

A FEW ROUNDS WITH GEORGE FOREMAN

How long do you think I would last in a fight with former world heavyweight boxing champion George Foreman? I figure I could last at least three seconds. If I ran fast.

As most of you know, the International Boxing Hall of Fame and Museum is located near Syracuse in Canastota, home of former world champion Carmen Basilio. Each year there is an induction ceremony for four to five world champions and other outstanding stars of the boxing world. The ceremony is always preceded by a big parade through the village of Canastota.

During the time I owned the Zimmer Car Company, I received a call from the Hall of Fame. This year, the big "star" to be introduced was George Foreman. Would I drive George in the parade in one of my Zimmer Golden Spirit motor cars?

I said yes right away. I just happened to have in stock as my personal Zimmer, a fabulous four-door Zimmer Golden Spirit convertible. I had a custom-made seat, more like a throne, to put in the middle of the back seat that would raise George up for the parade ride.

A few days before the big event the Hall of Fame organizers called back. There was a problem: they had a tradition that the person who volunteered the most hours at the Hall of Fame the previous year drove the "star" in the parade. I said no problem, the volunteer can drive; I'll sit in the front passenger seat.

The morning of the parade I met the driver. He drove the Zimmer to the place where we were to pick up George. They were having a reception for him...at a funeral home. George Sr. and George Jr., George III, and George IV all came out to see the Zimmer. The boys were all large young adults. I was introduced to George Sr., who marveled at the car. We chatted for a few minutes. George wanted all the Georges in the car for the parade. There is no way all four could get in the back seat, especially with the "throne" seat. I said no problem. One of the boys could take my seat in the front. George Sr. said, "No way! None of my boys are taking Mr. Zimmer's seat!" So we started to argue about it.

As we were arguing back and forth, someone said, "The parade is ready to start. You need to get going." So I pushed George Sr. in and up on the throne and before we could exchange punches, I pushed George Jr. and the III in the back and grabbed George IV and pushed him in the front seat and said, "Let's go!"

I was walking next to the car. We were surrounded by security people to keep the crowd back from George and the car, but I was allowed to walk alongside. We went down the street, waving to the crowd. All the Georges were waving, and George Sr. and I were chatting.

George loved the car and thought he might buy one. I gave him my card and told him to call me. Alas, I never heard from him. Perhaps if I had installed a BBQ grill in the trunk (a Foreman grill, of course), I could have made a deal. Anyway, I sold cars to other big-name celebrities. You can't get them all.

ANOTHER ALMOST SALE

I got a call from Grammy-winning singer Lou Rawls, who owned two cars made by the original Zimmer Company. He had some questions. After that initial contact, whenever he was doing a concert in the area, there were two front-row center, comped seats for Shirley and me, and we would have dinner with him after the concert.

One day he called and said, "You know I got married last year and now we have a new baby. I love my Zimmers, but they're two-door sports coupes.

Grammy winner Lou Rawls owned two Zimmer Golden Spirit cars. He chatted with Art and Shirley about the new 2002 Zimmer line in this photo.

With a family, now I need a four-door sedan. I'll give you my two Zimmers (worth about $55,000 each) for one new four-door." The four-door was priced at $160,000. I said we could probably make a deal, but that he would need to put in a few extra dollars. He said, "Okay, I'll call you back in a couple of weeks." I never heard from him again. Sadly, two months later, he died. Later his wife called me for advice on selling the two Zimmers.

My jailbird pen-pals

Over the years, thanks to the New Times or the Zimmers, I corresponded with people in jail. Inmates, usually from Auburn Prison, would have copies of the New Times. They would request a free subscription or to run free personal ads for a wife. Most people would just toss such letters away. But I always wrote back. I would give them a subscription, but no ads. Prisons all around the country would have car magazines in their libraries. Inmates would see my Zimmer ads and write to me, requesting a Zimmer calendar or catalog. I always replied.

Some would tell me that when they got out, they had a big stash of money somewhere and the first thing they would do would be to buy a new Zimmer. A couple of people I heard from regularly were on death row. Of course, all were innocent, or so they told me.

Most of my friends thought I was crazy, if not for writing to prisoners then for many other reasons. One day I got a letter that began like this: "My husband, the killer, he loves Zimmers. His 65th birthday is coming up and all he wants is a red Zimmer convertible. We can't afford one, but he would do commercials for you in exchange for one."

And a real killer

For you more mature people, you may remember that there was a 1950s rock-and-roll star, Jerry Lee Lewis (*Great Balls of Fire* and other hits), and his nickname was "the Killer on the piano." It was his wife—his fifth, I think— who wrote to me. When Shirley did an Internet search, the wife looked like a young Farah Fawcett Majors—hair and all. She had her own TV show and

The Hamilton 4th of July parade has always been a favorite of ours. I walked along as one of my convertibles turned heads in the 2003 parade, above. The parade grand marshall sitting in the back seat was local resident Lois Lee Clark. The driver was high school classmate Dick Chapin, and my mother, Edna Zimmer, was in the passenger seat. It would be the last time she ever rode in a car.

was quite a celebrity on her own. We wrote back and forth several times. My annual ad budget was about $5,000 and the car he wanted was about $130,000. In my office, I had a very large blown up photo of a red Zimmer convertible. It was beautiful. I took the photo down and wrote across the bottom: "To my friend Jerry Lee, who deserves a car like this." I signed it "AZ, president, Zimmer Motor Company." I took the photo with inscription down to Syracuse Blueprint and gave it to my friend Israel Hagan, who worked there. Israel is a great musician and has his own well-known band, Stroke. I asked Israel to have the photo framed up in the fanciest, most ornate, expensive frame they had. When done, it looked spectacular. Then I sent it via UPS to the Killer's wife.

A few weeks later I got a letter back from his wife. Jerry Lee loved the photo, and it was hanging in a place of honor over their fireplace. I wonder where it is now, as Jerry Lee has had one or two more wives.

I had other interesting experiences with my Zimmer Motor Company that involved His Royal Highness the prime minister of Kuwait; Uday Saddam, the "bad son" of Iraqi dictator Saddam Hussein; Willie Nelson; Shaquille O'Neal; Liberace; Dion (Dion and the Belmonts); and a Saudi prince. I'll give you a few examples.

Uday Hussein

I got a call from a reporter at a radio station in Oswego. He said that he was watching CNN and saw a report about a group of Marines with a CNN news crew entering Uday Hussein's palace in Baghdad during Desert Storm. There in the courtyard of the palace were about six luxury cars: a Lamborghini; a couple of Rolls Royces; and, he thought he saw two Zimmer Golden Spirits. The reporter had attended my big Zimmer press party at Syracuse Stage and recognized the car.

A flood of messages started to come in from news outlets around the world. How did Uday get the Zimmers? Did I sell them to him? Am I a terrorist sympathizer and/or part of Hussein's government?

Uday, the son of Saddam Hussein, was an even worse person than his father or other slightly less "bad" brother. Uday had a reputation that when he saw something he liked, he just took it. If the owner protested, Uday just shot him dead.

From the photos, I recognized one of the cars as one that I had sold two years before to a businessman from Amman, Jordan. How it got to Uday, I do not know.

Also, there was a newly constructed wall right behind the Zimmer. The Marines broke into it and found about 300 million dollars in American cash. I wonder where all that was from, and where it went.

Several years later, another photo appeared in the newspaper. There were about eight cars sitting out in the desert with a fence around them. The cars looked beat up and were half-covered by blowing sand. Two of them were the Uday Zimmers.

Sometime after that, people from Saudi Arabia were in my New Times office to talk about buying a Zimmer. We talked about the Uday Zimmer. They mentioned that they were going to Amman, Jordan soon. I had not heard anything from my contact there in years. So I suggested that they try to look him up to see if he knew how Uday got the Zimmer. Later, I got a message

Meet the Zimmers

Three years ago, Art Zimmer, in the foreground, saw a car with his name on it. Now he owns the company and announced Tuesday he will begin building Zimmers in Florida. The Golden Spirit will go for about $70,000. See story in Business, Page B-9.

STEPHEN D. CANNERELLI/The Post-Standard

He Liked the Car and Its Name; Now He'll Try to Sell Zimmers

■ Why buy a Zimmer? Because it'll be easy to find in the parking lot.

By TONY FONG
The Post-Standard

It was a few years ago when Art Zimmer came across a curious car in front of Sam Dell Dodge. Long, slightly awkward-looking but certainly eye-catching, it grabbed Zimmer's attention not only because of its looks.

It also bore his name.

Tuesday, Zimmer announced that the car company with his name on it was now, indeed, his own. With two classic Zimmer Golden Spirits outside the Syracuse Stage — including one once owned by Liberace — Zimmer announced the creation of Zimmer Motor Car Corp., headquartered in Syracuse.

The Zimmer that Zimmer saw in front of Sam Dell's lot in 1994 was one of only 1,500 original Zimmers manufactured between 1980 and 1988 before the original company, owned by Paul Zimmer, (no relation) went bankrupt.

About a year and a half ago, Zimmer said, he bought a Golden Spirit at the behest of his wife, Shirley. Thus began a process that contin-

resurrect," Zimmer said. "I started from scratch. I started a new company."

Together with some former employees of the old Zimmer company, they've begun operations with a makeshift factory in Pompano Beach, Fla., and the corporation housed in the Syracuse New Times building on West Genesee Street. Zimmer is the publisher of the weekly paper.

The first new Zimmer motor car, the Golden Spirit, available in a two-door, four-door or convertible, is expected to be finished in Octo-

---

■

"Somewhere in the United States, there's 30 or 40 people each year that will be interested in buying this car. If there isn't (a market), then we'll make a few of these cars, say it was fun."

ART ZIMMER
Zimmer Motor Car Corp.

---

ber. At full speed, Zimmer said, the factory will manufacture 30 to 40 cars in a year.

At around $70,000, the Zimmers are priced to be competitive with Jaguars, Porsches and upper-end BMWs.

For sure, the Golden Spirit is not for anyone trying to move around incognito. The fact that Liberace owned one is perhaps an indication of the aesthetics of the car.

"I've seen a couple of them around town and I always thought they looked neat," said Donnie Sweazey, an auto dealer in Salt Lake City who was approached by Zimmer to be a Zimmer dealer. Sweazey, nonetheless, said the car has a limited market because of its price and the difficulties there would be in getting replacement parts for it.

Although under the hood the car is a Mercury Cougar at heart, the exterior looks more as if it materialized from an F. Scott Fitzgerald novel.

At 18 feet long, it takes up ample parking space, has chrome-plated exhaust pipes curling out of the side of the engine and a golden eagle hood ornament.

Standard features include a padded opera roof and opera lights, a hand-finished German leather interior and hand-finished wooden steering wheel.

In the end, Zimmer said, it is the uniqueness of the car's appearance that is its selling point.

"As you know, if you go out and

Both of the cars in the picture were built before I bought the company. Shirley and I bought the one in back, a 1987 Zimmer. This article appeared on the front of the business section of my competitor, the Post-Standard, and also appeared in the Herald Journal from them. The businessman to whom I had sold the car (actually, I sold him two Zimmers) was now bankrupt and destitute. He had no idea how Uday had ended up with the Zimmer, but the other Zimmer I had sold to him was in the Jordanian Royal Palace. It was seen being driven around by Queen Noor al-Hussein, the American, Lisa Najeeb Halaby, who became queen of Jordan in 1978 when she married King Hussein.

THE SAUDIS

The people from Saudi Arabia who were in my New Times office were there, I thought, to buy a Zimmer. When they arrived, they said that they had to leave by 4 p.m. We sat and talked for several hours. I didn't push; I just followed their lead. Not a word about buying a Zimmer car. At about 3:54 I was thinking: no Zimmer sale here. Oh, well, I've had a nice chat with some interesting people.

Then suddenly the lead guy said, "Oh, about those Zimmer cars, we will take two new ones. Also we saw one in the parking lot when we came in." I said, "Yes, it is mine that I drive." "What do you want for it?" he asked. I tossed out a number. He said, "Ship it to me tomorrow." In that last six minutes, we finalized the deal for three cars—about $500,000—and away they went.

That was possibly the best hourly rate I have ever earned.

A MONSTER ASSIGNMENT FOR THE ZIMMER

One day during the time I owned the Zimmer Motor Car Company, I got a call from a lady in California. She said that she was the producer of a TV show called Monster Garage. I was familiar with the Monster Garage show. It was broadcast nationally on the Discovery Channel and was quite popular with several million viewers each week. The show had been on for a couple of years. On the show, each week they assembled a team of auto experts who were given a crazy, wild assignment to take a motor vehicle, tear it apart, and convert it into something completely different, with the exterior still looking like the original vehicle. After conversion and all, it had to be able to still be driven down the road. They filmed the entire process all week and then edited

Zimmer cars always attracted interesting people. [Top] Our friends, Jackie and Charlie Abrams, met with Donald Trump; [left] racing legend Mario Andretti discussed Zimmer cars with Gary Hendrick; [below] I showed off a 2004 model at the Turning Stone Resort and Casino in Verona, NY.

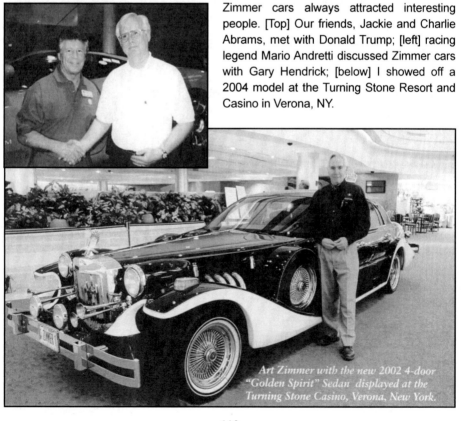

Art Zimmer with the new 2002 4-door "Golden Spirit" Sedan displayed at the Turning Stone Casino, Verona, New York.

it into one hour-long show. The team had to complete it on time—in one week—and on a predetermined budget. If they succeeded, they all got some very substantial prizes.

The deal was that they wanted to do a project using a Zimmer Motor Car and wanted me as part of the team as a representative of ZMCC. I would get a free round-trip, first-class flight to LA, stay for a week in a fancy Hollywood hotel–all expenses paid and $500 extra spending money... and I'd get to rub shoulders with some Hollywood stars. If the project were successful, there would be some nice prizes, too.

I said, "YES, I am ready to go." She said, "Okay, you are on. What automotive skill shall I put you down for? I said that I owned the company. She said yes and again asked what skill. I owned the company, but had no automotive skill (electrical, welding, body work, hydraulic, etc.). She said that she was sorry, but they required all participants to have a working part in the project. So I said that I had the perfect person for her: Sam Vigliotti. Sam owns Sam's Auto Body in Syracuse. His company manufactured the cars for me. I told her that Sam had just about every automotive skill that she needed. So Sam went to California and had the great trip and the time of his life.

One of my first concerns was that they would want me to donate a Zimmer to them for the project. But this is a big-time national production company, and they had already purchased a Zimmer. The assignment for Sam and his team was to turn the Zimmer Golden Spirit 2-door sport coupe, into a wood splitter that would split large logs into fireplace wood. I figured that when they were done, one cord of firewood would cost about $500,000.

Sam's team completed the job on time and on budget. A couple of months later the show was broadcast nationally. We threw a big party at a local restaurant, at the former site of my old friend, the Schnitzelbank, and we all watched the show. Sam and his business, Sam's Auto Center on West Genesee Street, got a million dollars' worth of publicity.

The wood splitter Zimmer was on display for a couple of years in Long Beach, California. I'm not sure where it is today.

BEAUTIFYING THE ROADS OF KUWAIT

One day I got an e-mail from a person who claimed he was the chief of staff in the palace of his Royal Highness, the Prime Minister of Kuwait. I would regularly get calls and messages from a lot of people who wanted a Zimmer Motor Car, but a lot of it was fantasy and pie in the sky.

This e-mail was also a bit suspect, as the name was a very long German-sounding name. What is he doing in the royal palace? I always treated every inquiry as a serious one and would follow it to the end...frequently a dead end.

It turned out that the e-mailer truly was the chief of staff in the royal palace, and his Royal Highness wanted to buy two Zimmers. He wanted the biggest and most expensive ones that I had, almost $200,000 each. We exchanged messages for a few months, working out details. One thing I never did, or do, was/is to push hard or get aggressive on sales. You want it? Just send the money. I can't chase people. I only respond to their messages.

December arrived, and I was getting ready to leave town for three months. All the other businesses functioned well without me. Is it because I really have nothing to do, or because I organize everything so well? Probably some of each. However, with ZMCC, when I went away, it pretty much closed down. Even though it was a million-dollar-a-year-business, it was really just a little side hobby that I didn't treat too seriously. However, I did send the chief of staff a message, saying, "If his Royal Highness really wants a Zimmer, order it now, or wait until next spring." I received no response, and away I went.

In the spring I returned to the office, where a message from the palace awaited me. The message said, "Dear Mr. Zimmer – sorry to inform you, his Royal Highness passed away in January." I said to myself, if I had only been a little more aggressive, I could have received a deposit and made the sale last December. An extra $400,000 sale would have been nice. However, the next sentence was, "The new prime minister wants two Zimmers. Let's make the deal." Soon money was wired into the ZMCC bank account. (I never sold a car without payment up front.) A few days later, I got a call from the manager of M&T Bank, where the Zimmer account was. The banker said that a high-ranking official from the CIA wanted to know about all this money coming from the Middle East into Mr. Zimmer's account. Yes, even back then, Big Brother and the Chinese knew what everyone was doing.

Just by coincidence, that morning I saw a television report that then-President Bush was in Kuwait. That evening he was having dinner with his Royal Highness, the Prime Minister. I said to the bank manager, "Tell the CIA if they have any questions, ask their boss (the President), as he is having dinner with the person who sent me the $400,000 (today equal to almost a million)." The manager said, "I can't tell them that." I told him that he would have to because that was all I had to say on the subject. I don't know what he told the CIA, but I never heard another word on the subject.

THE FRANKLIN AUTO MUSEUM

The fact that I owned the Zimmer Car Company probably led to a call I got from a member of the National Franklin Automobile Museum board of directors who lived in Central New York. The museum itself, he said, was in Tucson.

A little history. All Franklin automobiles ever manufactured were built in Syracuse. From 1900 to 1934, Franklin became a large and successful manufacturing company of luxury and innovative cars, and a major Syracuse employer. Its factory on South Geddes Street was several city blocks long. At its peak they employed almost 10,000 workers.

The Franklin auto was unique. It had an air-cooled engine and was very expensive. It was considered to be just about the finest luxury auto manufactured in its day. With the stock market crash of 1929 and the Great Depression that followed, the market for the Franklin luxury car dried up. Its leaders tried to save the company with a cheaper car, but by 1934, it was all over. Many Franklins remain today in highly prized antique car collections. The Northeast Classic Car Museum in Norwich, NY has almost 100 Franklins in its collection.

For years, the National Franklin owners' club has had an annual trek or convention in Cazenovia. Two hundred Franklins descend on Cazenovia for a week every August. As part of their activities, all the cars parade to the original factory site on South Geddes Street in Syracuse to pay homage to their birthplace. There is a large billboard on Geddes marking the spot. The

Onondaga Historical Association displays a very early Franklin auto at their Montgomery Street headquarters.

My caller said that the National Franklin Museum needed to expand and could not do so in Tucson. The Board was looking for a new location. Some board members thought that the museum should be in Syracuse, known as Franklin city at one time. When I manufactured my first Zimmer in Syracuse, it was put on display in the lobby of the Turning Stone Casino in Oneida County, next to a 1934 Franklin. It symbolized the last auto to be built in Syracuse beside the latest car to be built in Syracuse.

The board of directors was soliciting bids from various cities for the new museum. He sent me the bid requirements, which included the donation of a large piece of desirable land for the museum. This could be a wonderful project for Syracuse, with a major economic development impact on the economy, as several thousand people each year would come from all over the country to visit the major new attraction.

I was in full agreement that the one and only location for this major project was in the Syracuse area. I agreed to head up the project. As a Chamber of Commerce member and chair of three of its committees, I confidently went to the Chamber to line up their support and help...and was surprised that they had no interest in the project.

Next I went to the city of Syracuse economic development office. I was shocked; they had no interest. Shame, Syracuse, shame on you! I then went to Irwin Davis, the executive director of the Metropolitan Development Association (MDA). He was super excited, calling it a great project. He was on board 100%. Fact is the MDA did more than I did before it was all over.

I organized a committee and the search was on for a desirable, free piece of land we could get to donate to the museum. I recruited Nick Pirro, Onondaga County Executive. Nick was very helpful, as the county owned several pieces of land that might be possibilities. I also recruited a couple of people from Cazenovia because of the annual Franklin trek held there.

We ended up with about five possible spots in Syracuse and two in Cazenovia. We hosted a meeting of the museum site selection committee. They toured our possible locations. We presented a detailed bid to them with other incentives. Our slogan was, "Franklin Come Home." They were very impressed and pronounced Syracuse their leading candidate.

The site they selected as the best for us to concentrate on was near Long Branch Park, at the north end of Onondaga Lake. The land was owned by the county and was unused park land. It was adjacent to the Syracuse University rowing crew's boat house.

We finalized the proposal and submitted it to the Franklin museum board. They planned to meet in August in Cazenovia and finalize approval. They said Syracuse would be their choice.

Days before the meeting, I got a call from Nick Pirro. Nick said, "Art, I'm sorry to tell you. You can't have the land; the deal is off." I called the president of the museum board to plead for more time. He was sorry, but he said the board would vote on schedule. Syracuse was out.

I quickly informed the committee. The person who had procured one of the Cazenovia sites asked if we could submit a quick counterproposal on that location. I said, let's go for it. We did, and the board voted to locate the new museum on a piece of land on Route 20, about one mile east of Cazenovia. I was semi-happy.

What had happened to the Syracuse site? I later found out that Bill Sanford, the SU crew coach and chairman of the Onondaga County legislature at the time, the second most powerful politician in the county next to Nick Pirro, decided at the last minute that he might at some point in the future want to expand the SU crew headquarters onto that land. He had put on pressure to withdraw the county's offer to donate the land to us.

But the museum was coming to Central New York at least, reasonably near the original home of all Franklins. A big sign went up on the land in Cazenovia: "Future Home of the National Franklin Automobile Museum."

About a year later, there was still no activity at the site. I asked the museum people for an update. The museum curator, who was also a member of the board, had decided that he did not want to move the museum out of Tucson. He threatened the board with a lawsuit. Not wanting to get into a legal hassle, the board caved.

After all the effort and excitement, the museum stayed in Tucson.

[Top} Mary Lou and me, all dressed up for the junior prom in 1955.
[Bottom] My first car, my beloved 1949 Hudson, was the backdrop for this picture of the two of us outside her house, also taken in 1955.

{Top} My old friend Bill Steene, and his wife, in 1990.
[Bottom] James Earl Jones, center, was the featured guest at the 2006 Syracuse Film Festival. At left is SFF board member David Schnuckler.

Clothes really do make the man. My New Times staff gave me this ascot, and I used it and the nametag to advertise two of my businesses at once. On several occasions I made a sale or a sales contact when someone would say. "I didn't know you owned these businesses!"

Among friends at Coleman's: (from left) Peter Coleman, Beth Coleman, me, John Murphy, Dick Flaherty, and Jerry Willis. September 2009.

One of my favorite promotional images for Zimmer Cars. This one was sold to a businessman in Amman, Jordan, and later ended up in the hands of Uday Hussein.

Shirley and I work the phones at a WCNY fund-raiser in December 1998.

My cute co-narrator and I enjoyed hosting the "Cruizin'" performances.

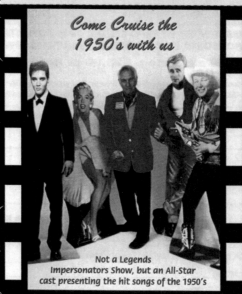

Above: A playbill. Opposite page: Cast members and a shot of the magnificent set for "Cruizin'," created by Dennis Calkins.

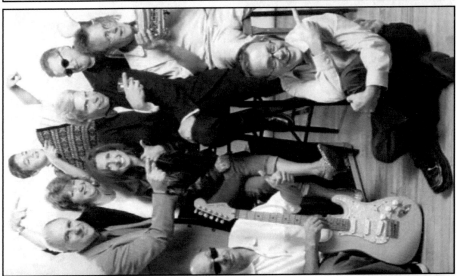

25

1984 - 2009

This appeared in the New Times on the 25th anniversary of my ownership.

Dick Flaherty and I ride the range at Dick's farm on the Tug Hill Plateau in 2003.

Shirley and me in 1988 on the 32-foot cabin cruiser on 'Lake Zimmer', our comfortably sized private pond near the Otisco Lake home.

Our lovely Sentinel Heights home. The view from the ground rivaled the view from the air.

At the lodge in Vermont in 2012, 42 years after I purchased it on behalf of the Onondaga Ski Club. Left to right: Dick Flaherty, Dona Flaherty, me and Shirley. *Photo by Earl Alger*

The cadets march prior to a football game between Navy and Syraucse that Shirley and I attended a few years ago. A very impressive sight.

I checked out the castle of King Ludwig II of Bavaria, located in Neuschwanstein, Austria, during our European tour. I was just looking for a few design ideas for our Hamilton house. Unfortunately, local zoning regulations forced us to make a few changes.

The church in Salzburg, Austria where my friend, Maria Von Trapp, was married.

Shirley on our honeymoon, at Sonnenberg Gardens in Canadaigua.

On another trip, we visited the beautiful beaches of Corpus Christi, Texas.

'The King' serenades Shirley at her surprise birthday party at least 25 years ago.

With Debbie Reynolds, one of our favorite stars, at her resort in Las Vegas.

Managing partner Bob Linn speaks at the mic as I am honored with the Ernst & Young Entrpreneur of the Year award in 2003.

2001 ZIMMER "Golden Spirit" convertible, only $95,900.00.

One of my favorite Zimmer models. I sold this very car to Shaquille O'Neal.

A labor of love for me is this community service project that Shirley and I have produced for the last five years.

It includes a detailed map of the village of Hamilton and Colgate University, and it has extensive lists of local businesses and points of interest. Each year, the publication comes together over four months aided by an all-volunteer staff. Dozens of area businesses stock it, and the initial printing of 10,000 copies runs out in the first 10 months.

Home Sweet Home(s)

Custom-made stained glass windows Art had made as a surprise present to Shirley. The windows have travelled with us to each of our homes, including Hamilton.

After I left Hamilton and moved to Syracuse, I lived in a series of rented apartments, eventually owning and renovating the places. I sought a place to stay and keep my belongings while I did most of my "living" elsewhere. After I met Shirley, all I wanted was to make a home with her where she would feel happy and completely loved. Wherever we've lived, we have always felt we were living in our "forever" home.

1987-1997
OTISCO VALLEY ROAD - THE FARMHOUSE

Our first home in 1987 was a large 150-year-old farm house atop a hill overlooking the Otisco Lake Valley. A wonderful location with a fabulous view. Our cow neighbors outnumbered the humans. We owned about 20 acres of land and had no close neighbors. For kids raised in rural settings, it felt like home and was just what we wanted.

After a couple of years we got into detailed discussions about our future. The 35-minute commute each way to our office was a pain. But to move into

Art and Shirley's first home. Note the 'cabin cruiser' on their 'private lake'.

the city near the office would require having neighbors, still a no-no for us. So we decided to stay in the farmhouse and fix it up.

One of our best employees at the New Times, Jill Hutchinson, told us that her husband, Tim, was a contractor. In time we learned that he was not "just" a contractor, but a master craftsman who did superb work.

So each year we selected a room at the farmhouse and had Tim Hutchinson rip it out and rebuild it. Over the years we added bathrooms, expanded rooms with dormers, and added an oversized three-car garage, a large deck with an ornate gazebo, and a laundry room.

One year, we decided to completely remodel the kitchen. We finalized our plans with Tim and then told him that we were going to Europe for six weeks. We asked him if he could have the remodel done when we got home, and he did!

After ten years we had a beautiful showplace in the country and planned to live there until we moved to assisted living. We also created a large pond in the side yard, complete with a white sand beach, for swimming and winter ice skating. We mounted a 32-foot cabin cruiser in the pond that became quite the tourist attraction. That's not saying a lot, as there are no *other* tourist attractions in Otisco.

1997-2010
Sentinel Heights
The Big House

One day I took a different, scenic route home from Syracuse and drove through a sparsely populated area called Sentinel Heights, near Lafayette Country Club. I saw a sign: **For Sale, 30 acres with a 50-mile vista.** There were no houses in the area and it was only six minutes to downtown. What a great location, I thought.

I didn't mention my drive to Shirley, but I called the number on the sign and met the owner at the property. The area was undeveloped because it was dotted with steep cliffs, big rocks, had no services, and wasn't suitable for development. The area was a jungle and the 30 acres were in the middle of a 500-acre forest.

A few days later I asked Shirley to go for a walk in the woods, something we did frequently, either in our own backyard or at Highland Forest. I drove around for a while and ended up in Sentinel Heights. Shirley was totally

The Sentinel Heights house had sweeping views of the city of Syracuse all the way to Lake Ontario, 50 miles away.

confused. As we headed into the woods there was no trail and it was difficult going. We soon came to a small clearing the owner had showed me.

From there you could see the entire city of Syracuse and, beyond that, out 50 miles to Lake Ontario. And yet we were only a three-minute drive to Route 81 and six minutes away from downtown Syracuse. I said, "Shirley, what would you think if we bought all this land, designed a new home, and hired Tim to build it?"

Her answer: "WHAT?"

Two weeks later we closed on the land.

This was going to be a huge project; with Tim Hutchinson we developed a five-year plan. Each year we would do a major job—building a private road into the middle of our land; clearing an area of the jungle; drilling a well; trying to put in a septic system and leach field on a rocky cliff; excavating and putting in support pilings for a 13,000-square-foot building; and bringing in underground utilities.

We figured we had plenty of time, as it would take several years to sell the farmhouse. I had what real estate people call the worst case to sell: the most expensive home in its area. Anyone who could afford the home would not want to live in the middle of a herd of cattle; they would buy over the hill in Skaneateles.

Five weeks later we received a purchase offer that was at our asking price. Suddenly our five-year plan went out the window. Except now we did not *own* a window. We quickly rented a house in Lafayette. Nine months later, we moved into our new home that we planned to stay in until we moved into that assisted living facility.

One big question: Exactly where to clear the forest for the house in order to have the best view? Our friend Dennis Calkins, who I now suspect is half monkey, started to climb trees to pick the best view. Our friend Dick Flaherty used his four-wheel drive truck to haul a tall cherry picker up the hill to try to spot the best location, but most of the hill was inaccessible.

Then there was the question of where a road could be built, and where a leach field could be installed. The final building site was only 100 feet from where Dennis had suggested.

Shirley and I designed the Sentinel Heights house ourselves, and drew our own blueprints, using an architect only to get a building permit. We designed for maximum entertainment space: a formal dining room with crystal chandelier and sit-down dining space for more than 40 people. It was to be a marketing tool for the New Times. It served that purpose very well.

One time our kitchen was the "studio" for a television spot for Syracuse University's college for part-time students, University College. The script called for five adult actors and a 9-year-old boy. There were production people, a director and several producers, and visitors throughout the day. All the cars and trucks could unload right outside the back door and then park. Everyone fit very nicely in the great room, dining room, and kitchen, with space on the porches and outside for breaks and lunch.

We heard about all this secondhand; early in the morning we packed up what we'd need for the day and went to work, warning the cats to stay in the basement out of the way.

While we lived in the Sentinel Heights house, I got a call from a lady who Tim Hutchinson had given my name as a reference. Tim's work was superb and, unlike many contractors, he was always done on time and on budget. I asked if my caller would like to come up and see Tim's work. She was very interested and wanted to see our home.

At the time of her visit, Shirley was tied up at a meeting. I gave Tim's client a full tour of the house; she loved it. A few weeks later, Shirley had appendicitis. I took her to Community General Hospital's ER. The doctor on duty to treat Shirley was the person who had toured our house! I knew her name, but not that she was a physician. She smiled and said, "Shirley, you have a beautiful house. I've been all through it." Shirley, lying there in pain, was mystified.

2011-present
HAMILTON
ACTION CENTRAL

Several happy years in the new "big" house, and I was approaching 70. Shirley and I were each working over 70 hours a week, and we started to think

Our new home in Hamilton, situated on 10 acres of woods and stream. No close neighbors, and it's three minutes from the center of the village.

about retirement. The house out in the woods with no neighbors was great. But now, we thought it would be nice to live in a village where we could walk to "everything."

We wanted to remain in Central New York, as it is by far the best area in the world to live. After researching all the villages in CNY, we found they are like most other villages in the country these days; you could walk to everything but there is not much to walk to: some empty storefronts, few services, and a WalMart at the edge of town.

Then we discovered Hamilton—or perhaps I should say *re-discovered* Hamilton—the most vibrant, complete little village you could imagine. I had always liked living there; I just didn't want to work on a farm for the rest of my life. Or live on one. So, what topped off our delight? We found 10 acres of vacant land right in the center of the village. The land was a jungle and a swamp, the worst eyesore in the village. We hired Gerry Chesebro (Murray's brother) to clean it up. It took almost four years. Gerry transformed it from a long-time village embarrassment into the most desirable building lot in the world, where we built our current home.

We built a new (and smaller) house with no close neighbors. The lot included woods and a stream. It's a five-minute walk to 16 restaurants, one liquor store, a 24/7 mini-mart and gas station, a dozen stores, boutiques, six salons, a large regional hospital, no empty storefronts, no WalMart, a brewery right in the village, and a little school called Colgate University with all kinds of culture, entertainment, and sports events. It's basically a five-minute walk to everything.

Of course, our first thought was to ask Tim Hutchinson to work his magic once again. But the cost and travel would have been prohibitive.

Our neighbor, Sam Cooper, remembers when the new house "arrived": "Five years ago, I learned that I was going to have new neighbors, Art and Shirley Zimmer. One morning I noticed ten-wheeler after ten-wheeler unloading fill in the lot across from my house on Eaton Street in Hamilton. Speculation and rumor ran rampant in the neighborhood that the mysterious new owner was an automotive genius who had decided to move his company from Syracuse to Hamilton because he had 'roots' in the community. The anticipation among the neighbors was that it would be a small building to house replica cars similar to the long-retired Duesenberg roadsters of yesteryear. I expected that we would likely see a wealthy client or two arriving in a Rolls Royce to order a new car.

"One afternoon while sitting on my porch, I noticed a stranger pacing back and forth across the road. He wore a bright red plaid flannel shirt (which as time went on I assumed was his favorite, as he seemed to wear it almost daily), with shirttails flapping in the wind. Back and forth he went, looking here and then there, checking the small ditch along the edge of his property line, and stopping to wave to just about anyone who drove past. Could this mystery man be the new owner whose car-building factory was going to compete with Colgate as the largest employer in the Village of Hamilton? The stranger exhibited nothing pretentious in appearance or even a hint of being the next Henry Ford. The temptation to be the first resident with knowledge of the Mystery of Eaton Street made me walk across the street to find out more about the man in plaid. And so I met Arthur Zimmer.

"For the next hour, Art regaled me with details of how hard work, a little luck, being at the right place at the right time, and having been raised on a farm on the edge of Hamilton all contributed to motivate him to seize all opportunities that presented themselves. I learned that Art's entrepreneurial drive led him to own the Zimmer Motor Car Company, while at the same time he bought a nearly bankrupt weekly newspaper and turned it into a thriving business. When I asked Art what prompted him to buy the Zimmer Motor Car Company, his reply was, 'Wouldn't you buy a car company that had your last name?' Actually, there IS a Cooper, but the company is not for sale! And owning a newspaper? Art said that one of the fringe benefits associated with owning your own newspaper was that he could appoint himself as the ski columnist and could report on many of best ski resorts around the world.

"Even with all of his entrepreneurial successes, however, I soon learned not to ask Art how to turn on a computer, or make a call on a cell phone, or ask him to change the channel on his LED television. Without Shirley, Art would still own a rotary telephone, would be listening to a transistor radio, and possibly the Syracuse New Times would still be using handset type.

"I will always picture Art as Hamilton's version of a modern-day 'Luddite.' Ned Ludd, who was an 18th-century factory owner, was once the wealthiest textile producer in England. However, Ned refused to import the latest weaving machine machines while his competition sprang to install the technology. Ask Art how to use the Internet, or what an App is. He will be the first to tell you Shirley is the one who knows about such things. Let us just say that if you were to give Art a hammer and screwdriver, he could build anything. Ask him about adding a name to your cell phone directory, his answer would be to 'Ask Shirley.'

"I remember Art was so proud of his most recent success at installing 16 solar panels on his house. It was one of the first in the village to have such advanced technology. I was in awe. 'Art, I cannot believe you, Mr. Ned Luddite himself, installing solar panels on your house?' 'Yes,' Art replied, and proceeded to point out the 16 small lights he had attached to his roof's edge, each with a two-inch solar-powered battery as he added with a grin, 'I said they were solar panels, but they were just not the size or wiring that you were thinking.'

"With Art, what you see may or may not be what you get. When you are with Art you never know what new adventure is just around the corner, but you know it will be different."

Dick Flaherty swears that I'm being disingenuous about "technology." "Art isn't a tech guru, but look at what he has done in his life. I swear he had the first 'answer machine' on his North Syracuse phone number for his real estate business. But people would hang up when they called and got a 'machine.' So he educated people to leave a message by having the recording say: 'Leave a message for 'Homer'. For some reason people stopped hanging up and would leave a message."

We plan to live in the Hamilton house until we move into that assisted living facility. Or a cemetery.

When we were looking for a place to spend eternity together, we found a nice little country cemetery about two miles outside of Hamilton, the Smith Valley Cemetery in Randallsville. Deciding to continue our tradition of not having close neighbors, we bought ten burial plots instead of two, with plans to be buried in the center of the ten, so for eternity we will have no next-door neighbors.

When the cemetery association realized I was now the largest landowner in the cemetery, they elected me to the board of directors. At my first meeting, I said I thought the cemetery would soon run out of space to sell burial plots, and the source of income for upkeep would dry up. When that happens to a cemetery, I told the other directors, it goes out  of business so to speak. It becomes an overgrown, abandoned junkyard. You see such abandoned cemeteries all over the country.

By law, when a cemetery association ceases to function, the town where the property is located must take over its maintenance. This might work for a short time, but in most cases the town does not have the funds or interest to continue keeping the property up.

Of course, I also had a solution to present. I suggested we ask Colgate University to donate some land they owned adjacent to the cemetery.

The land had been donated to Colgate by Philo Parker in his will. Parker was a multi-millionaire who had been president of Standard Oil (Esso)

Company. The other board members just smiled and said, yes, they had approached Colgate about the land and the answer had been NO.

So I asked permission to pursue the request, and they said okay. I wrote another letter to Colgate and several months later got the same answer. No.

But I didn't become successful by taking no for an answer. I did some additional research and wrote another letter. Four months later I got a phone call from Colgate Vice President Joanne Race Borfitz. Yes, Colgate would donate five acres of land to the cemetery. That extra space will keep the cemetery growing, and funded, for over 200 years.

I'm sure that in 2214, if members of the cemetery association board approach Colgate University and show its trustees this chapter, they will find a way to deed a few more acres to our cemetery.

You're welcome, board members of the future!

~8~

Rudy

My friendship with Rudy Stefanovic was one of the most rewarding adventures of my life. Meeting and getting to know Rudy was an experience that was as unusual and exciting as you could get.

First, let me tell you about his background. Rudy was born into a well-to-do family in Yugoslavia. Rudy's father was a high-ranking government official. Rudy had a very good early life. One of his interests was tennis, and he became a very good tennis player. Rudy considered a career as a tennis professional. When Rudy was about 17, the Nazis marched into his town, killing people at random.

Rudy's father, along with other government officials, fled into the mountains to conduct the resistance to the Nazis. They fought during the entire war and assisted American troops to help win the war. During the war there was an opportunity for Rudy's family to leave Yugoslavia. However, his father would not leave, and his mother would not go without her husband. Eventually Rudy was captured by the Nazis, marched to a German concentration camp,

Rudy Stefanovic at our Otisco home.

and forced to work in a factory. Rudy's mother and sister remained in their village under harsh conditions.

Rudy planned to escape, but he knew that as soon as he was out of the camp the streets were full of Nazis. The Nazis stopped people to check their papers. Without proper documents, he would be shot. So Rudy taught himself to speak German like the locals. By the end of his life he taught himself seven languages.

Rudy thought if he could speak German like a local, he would not raise suspicion and it would aid his escape.

It took several years. He escaped and started to make his way across the country toward Yugoslavia. The journey took more than a year and included many harrowing experiences, including near death and starvation. In 1994, we took Rudy to Europe and travelled to some of the places where he had been at this time. Rudy's comment was that, the last time he was there, he hadn't known if he would ever eat again, let alone when.

As Rudy got to Yugoslavia, he started to see the red star flag and discovered the Communists from Russia had invaded the country. The Communists defeated the Nazis and set up a new brutal dictatorship government, treating the people worse than the Nazis had.

Rudy's father and other government officials had fled back into the mountains and now were fighting the Communists. Rudy knew that to go home would mean his being killed, so he worked his way over to Italy and finally to Rome. Rudy got a job as a waiter in Rome.

One day, Rudy picked up a newspaper. There was an article with photos. The Communists had captured his father and other officials and had executed his father, mother, and sister. Of course Rudy was devastated—this, in addition to the hardships that he had endured for many years.

On top of all this, Rudy was soon informed that Italy had made a deal with Yugoslavia's Communists under which, in exchange for some land, Italy would send all Yugoslavian citizens in Italy back to Yugoslavia. Most, including Rudy, were targeted to be executed upon their return. This was around 1947.

Thanks to some connections that Rudy had, he got passage on the first ship leaving Italy. It was going to Argentina, and there Rudy spent the rest of his life.

Fast forward to 1986. Rudy worked the intervening years as a waiter and maître d'. I met him in 1986, shortly before I met Shirley in January 1987. He was a native of Serbia, working as a waiter at a remote ski resort in the Andes Mountains in South America. It was the restaurant where I ate during my visit. Luckily I liked the food; the ski area was so high up in the mountains (I skied at 14 to 16,000 feet) that there was only one restaurant.

Rudy had a smooth, elegant European air to him. We became fast friends and after the first week I asked him if he ever thought of coming to the U.S. He replied that his dream had always been to visit the U.S., but that he could never afford it or do it on his own. Just getting a visa would be difficult. He had once put his name on a list to emigrate here, but was told it would have taken 19 or more years. "Okay," I said, "I'll bring you to the U.S."

With me as a sponsor and a place to stay, he was able to get a four-month visitor's visa. I sent him money for airfare and supported him while he was here. I brought him back four more times, two after Shirley and I married. We talked to an immigration lawyer to see if we could get Rudy full-time into the U.S. We were unable to do so.

Rudy spoke seven languages and Shirley was fluent in Spanish. She had taught Spanish in the North Syracuse School District for 17 years, and by then was an administrator in the district. She no longer got to use her Spanish much, so they enjoyed conversing in Spanish all the time. And I never knew what was being said.

The first time Rudy was in the U.S., he spent a few weeks at the Vermont Bavarian Haus hotel. Rudy was there when it burned down. He also spent a few weeks at the Vermont Austrian Haus hotel in subsequent years. He was a big hit at the hotels. There were guests at each resort from various countries. The international guests were very impressed when Rudy would talk with them in their native languages.

An exciting life

Rudy had a very good friend in Argentina, Pedro Buscaglia, who was the national minister of education under President Peron, and had worked often with Eva Peron (Evita). Rudy had at one time worked for Pedro's mother as a gardener. There were some very interesting stories there.

Rudy liked to gamble a little and for some reason he always dreamed of going to Caesar's Palace in Las Vegas. Rudy said that if he had the money he would live in a penthouse at Caesar's. One year, Shirley and I took Rudy to Las Vegas for a week. We all had a great time, and Rudy loved it.

Rudy had lived in Rome for about two years and knew the city well. He had good friends there who had helped him escape. Over the years, Rudy had lost contact with them, but always dreamed of going back for a visit. In 1994 Shirley and I took a six-week trip to Europe, and Rudy went with us. The week in Rome was fabulous. Rudy was our personal guide and showed us the "inside" of the city—through his eyes. Unfortunately, all the people Rudy had known from long ago were gone. Rudy could find no information on any of his friends.

Shirley and Rudy both enjoyed watching tennis on TV, so I arranged a trip to Stratton Mountain in Vermont, where there was an international tennis championship. I also invited my mother. My dad had passed away the year before. My mother, in her 80s, had trouble navigating stairs, so I got her handicapped seating at the matches. I did not tell Rudy or my mother where we were going. We just told them each to pack a bag, as we would be away for a few days.

There were several international tennis stars at the event from Spanish-speaking countries. They included Conchita Martinez and Arantxa Sánchez Vicario. The handicapped-accessible seats were right down front, court side. They were so close to the court that Rudy and Shirley had a great time talking in Spanish with many of the world's top tennis players. It was a wonderful experience for us all.

Another time we took Rudy to New York City. Madison Square Garden was hosting the end-of-season world championship tennis matches. After the matches, we walked around New York City for a couple of hours. As we came back to the Garden to get our car, we were near the back entrance just as Martina Navratilova walked out. Martina was a world champion, but not a favorite of Rudy's, as she was Czechoslovakian, while Rudy was Serbian. The two factions had been fighting off and on for a thousand years. As Martina approached us, Rudy greeted her in her native language. Martina was taken aback, but pleased, and stopped and chatted with Rudy before getting in the limo to leave. It was quite an exciting moment. It felt like one of those times when you realize that sometimes two people talking can bridge huge cultural chasms.

In 1991, our friends Al and Thalia Vizgaitis, the couple who set Shirley and me up for our first date, asked us what Rudy was going to be doing the next few weeks until he needed to return to Argentina. Shirley and I had planned for Rudy to hang out with us. I was running about five or six companies at that time. Al and Thalia asked if Rudy would like to live with them and help take care of their newborn baby girl. As Rudy had never married or had a family, we did not think that he would be interested. However, we asked him. Rudy said, "Well, I've never done anything like that, but you always have to be open to doing new things. Sure, I'll try it." In fact, in 1994, Rudy returned to spend time with us and stayed with the Vizgaitis family to help with their second child!

Even between his visits, we would find ourselves reminded of him. The very successful Syracuse International Film Festival that I talk about elsewhere in this book was organized and run by Owen Shapiro and Christine Fawcett Shapiro. Another person who was very involved in the film festival was Pedro Cuperman, founder and director of the Point of Contact gallery, and on staff at SU.

One evening at a fundraising cocktail party for the film festival at the Century Club, Shirley and I were talking to Pedro (Shirley and Pedro were chatting in Spanish), when Pedro mentioned that he was from Argentina and had lived in Buenos Aires. We said that we had a friend from Buenos Aires (a city of several million) whose name was Rudy. We did not say his last name. Pedro said, "Rudy Stefanovic?" "Do you know Rudy???" we exclaimed.

"No," Pedro said, "but my sister who lives in Buenos Aires has frequently talked about her friend Rudy... Stefanovic!"

We loved the adventures Rudy had with us. And considering the amazing life he had already had, we thought it could make a very interesting book, and perhaps movie, and set him up financially for life. His stories were interesting and exciting with lots of drama.

We talked him into writing out his life story in Spanish. He did so with paper and pen, about 100 pages. I had it translated and typed in English. That's when we discovered that his writing was dull and did not convey how amazing his life had been. All the facts were there, but it lacked the humor, excitement, and drama that his stories had when he would tell them to us.

As Rudy finished the book, it was time for him to go back to Argentina. My plan was to bring Rudy back the next year and hire a writer. Perhaps Walt Shepperd, who worked for me at the New Times for about 25 years and was the only person to be named writer of the year twice by the New York Press Association, could take Rudy's book, sit down to hear Rudy's stories in person, and rewrite it into a riveting biography. I thought that we could have ended up with a best-seller.

Rudy never came back. He got sick and died before he could. I still have his manuscript and often wonder about doing something with it. I feel a little better about this unfinished saga now that I've written about him here.

~9~

Shirley

I didn't find her until I was almost 50; the past 28 years with Shirley have been the best years of my life.

On our first (blind) date, Shirley and I drove to a restaurant to meet Al and Thalia Vizgaitis, who had fixed us up. We were amazed to find out that we grew up just a few miles apart. Our parents knew each other quite well. My dad had done business with Shirley's dad for years. Shirley's dad was the manager of the milk processing plant in Eaton where my dad shipped his milk every day. This might be my most important "small-world" experience!

Engagement Announced

Shirley Sherburne and Art Zimmer have announced their engagement.

Miss Sherburne is the daughter of Mr. & Mrs. Ray Sherburne of Eaton New York. Mr. Zimmer is the son of Mr. & Mrs. Carl Zimmer of Hamilton, New York.

Miss Sherburne is a graduate of Morrisville-Eaton School and Ohio State University. She was formerly a Spanish teacher and is currently District Coordinator of foreign languages for North Syracuse Central School.

This summer, Miss Sherburne is on an extended tour, visiting New Zealand, Australia, Tonja and Hawaii.

Mr. Zimmer is a graduate of Hamilton High School, an Eagle Scout and former scoutmaster with troop 15 Boy Scouts and a veteran of the U.S. Army. He is currently an independent businessman in Syracuse and owns and operates various business enterprises including: hotels, restaurants, printing, publishing, real eastate and Graphic Arts companies. He is also the publisher of the Syracuse New Times Newspaper and a former Mid-York employee. The New Times is the largest weekly newspaper in up-state New York.

A late summer wedding is planned. They will make their home near Tully, N.Y.

Steppin' Out

The Shirley Sherburne–Art Zimmer Wedding

Aug. 29, 1987, Imperial Ballroom, Hotels at Syracuse Square

*T*he *New Times* isn't too hip to show up at its own party. Or yours. From time to time, we'll feature our readers when they're steppin' out. And what better place to start than the publisher's wedding? We know who signs the checks.

Shirley and Art schmoozing.

Herald society columnist Jackie Coley.

MICHAEL DAVIS PHOTOS

In Shirley's words:

"In January 1987 Art met me ('the most wonderful girl in the world,' according to him), not immediately recognizing me as that little eight-year-old waiting for the school bus in front of the milk plant when he was in high school.

"To celebrate the day we met, January 23, 1987, Art and I recognize in some way the 23rd of each month. The first year, Art gave me a rose for the 1st-month anniversary, two roses for the 2nd-month anniversary, and so on throughout the first 12 months. OK, after a dozen months and 78 roses, the roses were history. The celebrations continued and do to this day. We take turns planning the day and surprises, recognize the day with cards or special messages. Wedding anniversary celebrations are similar in that we take turns planning something special.

"The first few years, Art and I went to the Finger Lakes frequently, as it was close enough and held special meaning for us, since we went to Geneva-on-the-Lake for our honeymoon. One time, I surprised Art with a trip to a BnB near Naples. It was down a winding dirt road. Art was truly perplexed and wondered where in the world I was taking him. The ambience in our suite was interesting, as there was a stuffed white peacock perched on the side of the hot tub.

"Art told me once that he would love to drive a Zamboni ice-clearing machine, like Snoopy in the Peanuts comics strip. He has surprised me with so many wonderful trips, shows, and more, I thought how great it would be for him to drive the Zamboni that clears the ice at Syracuse Crunch hockey games.

"In the summer of 1995, we were at a friend's 70th birthday party; then-County Executive Nick Pirro was also a guest. We started to chat, and I told Nick how I dreamed of surprising Art with a Zamboni drive. I thought it was casual talk...until September, when Nick called and gave me the details of how to set my plan in motion!

"One November afternoon that year, Art and I 'just happened' to be walking in downtown Syracuse near the Civic Center. As we approached the War Memorial, I suggested to Art that we go inside to get warm. He had no idea that I had tickets for a Syracuse Crunch game that afternoon. Several friends were waiting to join me in the stands as he drove the Zamboni to clear the ice.

"It took some convincing to get him inside. We walked to the ticket gate, and Jerry Gallagher, the executive diretor of the War Memorial, was there to meet Art, who still had no idea what was going on. Jerry took Art 'backstage' to show him where to be at halftime. I

met him at our seats, where he was again surprised to see that a large crowd of friends was there to watch his drive! It was the first and only time a non-union 'civilian' drove the Zamboni during a hockey game at the War Memorial. Art was so surprised. The look on his face as he cleared the ice conveyed pure delight. I'm so grateful to Nick and Jerry for making it possible for me to surprise Art."

Shirley and I always seem to find such interesting coincidences like the "milk plant connection," or they find us. After that first-date discovery, others soon followed. When she met my parents, I had told my mother that Shirley was very involved in the foreign language profession. As a Spanish teacher in North Syracuse schools, and later the foreign language department chair,

Shirley regularly went to conferences and meetings in the northeast. My mother said, "You may know Art's cousin, Helene." Shirley, astonished, exclaimed, "Helene Zimmer Loew? Helene is Art's *cousin*?"

Shirley and Helene had roomed together at conferences. One time when she had forgotten to pack an outfit for a formal banquet, Helene loaned her what she describes as a beautiful designer dress. Who knew that she would have known my cousin from Connecticut and seen her often

Art and Shirley's wedding picture taken in backyard of their new Otisco home.
Photo by Norma Jean Young

over the course of her foreign language education career. I had not seen Helene for 60 years, not since my family moved from Connecticut to New York, when two years ago many of our family members gathered in Hamilton for a reunion.

Shirley's friend Marcia Ferber remembers when she met me, soon after Shirley and I started dating.

"Shirl and I were already friends when they 'lucked-out' and met. Many of the stories I could tell are so specific to location/event and the folks involved that they would make little sense to anyone else ('convicted

Shirley as a senior at Albany State in 1968 (left) and in 1985 (right), two years before her blind date with me.

Photo by Pictures With Pride

felon,' indeed, Mr. Zimmer!!) It took me a while to acclimate to his very dry sense of humor but I get it most of the time now. The aspect of Art's personality that impacts my life in the most positive way is his willingness to initiate fun events and/or trips that include me. He and Shirl could go on their own, but his generosity in including me is just the coolest."

One day shortly after Shirley and I were engaged, we were at a fund-raiser at downtown Sibley's department store (Remember Sibley's?). I was a celebrity bartender for the event. Shirley introduced me to her very dear friend who she had not seen in several years, Harriette MacDowell.

Harriette was a very successful business woman, but she and Shirley had lost touch over the years. As a surprise for Shirley, I invited Harriette to the farm for dinner. They rekindled their friendship, and we frequently spent time with Harriette for several years until, at a young age, she died of cancer. Back to the surprise dinner. Harriette was in the living room, and we heard a surprised gasp. We hurried in from the kitchen to find Harriette was holding our framed marriage license that included my birth date and place of birth on it. Harriette exclaimed, "I don't believe it. We have the exact same birthday, right down to the year, and we were born near each other in Connecticut!"

My birthday friend for several years, Harriette MacDowell.

From that point on we included Harriette in all of my birthday celebrations. Every five years, we had a big party to celebrate our mutual big milestone. Birthdays have never concerned or bothered me. I could never understand why people got hyper about passing 40 or 60 or 65. I just keep rolling along, business as usual. Now at 78, it's just another day.

So much of life is just a proper mental attitude.

COME AWAY WITH ME...

The year after Shirley and I were married, we took a ski week in Canada. Every day was about 20 degrees below zero, so we decided to start spending winters in warmer places.

In the next few years we traveled to Hawaii, Acapulco, took a six-country tour of Europe, and, in the Caribbean, visited Aruba, Barbados, Curacao, Grand Caymans, Bahamas, Key West, and several other islands on three cruises.

Other cruises we took include sailing down the Pacific Ocean and through the Panama Canal to South America, a cruise up the Mississippi on a Mark Twain-era paddle boat and a train trip across Canada, followed by a cruise to Alaska. And we drove across the U.S. five times. As I write this, we just got back from a tour of the western U.S. National Parks that the government shutdown cut short for us a year and a half ago.

We've taken several trips to Montreal, Quebec, Toronto, and Ottawa, Canada. Many short jaunts to the Thousand Islands, Adirondacks, and Finger

Lakes. Lots and lots of trips to Vermont for business and pleasure. Several trips to NYC for the Big East basketball tournament. A trip to New Orleans for the Sugar Bowl the year SU was in it. Trips to Penn State and the Meadowlands and Baltimore for SU games, plus about a dozen two- or three-month trips to Florida for the winter, staying in places all over that state. We've visited about 40 states, including Alaska and Hawaii.

Before I met Shirley, I joined the U.S. Ski Writers Association, as I was the Ski Editor of the Post-Standard, then Ski Editor for the New Times. As a ski writer, I took trips year-round almost every month for six years, from long weekends to four weeks, traveling to most every ski area in the U.S., all over Canada, six trips to Europe, and a fabulous August ski trip to South America—Argentina's Andes Mountains (their seasons are opposite of ours). That trip included a week in Buenos Aires and a week in Rio de Janeiro.

I don't know how I have had the time to run 11 major businesses and have a busy social life.

TRAVELING THE WORLD

Over the past 28 years, Shirley and I have worked long hours running as many as seven businesses at the same time, putting in 70-80 hours per week, seven days a week. Coupled with that extensive workload was careful advance planning that allowed us to travel extensively and see a lot of the world.

Prior to our meeting on that blind date, Shirley had traveled around the U.S. and lived in Spain and Colombia. I had traveled and skied throughout the world, including South America, Europe, Canada, and the U.S.

Sometimes we muse that the ground we have covered is amazing for a couple of country kids from Eaton and Randallsville. But really, it's nothing more than most anyone could do if they are willing to work hard and plan carefully.

Fifty Years in the Salt City

When I first hitchiked to Syracuse with only $18 in my pocket, I would have felt fortunate to find a paying job (I did) and a place to live (I did). But I also knew that I wanted to make a "difference," to control my own destiny. This was before my retirement, at age 31, from being an employee; even working for other people, I wanted to feel that I was writing my own future, and helping other people write theirs.

That instinct figured in my joining the Onondaga Ski Club and starting to invest in real estate. And later, it influenced my decision to buy the Syracuse New Times. As a publisher, I had influence and money to spend. Deciding how to use those resources shaped my 50 years of community involvement in the Salt City.

NEW TIMES AWARDS

Of all of my awards, I am most proud of the 250-plus national and regional awards presented to the New Times when I owned it. It tickled me that the farm boy who failed English for four years was now the owner/publisher of the largest weekly newspaper in New York, outside of New York City.

An association called Free Community Papers of New York (FCPNY) gives out an annual award for overall general excellence, covering all aspects of a newspaper's operations. No paper had ever won it more than twice. Then my New Times won it every year for 13 consecutive years.

Why am I proud of all these awards? Why did I fight to qualify for them and then win them? Some people (usually the losers) would say I'm an egocentric maniac. Perhaps I am. But I also created a public persona: I was the SNT and the SNT was me. Awards gave us a million dollars' worth of free advertising; it was all marketing. Coverage of many awards was even carried by my competitor, the Post-Standard. And my friends at the Business Journal Newspaper printed a lot of it. Bernie Bregman, the now-retired marketing genius at the Business Journal, taught me much of what I know about marketing.

As a publisher, I was invited to every news conference and every announcement. And I could be of value to causes and goals I cared about.

Art with a few of his favorite awards presented to him over the years.

Long-time New Times editor Mike Greenstein agrees:
"Support of community events and initiatives was definitely Art's
major achievement with The New Times. The paper has credibility in
the arts communities, and the paper's publicity and services could help
to establish festivals such as Jazz Fest and Blues Fest, awards for music
like the Sammys, SALT, and more, plus Street Painting, the Syr-Haiku
Poetry Contest, athletic events, and more. All of these co-sponsorships
made the paper more visible and more 'establishment' during his tenure
as publisher."

And my first editor, Roland Sweet, adds,
"Art was a legitimate community and cultural booster who brought
financial stability and even a measure of prosperity to the paper."

The Syracuse Area Live Theater (SALT) Awards

Soon after buying the Syracuse New Times, I decided that, since the
weekly was the primary medium covering live theater, we should sponsor an
annual awards show, much like the Oscars and Tonys, which would honor
local productions and actors. Another great marketing tool for us as well as for
local theater. The year before Paul Harvey, a respected local theater person, had
tried to organize such a ceremony and failed under a hail of bickering and hard
feelings among the various community theater companies.

I took my idea to my editor-in-chief, Mike Greenstein, and theater critic,
Jim MacKillop. Both said, politely, NO. It would never work and the New
Times would be left in the middle with all the theater companies hating us.
They reminded me of Paul's unpleasant experience. I was new in the business
so I took their advice and dropped the idea.

Ten years later, I ran into Paul Harvey at a party and we discussed the
failed concept. I still thought it was a great idea. Once again, Mike and Jim
were opposed to it. So I sat down and designed how the entire process could be
done. I proposed the acronym SALT—Syracuse Area Live Theater—Awards.

Mike and Jim reluctantly went along with me, but they predicted it
would be a disaster and ruin the position the New Times had worked hard to
establish as the leading voice of live theater in Central New York.

I received the Founder's Award from current Syracuse New Times owner Bill Brod at the SALT Awards in October 2014.   *Photo by Michael Davis, Syracuse New Times*

No one could believe what happened next. That first year the entire theater community came together, many for the first time in the same room: the Syracuse New Times Theater at the Fairgrounds. We threw a red carpet gala, with gowns and tuxedos and limos. Actors and producers who previously were feuding embraced each other and applauded and cheered when their rivals won an award.

After a couple of years, SALT outgrew the New Times Theater and I moved it to Syracuse Stage. We outgrew that venue and I moved it to the Syracuse Palace Theater. It continues to thrive.

Even today, Jim MacKillop and I joke about his early opposition. Now he is SALT's biggest fan. And guess what: every year the Post-Standard does articles with photos and credits me and the New Times for getting a great tradition rolling.

CHILDREN'S MIRACLE NETWORK

Today, the Children's Miracle Network (CMN) is one of the best known and most successful nonprofit fundraising organizations in the world. An international nonprofit organization that raises funds for children's hospitals, medical research, and community awareness of children's health issues, 30 years ago the Network was an unknown fledgling group with a chapter trying to get off the ground in Syracuse.

I met Karen Williams, CMN's local organizer, through a skier friend, as Karen and I were both avid skiers. Karen told me about the new nonprofit she was trying to get started, but the process was very slow. Karen asked me if the Syracuse New Times and I could help.

It sounded like a good concept to me, so I signed on. At that time, Syracuse's daily papers and local television stations would not help them at all. So I put the power and prestige of the New Times behind the Network. The New Times donated advertising space to them and published some nice articles about their work and the children they serve.

I acted as a business volunteer consultant for the organizers. As one of their first fundraisers, the New Times sponsored a ski race at Labrador Mountain. When we advertised the ski race to benefit the Children's Miracle Network, no one knew what that was. With my connections in the ski world and the promotional articles in the New Times, the ski community turned out in force.

Over $250 was raised at the race, and the New Times donated a matching $250. Thirty years ago, $500 was like $5,000 today, and it was the first big local donation they received. Today almost no one remembers that the New Times and I were instrumental in the early success of the Children's Miracle Network in Syracuse.

In subsequent years, the New Times worked with CNY school districts to publish students' writing and art work in an issue called Kids Times, a publication for and by students, printed in the spring. The New Times donated the proceeds from the paid advertising in Kids Times to the Children's Miracle Network for several years.

SYRACUSE INTERNATIONAL FILM FESTIVAL

I was a charter member of the organizing group for the Syracuse International Film Festival (SIFF). I stayed on the Festival board until I moved to Hamilton. Now I'm on the Hamilton International Film Festival Committee for this annual August event that is growing every year at Hamilton's movie theater. The New Times was an early financial backer of the SIFF and published its official program for years at no cost to the Festival.

THE SAMMYs

The New Times published the program for Syracuse's annual Jazz Fest and was a major sponsor each year as it grew into a venerable annual event.

Jazz Fest's director, Frank Malfitano, then-director of the Landmark Theater in Syracuse, approached me about a new idea he had. He envisioned a music awards show, sort of a local Grammys: "I've been working on it for two years and it's going nowhere; would you help?" he said.

The New Times and I took over what would become the SAMMYS (Syracuse Area Music Awards). The SNT and I put up the money to get it started, organized a board of directors, printed programs, and got it off the ground. Frank remained the public face of the event, and the New Times and I made it all work behind the scenes. Every board meeting for 16 years was held in my New Times office. New Times employees made up the majority of the board and for about ten years, a New Times employee was the board president.

SYRACUSE CHAMBER OF COMMERCE

After I bought the New Times, I joined the Syracuse Chamber of Commerce and was an active member. I chaired three major committees at the same time, the only Chamber member ever to do that. I created several programs that are still operated by the Chamber, part of CenterState CEO today. One of the committees I started to chair was inactive at the time. It was called Buy Local. Soon the Buy Local committee meetings were attracting 100 members, more than some Chamber events.

My Buy Local committee started a little trade show, the Local Business Show, for locally produced products; the second year we outgrew the Chamber facilities. The Chamber took the show out of the committee's hands, and I continued as an advisor. It continued to grow, and the Chamber hired Center Stage Events to run it. It kept growing, taking over the biggest building at the State Fairgrounds.

A few years ago, the Chamber took management of the show back in-house and renamed it Business Showcase. It fills the downtown OnCenter each year. I'm willing to wager that no one currently at CenterState CEO remembers that I was the founder of their big annual show.

As publisher of the New Times, I was the Chamber's Member of the Year once; the New Times was a finalist for Business of the Year seven times. No other member company ever became a finalist more than twice. But with 2,000 companies in the Chamber, some with more than 1,000 employees, it was hard for a small company to actually win. After the New Times lost to Marcellus Casket and then to Stickley, I pointed out that, since small companies make up over two-thirds of the Chamber's membership, there ought to be two categories for Business of the Year: one for large and one for small businesses. Then, when a nonprofit organization with 50 employees and over 2,000 volunteers won the Small Business award, I lobbied for a nonprofit category to be created and it was. We still didn't win, but I'm glad to say the Food Bank did.

Bernie Bregman and Ellie Hayman (she was the top realtor in CNY for 20 years) are two people I admire the most and try to emulate in all my business dealings. Ellie recalls that she and I met through the Chamber of Commerce:
"I met Art in the 1980s through the Chamber; it was love at first sight! It honors me that he cites me as one of his 'business gurus.' We have all had such good times together, but have you noticed how when someone does something great for someone you love, it stands out? Art arranged for my significant other, Jack Mesnick, to enjoy a ride in a fabulous Zimmer car. This was during a party at 'the big house', Art and Shirley's lovely home on Sentinel Heights."

Pictured above L to R: Bernie Bregman, me... and Bernard Bregman. I have developed 13 companies—many from scratch—into successful and profitable businesses. Most of that success came from lots of hard work and aggressive and unique marketing. People would say "Art, you are a marketing genius". I answer, "No, Bernie Bregman, my mentor, taught me all I know. Bernie and Realtor Ellie Hayman are the true marketing geniuses of Central New York."

USA TODAY ENTREPRENEUR OF THE YEAR COMPETITION

For several years, USA Today and Ernst and Young, the national accounting firm, sponsored an annual national Entrepreneur of the Year award. Ernst and Young nominated me as the owner of a New York State business, one of over 20,000. I was a finalist but didn't win the top prize. The next year (2002) I asked Robert H. Linn, the director of the upstate branch of the Ernst and Young Agency, about being nominated again. He said no one got put up more than once. I pointed out that the true mark of an entrepreneur is persistence. So I became a finalist again. In 2003 I won it all, becoming New York State's Entrepreneur of the Year.

Shirley and I went to Palm Springs, California for the National Finals, hosted by Jay Leno. Other finalists were people like the founder of Jet Blue

Robert Linn presented me with the Entrepreneur Award.

and the founder of Whole Foods. Needless to say, I did not win. But we had a thoroughly enjoyable time as nominees.

2003 Ernst & Young National Entrepreneur of the Year Award - Art's Speech

Tonight this award is not for Art Zimmer, this award is not for the wonderful staff of the Syracuse New Times newspaper. This award is not for the unique and exciting Zimmer Classic Motor Car Company.

Tonight, this award symbolically goes to all those out there starting out with less than a dollar and a dream.

Tonight, this award goes out to all the Horatio Algers who started poor and did it on their own, to those without the education or fancy college degrees. This award is for all of you who pulled yourselves up by your own boot straps to become successful entrepreneurs, of the old school.

This award is for all of you who achieved your success through hard work and perseverance with no well-connected family or friends to open doors for you.

This award is for all of us entrepreneurs who have not asked for or received a penny of corporate welfare, called government assistance, in any way.

And most of all, this award is for the spouses who stand beside us, not behind us, to make it all worthwhile. This award is for my wife, Shirley S. Zimmer. Thank you.

MY CRYSTAL BALL

Central New York's chapter of Sales & Marketing Executives (CNYSME) sponsors the Crystal Ball award each year. The Crystal Ball is given to a top marketing executive in the Syracuse area. After being nominated several times, I asked a friend on the committee if I was ever going to actually win. He explained the award is given out at a banquet, their biggest fundraiser for the year, so they tend to give it to an executive from a big company who will bring lots of people to the awards dinner. Even though I felt I was more qualified than several previous recipients, my company was small; the New Times had only about 80 employees, compared to companies with thousands of people on staff.

The program from the CNYSME's Crystal Ball Award in 2005.

So in 2005, I sat down and wrote a 14-page single-spaced letter listing everything I had ever done in sales and marketing, starting with the Hamilton Boy Scout Troop that had 14 members when I joined and 52 when I left. I didn't know what marketing was in those days, but I knew how it worked. The Crystal Ball nominating committee members were unaware of most of my background. I sent a copy to each one of them.

My friend on the committee said that when they read the letter, they had to give me the award. I told them to change the venue for the banquet from the Sheraton University Hotel to the OnCenter, as I planned to outdraw the big boys. They changed it to the OnCenter and, thanks to my friends, associates, and acquaintances, attendance at my banquet equaled or exceeded all others.

My marketing idol, Bernie Bregman, who is the greatest and most creative marketing person in all of CNY, said, "I'm glad that your banquet actually exceeded their budgeted expectation, as I was pushing the committee to give you the Crystal Ball."

ART'S ACCEPTANCE SPEECH FOR
THE CRYSTAL BALL AWARD 2/10/05

Thanks, Y'all:

If I were to list all the people I should thank, we would be here much too long. So, I wish to thank just three people or groups of people.

First and foremost I give profound thanks to the one person that makes all I do worthwhile. The person that gives me full and complete support on every crazy, off-the-wall idea I come up with. The person that pushed me into starting the Zimmer Motor Car Co. and the musical show, Cruizin' thru the 50s. The person that does not stand behind me but stands beside me, Shirley S. Zimmer. Let's have a standing, rousing ovation for Shirley.

Of all the things I've done in my life, the smartest thing I ever did was to marry that girl, thank you Shirley (kiss).

Secondly, I wish to thank all the past recipients of this very prestigious Crystal Ball award. These people have set a high standard of excellence in the community and in the profession of Sales and Marketing. People like the founder and first recipient of the Crystal Ball, Doc Swartz. Doc, stand up and take a bow.

I feel humble and inadequate being in the company of these past recipients.

People such as the Audis of Stickley fame, and Mayor Tom Young. I worked with Tom for many years when he ran the New York State Fair and I was director of the big ski show for 16 years.

And another past recipient, Bob Congel. I say this to you, Bob Congel, it is time to kick some ass and get Destiny built. Central New York needs it.

The list of Crystal Ball recipients goes on and on and I thank them all for setting such a fine example.

And third, I wish to thank in advance all the future recipients of the Crystal Ball Award. The example you will set in the community and your chosen profession of Sales and Marketing will be one that will make me proud to have been a Crystal Ball recipient. I would like to hold myself up as a role model to all of you in Sales and Marketing, and encourage you to live by these three rules that have guided me.

Rule one, Sell, Sell, Sell, everywhere, all the time and be aggressive about it.

Rule two, Market and promote all the time, everywhere, and be creative about it.

Rule three, Network, everywhere, all the time and be both aggressive and creative about it.

The proof that these three rules work are in people like myself and Ellie Hayman and Bernie Bregman (Bow) and all the past Crystal Ball award winners.

And so, in closing, the Sales and Marketing Executives Association would not consider me worthy of this wonderful award unless I practice what I preach. That is, to sell, market and promote, and network at every possible opportunity. So when you are ready to buy a new car, please purchase a Zimmer Motor car, they are only $150,000.

And as you cruise around town in your new Zimmer, stop at one of our 650 outlets to pick up a copy of the Syracuse New Times newspaper, the most popular paper in Central New York.

And if you have children or grandchildren, pick up a copy of Family Times, the only parenting guide magazine in Central New York.

And if you EAT, pick up a copy of Dish, the only official dining guide in Central New York.

Then park your Zimmer at the New Times Theater to attend the smash musical show, Cruizin' thru the 50s and 60s II

Thank you all, and good night.

CRUIZIN' THRU THE '50S
ON CRUIZ CONTROL

For several years in our travels, Shirley and I had seen several shows about the 1950s era. I always criticized them as not really portraying the 50s properly. One day, after seeing one such show on TV, I as usual sounded off to Shirley. I guess she had had enough. She said, "Would you stop criticizing them or do something yourself that's better."

I had about three seconds for a comeback. Without thinking about it in advance, I said, "Okay, I will."

Shirley said, "What?"

I thought I could toss out a quick answer and then forget about it. I said, "I'll write a musical play." She said, "You don't know how to write." Well...true. She said, "You know nothing about theater."

Well... no. So now I had to do something.

I arranged to rent the theater at the New York State Fairgrounds and have its name changed to the New Times Theater as a marketing strategy for the SNT. I called a press conference at the theater and was surprised when 200 people showed up. Usually six to eight people attend news conferences in Syracuse. No one but Shirley and I knew what the announcement was to be.

I announced that I planned to do a musical play. Shirley had come up with a name: "Cruizin' Thru The '50s." One reporter asked if it was all written and ready to go. I admitted I had not written a word and really did not know what I was doing. Everyone thought I was kidding.

The next morning the New Times office manager, Kathy Fisher, came in my office. "What should I do?" she said. "People are calling for tickets to your show." I told her to just take their phone numbers and we would call them back.

A week went by and I still had done nothing. Wednesday night we went to a Chamber clambake at Hinerwadels'. I love steamed clams. After 16 dozen clams, plus hamburgers, hot dogs, etc., I woke up at 2 a.m., feeling fine. I said to myself, Art you had better do something about the musical play. I got dressed, went to my home office, and sat down with a tablet of yellow legal paper. I

Shirley and I acted as narrators for the show. Below: a poster for the production. We sold out every night for seven straight years.

Above: Dennis Calkins designed and built the set to my specifications. I wanted the entire band on stage for the entire show; It really showcased their talents. On the left side was the radio DJ booth; in the center was the theater marquee. To the right was the band, and a '59 Cadillac hovered over them with Elvis and Marilyn Monroe cruising in it. Farther right was the soda fountain, and the menu board displayed the informaiton for each song as it was being performed. All the way to the right was the jukebox with all of the "good songs" on it. **Below**: Wells Corey was the show's first 'Elvis'.

started to write. Six hours later, the first half of the play was done. Two nights later and six more hours of writing in the middle of the night, and it was done. (Eat your heart out, Neil Simon. It took that guy two years to write a play.)

Now I needed a director. As I don't know anything about theater, some friends recommended the head of LeMoyne College's drama department, who knows a lot about theater. We had a meeting. I gave him my handwritten script. Three days later we met again. He said, "This script just won't work; I have suggestions for changes." I said, "NO, it's my show; we do it my way. I don't care if it closes the first night." Out he went.

I then recruited Bob Brown, a well-known Syracuse actor and director, who was widely known for playing the title role in Salt City's Jesus Christ Superstar production. Bob said, "Okay, we'll do it your way." He signed up Jeff Unaitis as music director, the key person for a musical. Most of the credit for the success of "Cruizin' " goes to Jeff, and the very talented band and cast he put together. The show that was presented was 98 percent the same as what I wrote those two nights.

I was the producer and playwright. The show made history, selling out every performance for seven years. That was 63 performances, with a total audience of about 18,000, all in the New Times Theater at the State Fairgrounds in Syracuse. I also combined it with dinner in the room next door to the theater; for several years, 150 people came early for dinner each night before the show.

The huge success of Cruizin' was due to many factors, and there were many outstanding moments in the show. Start with the fact (in my opinion) that 1950s rock and roll is by far the best and most popular music in the world. People still flock to hear it. The script I wrote framed the 1950s in a way no one had done before, and people really liked it.

The first big credit for the success must go to Jeff Unaitis. Jeff was vice president of Time Warner and a very talented musician. I got to know Jeff when he played around town and frequently donated his musical talent to play at nonprofit fundraisers that Shirley and I attended. When Jeff agreed to be music director for Cruizin', he put together a very talented band, a cast of singers and actors, arranged the music, and made it all work. Without Jeff, I don't think that there would have been a Cruizin'.

The band members Jeff put together all came back to play every year. They really loved playing the 1950s music. They were all very talented, high energy, and really made the music come alive. They were so good that I made some changes to the script to give them some band-only musical numbers.

Here are a few of the high points:

We had some very unusual and beautiful sets that were designed by and actually constructed by Dennis Calkins. Dennis was for more than 40 years the art director of TV Channel 9, Syracuse's ABC affiliate, starting there even before the station went on air. Now retired, he has done some illustrations for this book.

Of course, you cannot have a 1950s show without an Elvis impersonator. We had two of the best: E. Wendell Conley and Nick Mulpagano.

Then there was Armand Magnarelli. Armand was a very popular politician. He had been New York State Director of Parks and for years performed in musical theater with the Pompeian Players, for many years the primary local live theater production company. By then Armand was getting quite elderly. You should remember the 50s hit novelty tune "Witch Doctor." They still play it on satellite radio Sirius XM channel 5. Bob Brown dressed Armand up in a grass skirt and a big African headdress. When Armand stepped out on stage to the music of Witch Doctor, carrying a spear, it brought the house down. One night his grass skirt fell down. Luckily Armand was wearing boxer shorts under it, so the performance didn't become x-rated. It brought the house down double. We asked him to let the skirt slip for every show...but he said no. It would stop the show for too long. Armand also performed a Hank Williams, Sr. number that brought tears to some eyes.

When Rod Ward, a member of the band, stepped out front and did a stirring rendition of Mack the Knife, for a moment everyone forgot Bobby Darin. All agreed that Rod's Mack the Knife was better.

Michael Connor was a classically trained opera singer and appeared in many Syracuse Opera Company productions. He was also the marketing director of the New Times. Michael could sing anything. He thrilled the audience with several solos and joined the cast for some numbers.

Carrie Berse had such a sweet voice, people just loved to hear her sing and always wanted to hear more. She was director of the Crouse Hospital Foundation.

What can I say about Elizabeth Fern? A great talent and a wonderful voice. One year after the show was over, she told us that she had been pregnant during the show. Only her first trimester, so it wasn't obvious. Two years later, Elizabeth called to tell me that she couldn't do Cruizin' that year because she was pregnant and would be near her due date at show time. Elizabeth didn't think that I would want a nine-months-pregnant lady waddling around the stage. I told her that, yes indeed, we wanted her in the show. We would just change a couple of her songs to numbers with a baby theme and actually play it up. Elizabeth reluctantly agreed.

This led to a very special performance. When Elizabeth first came on stage, her mother, who was in the audience, started to cry. Elizabeth was wearing the bright yellow maternity dress that her mother had worn when pregnant with Elizabeth. At first, the audience thought it was a funny joke, a girl singing baby songs with a lot of padding to look pregnant. However, it quickly became very obvious that Elizabeth was really nine months pregnant. For each performance, she was on stage singing, dancing, and kicking her heels

Moe Harrington, one of CNY's great theater performers. She appeared in every performance of "Cruizin'" as well as several other shows Art produced.

up. The entire cast was taking bets on which day Elizabeth would deliver. The problem was that we had no plan B for the second weekend.

The second weekend came, and there was Elizabeth up on stage performing. So we got through four or five performances. Sunday night, during the last number, Elizabeth was still up on stage kicking her heels up as high as all the others. Two hours later, she was in the hospital delivering her baby. When she said the show must go on, she really meant it.

Karin Franklin-King was a long-time popular TV talk show host and featured singer for the popular oldies band Golden Gate. Karin added a spark and excitement not only with her talented voice, but also the hula hoop demo and playing Name That Tune (remember that old TV show) with the audience.

Moe Harrington also appeared in several other shows that I produced. A long-time, very talented musical theater performer, Moe had done shows with Bonnie Nye, one of the top theater producers from many, many years ago.

Dana E. Sovocool is not only very talented but very versatile, with a strong background in musical theater in Buffalo, at Cornell University, and Syracuse.

That set Dennis designed and constructed had a theater marquis in the center. As we went through the years of the 1950s a young boy, Spencer Murphy, an eighth grader from Jamesville-DeWitt, would bring out a ladder and climb up and post the name of the Academy Award film winner for that year. He was all decked out in a splendid uniform, almost like an Army general. Remember when all theater personnel dressed like that?

Spencer was a talented musician, and sometimes, between his ladder gigs, he would sneak into the band and play instruments with them. Spencer's dad, also a writer for the New Times, was a talented musician and played in a band. After a couple of years, I thought that Spencer should have a bigger role and sing a song. When I called to talk to him about it, he said that he was sorry, but he couldn't be in Cruizin' that year. He had been selected to be in the New York State Jazz Band. It was a big deal, with the big concert in Albany on Cruizin' weekend. I don't know any kids, so I asked Spencer if he had any suggestions. Yes, he did. A boy at his school was interested in his stories about Cruizin'. So I arranged to meet Jeremy Wallace and his parents at Wegmans in DeWitt. Jeremy was a skinny little kid, with what I thought was not much of a voice. Both his parents were lawyers, so I figured I better be careful. I took the coward's way out and said that Jeremy would need to audition with Jeff Unaitis. So if necessary, Jeff would be the one to say no. Jeff said yes. Jeremy became a big hit and went on to appear in several major performances in various productions around Syracuse. Jeremy already has quite a career behind him. When he collects his Tony Award, I hope he says that he owes this high honor to Art Zimmer and "Cruizin' Thru the 1950s."

One day during the Cruizin' years, a lady came into my office and introduced herself. She was Lorraine Grande, a name that I did not know, as I had no background in musical theater. Lorraine wanted to be in Cruizin'. She said that she had been in shows years ago, but was now retired. I explained to Lorraine that the entire cast returned every year, and we had no place for any additional performers.

A few days later I mentioned this to Jeff Unaitis. Jeff jumped out of his chair. "Do you know who she is???" he yelped. "She is the most talented musical theater performer in the entire area." WOW! She wanted to be in Cruizin'...so we signed her up and made a place for her. Lorraine's first song was the Dusty Springfield number, "You Don't Have to Say You Love Me." When I first heard it in rehearsal, the hair on the back of my neck stood up, and I almost cried. I think Shirley did cry. Then something happened I had never seen before, and I go to a lot of shows; right in the middle of the show, when Lorraine finished the song, the entire audience rose in a long and enthusiastic standing ovation. It took quite a while to get them settled down so we could continue the show.

One year we added a new song. Talk about bringing the house down! I'm sure you all remember that famous duet, a gold and platinum record seller of Neil Diamond and Barbra Streisand performing, "You Don't Bring Me Flowers Anymore." Nick Mulpagano, our resident and very talented impersonator, dressed like, looked like, and sounded just like Neil as he moved slowly across the stage, singing that song. From the other side entered Moe Harrington, moving slowly, dressed in a long, elegant formal gown, looking and sounding like Barbra. It was truly a magical moment in local musical theater. People talked about it for years.

Neil Diamond and Elvis were just two of Nick's 'alter-egos', so to speak. A talented impressionist, he was an invaluable addition to the ensemble:

"When I think back on the Cruizin' shows, I have very fond memories of the new people I had a chance to meet and work with, and the opportunity to have the show tailored to fit my impersonation skills :)

"One moment stands out. In my dressing room were all of my props and costumes. Among them was a cowboy hat for my Hank Williams impersonation. Every night, I hung it on one of the big light bulbs (which I never turned on) above my mirror. One day, before I arrived, Art thought he would do me a favor and turn on ALL of the dressing room lights for me. Soon, the smell of burning cowboy hat filled the air, with smoke alarms going off and the fire department notified that there was a fire in the NEW TIMES THEATER! There wasn't any damage... wellll, except for my cowboy hat, which had a hole burned in the front. I wore it backwards for that show, and Art bought me another one. LOL!"

Another aspect of the show that people really liked was that I wanted everyone to know the song title and most importantly the name of the person who made the big hit of it, so they did not have to keep guessing. Since I did not want to take the time or slow the fast pace of the show with all these announcements, I had Dennis design and build a soda fountain for the edge of the stage. On the menu board we posted a big poster with the information as each song was performed.

I recruited Linda Pompo, a dynamic woman whom I got to know at the Chamber of Commerce. In the New Times chapter of this book, Linda relates the story of how we met. She expresses gratitude to me for my advice at that time, but her contribution to the success of Cruizin' more than paid me back. Linda wanted to be part of Cruizin' but was not a singer. For years, she would tell me the years with Cruizin' were the most fun of her life, and she did not lead a dull life, considering she was the mother of five grown daughters. Linda recruited a group of well-known area celebrities, so each night a different person was coming out on stage and posting the song boards. I can't remember them all. They included County Executive Nick Pirro, Chamber President

David Cordeau, State Fair Director Peter Cappuccilli, PEACE, Inc. Director Joe O'Hara, publisher and printer Victor Ianno, and TV-9 news anchor Nancy Duffy, also founder of the big Syracuse St. Patrick's Day Parade.

Another feature of the show that I created was a radio booth which I had Dennis build on the opposite side of the stage from the soda fountain. Several times during the show, the lights would dim and there would be a radio broadcast from the booth. The DJ in the radio booth would come on and give the news of the day. I had researched the big stories of each year (1950-59). Many stories were really funny and true. Like the year the mayor held a big press conference (1954, I think) to announce that he and the city engineer had developed a system to regulate the traffic lights that would for all time solve the traffic congestion problem downtown (ha ha). Another story was that they had plans that would forever solve the downtown lack of parking problems (ha ha ha).

Part of the news was the year that the Syracuse Nationals won the NBA basketball national championship and that the star of the team, Dolph Schayes, had set many records. One day, the DJ of the day, Phil Markert, rushed backstage to tell me that Dolph Schayes was in the audience. Phil wanted to stop the show and introduce him. Absolutely, YES, I told him. It was an extra big thrill for everyone. Each performance we used different DJs from various radio stations. Three that I remember are still on the air now: Ted and Amy and Gary Dunes.

Bob Brown was probably the best-known performer and director of musical shows around. Bob played Jesus Christ for about 20 years in the Salt City production of Jesus Christ Superstar. Bob toured nationally with several different productions and directed many shows. As I knew nothing about show business, I hired Bob the first year to be the director. The day before opening night, Bob said that he had to go to Philadelphia the next morning and would be gone all weekend. He told me to take over and direct the show and that he had taught me all I needed to know.

A few weeks later Bob told me that he was too busy to be director. So for the next six years, I was producer and director. Bob is still doing shows, and took over Salt City when Joe Lotito passed away.

One year we changed the script around, and part of it was a love story between Artie and Shirley, loosely based on me and Shirley. Two new people were added to the cast to play the parts. They were Mark Bell and Katherine Clare. Katherine was the daughter of my ticket-office manager, Tina Bilofsky. During the show, Mark and Katherine fell in love, married, and now have a family and are still entertaining. Just call us cupids.

One day Jeff came up with a great idea. Almost all theater companies, the night before opening night, do a full dress rehearsal, nonstop right through the entire show, just like opening night, except the theater is empty. Jeff said, "Wouldn't it be nice to have an audience for the dress rehearsal performances? We could call it 'First Opening Night.'"

The entire cast and band loved the idea. After thinking it over, I said, "Let's charge full price and donate all the money to local non-profits." Word spread quickly, and a couple of days later, I got a call from a lady in Camillus. She said that the Camillus Fire Department was closing. They had had a dispute with the village, and their funding had been cut off. They were broke and going out of business. They had had a couple of fundraisers and raised only a few hundred dollars. They needed at least $4,000 quickly or it was curtains for the fire department. I told her that I would give her the entire house. She would sell the tickets and keep 100 percent of the money. If she sold all the tickets, she would make about $7,000. She sold the show out, and the Camillus Fire Department was saved–thanks to Cruizin' and the New Times.

The next year, she called again. "You saved us, but we are still struggling financially. Could we have a few tickets this year?" she asked. I told her that I would give her the entire house again. If she sold it out, she could keep the $7,000. That should set them up financially. They did sell out.

For the next few years, we divided the tickets up among several nonprofits and church groups. For many charities, it was their biggest donation of the year. When we finally completed the Cruizin' run, we had raised over $40,000 for local nonprofits. I spoke with several local theater companies about doing the same. They all thought it was a great idea, but to my knowledge none ever followed through on it.

The Post-Standard and the Syracuse New Times were competitors, but I must compliment the Post's late theater critic, Joan Vadeboncouer. Joan was the theater critic for the Post-Standard for a long time. She always attended Cruizin' shows each year. Joan always wrote glowing reviews and always mentioned me and the New Times in her review. The Post-Standard always printed the names at her insistence.

One day I was talking to Jackie Coley, the longtime daily paper social columnist. Jackie wrote a very popular column every week. Jackie said that she was sorry my name was not in her column that week, as she had written about an event in which I was involved. She said that there were several editors at the daily, and it depended on which one was working when her column came out. A couple of editors would not allow any mention of my name or the New Times in the paper because they didn't want me to get any publicity. The other editors didn't care and left my name in her column. I considered all of that to be quite a compliment.

Over the years, almost all the performers in Cruizin' won SALT (Syracuse Area Live Theater) awards for their excellent work on stage. But there never was a SALT award for Cruizin'. As I was the creator of SALT, I thought it would be a conflict of interest to allow my show to win an award from SALT.

I went on to produce several other shows with Jeff and that very talented cast, both during its seven-year run and after. After the Cruizin' play was done, I did a 1950s dance party. Michael Davis, the New Times photographer (as he still is after 30 years), was in a band called the Coachmen. They were very popular and had been around for over 20 years. I hired them to play the dance party and insisted that they play only 1950s hits. I gave them a list of songs to do. They said that a few of my song selections would not work, as they needed a female vocalist and they were an all-male band. I suggested that they ask Elizabeth Fern to do those numbers with them. They said no, no girls in their band. I insisted and reminded them that I was paying them and Michael worked for me; do it my way. Finally they gave in. After the first rehearsal, they fell in love with Elizabeth. For the next couple of years, they played gigs around town, advertised as the Coachmen with special guest Elizabeth Fern.

The entire "Cruizin' Thru the '50s" experience was so improbable for me. I was an under-educated, reluctant farm boy from Randallsville (suburb of Hamilton) who had never written anything and had no experience or knowledge of musical theater. And yet I became a playwright, director, and producer of one on the most successful local musical shows ever (eat your heart out Andrew Lloyd Webber).

Yes, those years with Cruizin' were fun and exciting and brought us into an entirely new world of musical theater entertainment, right here at home. There are hundreds more people whom I should thank and mention, but space and memory won't allow.

A final note: I still have a display room of treasures from my past that features a very large fancy wall decoration created by TV-9 art director Dennis Calkins, depicting the Izitart Company, complete with an ascot installed in it. I also have several other very interesting and creative pieces of artwork by Dennis depicting the "Cruizin' Thru the '50s" musical shows, my landlocked boat on a pond in Otisco, and the Zimmer Motor Car Company. Shirley appears in the front seat of two of the Zimmer illustrations. Drop by when you visit Hamilton and I'll show you around.

DANCING WITH OUR STARS, SYRACUSE-STYLE

Dancing with the Stars became a big television hit. Arlene Stewart had the dream to produce a local version and use it as a major fundraiser for the renovation of an historic James Street mansion. After a period of time without success, she came to me and, much as we had for the SAMMYs, the New Times and I took the project on, organized it, put together a committee, and put money into it; the New Times was the first and, for a couple of years, the only sponsor.

I was sure that Channel 9, Syracuse's ABC affiliate that aired the national Dancing with the Stars show, would come on board in a big way. I could never understand why, but the station played only a minor role. The New Times did a lot and made it very successful: about $100,000 was raised over the first few years.

Part of that success was because I brought my long-time friend Bob Longo into the mix. Bob is better known as Bob Barker, the Hot Dog King of Syracuse. Bob is an avid dancer and former New York State ballroom dance champion. He was a big help in getting the program up and running for the first few years.

NOT TO SAY THAT I WAS ALWAYS SUCCESSFUL...

I did have a few failures. One was the creation of the SALTY awards-- Syracuse Area Live Theater Youth. It was to be a SALT awards competition for high school drama productions. It ran for three years, but the in-fighting and lack of cooperation among the high schools killed it. It was sponsored by Family Times, the parenting magazine created by the New Times, which became and remains the number one parenting magazine in CNY.

I kept trying to get Fayetteville-Manlius High School into SALTY, but was told NO, because someone there believed it was good teaching to tell their kids they were the best. For some reason this anonymous person believed that if students did not win the top awards, it would be bad for their self-esteem. I saw it differently. I pointed out to them that their sports teams played games, and sometimes lost. But the young athletes still knew they were good, and their collegiate sports scholarships showed that. But certain F-M administrators continued to work to torpedo the SALTY awards. This just in: as I write this in mid-2015, the Post-Standard and syracuse.com recently sponsored what they billed "the first annual" high school theater awards. And yes, Fayetteville-Manlius High School competed.

There's no shame in failure, especially when it comes to trying new or different things to benefit one's community. I like to say that I don't take NO for an answer. A final answer anyway. But sometimes the answer isn't really mine to take. And it makes the next success that much sweeter.

It IS a Small World

I am constantly amazed at how quickly time goes by.

As we mature, the years just zip by faster and faster. It seems like just yesterday that I was a skinny, under-educated, reluctant farm boy from Randallsville, wondering what I would do with my life. That was over 60 years ago. I thought that this was such a big world, but I have had many experiences throughout my life that showed me just what a small place it can be.

On our first (blind) date, the plan was for me to pick Shirley up and meet our mutual friends, Al and Thalia Vizgaitis, at a restaurant. They had fixed us up for this evening. As I drove, we chatted and were amazed to find out that we had grown up just a few miles apart. Our parents knew each other quite well. This might be my most important "small world" experience ever!

On our trips, we enjoyed many more such happy coincidences together. One day, Shirley and I were walking on the beach in Aruba. Shirley had a Syracuse New Times t-shirt on over her bathing suit. A couple walking by stopped us because of the shirt. They were from Camillus. As we stood there talking, another couple stopped; they were from Baldwinsville. It turned out that the Camillus person worked with Mike Hotaling (now living in Hubbardsville). Mike owned the insurance agency with which I had a lot of my business insurance, and worked with Carl Benedict (originally from Hamilton), the agent who handled my insurance.

Sometimes trips segue with other trips. We had spent a weekend at the Cranwell, a resort in the Berkshire Mountains of Massachusetts, with friends who owned a newspaper on Cape Cod. A few months later, we were in a hotel lobby in San Jose, Costa Rica, and saw a person wearing a hat from the Cranwell Resort. We stopped him and told him that we had been to the resort. He asked us a lot of questions about our stay there. Why was he so interested? He owned the resort!

Another time we were on a trip driving up Route 1 through Big Sur, the coastal highway in California, one of the most spectacular drives in the world. We were walking across a restaurant lobby when a voice said, "Hey, lady, where did you get your Chico's?" Chico's is now a national chain of woman's clothing that features a distinctive style of clothing. Back then, they were just on the West Coast. The week before, Shirley had gone shopping at a Chico's in Santa Barbara with Shirley Ronkowski. The second Shirley had worked with the first Shirley 15 years before in the North Syracuse Central School District. Shirley #2 had lived in California about 15 years. After much conversation, it turned out that the person who had called out to Shirley was the founder and owner of Chico's. He had sold the company but later bought it back and took it nationwide. We gave him a big sales pitch to open a store in Bob Congel's then-named Carousel Mall. I was acquainted with Bob and always admired how he got things done. I felt that I was like that on a smaller scale. People would criticize me, but I got things done while they sat on their hands and just complained. Today, Chico's has a store in Fayetteville and an outlet store in Destiny USA (formerly Carousel Mall). Probably not because of our campaigning. But one never knows.

One day we were at a local craft sale on the island of Barbados. A man selling native crafts was wearing a Syracuse University Orange shirt. He had traded for it and did not even know where Syracuse is. He was most happy to get a geography lesson about his shirt.

Soon after we were married, Shirley and I were at a Syracuse Symphony concert. By then Shirley knew all the details of my past. She knew everything about my life BS (before Shirley). A woman I had dated just before I met Shirley saw us in the lobby. As I introduced them, another woman who I had dated just before the first one walked over to us. I said, "I need to go to the restroom," and left. I never did ask Shirley what they talked about. She says she doesn't remember either, so I'm guessing it wasn't memorable!

One summer, Shirley and I, along with Dick and Dona Flaherty and Earl Alger, were at the Onondaga Ski Club lodge in Vermont, the property that I had bought on behalf of the club that it still operates today, 44 years later. We were the only ones at the lodge until Rod and Linda Ward arrived. I had not seen them in several years. Rod and Linda had been band members in "Cruizin' Thru the 50s."

Once we were in San Diego and took a day trip by bus to Tijuana. In less than an hour, we realized how dirty the border town was. A lot of the so-called local shops were selling bargain stuff that U.S. tourists were snapping up, much of which seemed to be from China. So we found a bar and sat down for a drink. A Syracuse University football game was playing on the bar's television. It would have been a fun way to pass the day, except Syracuse lost by about 48 points.

On several trips it seemed like every day, somewhere, we would see a UPS (United Parcel Service) truck. One day, we were in Venice, Italy, having lunch outside by a canal. Floating down the canal was a large UPS barge full of packages. We still laugh about that every time we see a UPS truck: they follow us everywhere!

The very successful Syracuse International Film Festival that I talk about elsewhere in this book was organized and run by Owen Shapiro and Christine Fawcett Shapiro. Another person who was very involved in the film festival was Pedro Cuperman, founder and director of the Point of Contact gallery, and on staff at SU.

One evening at a fundraising cocktail party for the film festival at the Century Club, Shirley and I were talking to Pedro (Shirley and Pedro were chatting in Spanish), when Pedro mentioned that he was from Argentina and had lived in Buenos Aires. We said that we had a friend from Buenos Aires (a city of several million) whose name was Rudy. We did not say his last name. Pedro said, "Rudy Stefanovic?"

"Do you know Rudy?" we exclaimed. Our long and interesting friendship with Rudy is detailed in another chapter of this book. "No," Pedro said, "but my sister who lives in Buenos Aires has frequently talked about her friend, Rudy... Stefanovic!"

OUR NATION'S CAPITAL

One of the highlights of our travels was Washington, D.C. We had three experiences there that stand out.

On one trip, we stopped in to visit with our Congressional representative, Jim Walsh. We had no appointment but knew Jim quite well back home, as Jim was a regular reader and fan of the New Times. The Congressman had the New Times cover on which he appeared framed and hanging on his office wall.

His staff kept asking what we wanted from Jim. We explained we were there just for a social visit. They were accustomed to everyone who came wanting something. Jim took us in his office and then gave us a lengthy behind-the-scenes tour through the entire capitol building. Jim even took us out on the floor usually reserved for members of Congress. It was a day to remember. Thanks, Jim.

Another time, we were part of a small group of newspaper owners invited to the White House for a private reception and a meeting with President Bush (the first one). We had complete run of the White House, no guides or restrictions, just not upstairs where the President and his family lived.

It was, as the kids say today, awesome to slowly wander around and soak up firsthand the history of the United States. Then President and Mrs. Bush came down to mingle and chat with us. It was a very exciting and, at the same time, humbling experience.

A year later, we had the opportunity for a return visit. This time President Bill Clinton was in office. Bill arrived so late that the Arkansas people who had arranged the meeting for the newspaper association were quite upset and worried that President Clinton would not show up at all. The First Lady did not. The previous year both President Bush and the First Lady were there, on time, and mingled with the conference attendees. President Clinton left as soon as he finished his remarks.

Even though I am often critical of big government, I must say that I was awed by these three experiences.

My international (almost) incident

There was a time when we were travelling to Europe when American money was really worth something on the continent. European businesses wanted U.S. dollars. The day before we left Syracuse, I went to the bank to load up on cash. I requested $100 bills to make it easy to carry.

The next day we were in New York City at the airport shortly before boarding a plane for Paris. We decided to get a quick slice of pizza. I went around the corner (Shirley couldn't see me) and ordered two slices. I told the cashier that all I had was $100 bills. The cashier said OK. Suddenly two police officers were behind me. The cashier handed the police the $100 bill. She had checked it; it was counterfeit, she said. The police told me that they were taking me "down to headquarters for passing counterfeit money."

"But officer," I protested, "my plane for Paris leaves in 15 minutes. Please call my bank in Syracuse – I got this bill there yesterday." This was, of course, before cell phones. The police said that they would call "from downtown."

Then one officer said, "Let's go down here." Down the hall we went, to a small branch bank where they had a more sophisticated scanning machine.

Shirley was wondering what was taking so long. She came around the corner, and I was nowhere in sight. She asked the cashier, "Did my husband just buy some pizza?" Imagine what she thought when the cashier told her what had happened.

Meanwhile, the police had discovered that the $100 was not counterfeit. I ran back down the corridor, grabbed Shirley, and jumped on the plane just as the gate was closing.

We didn't get any pizza until we got to Italy. And guess what: pizza in Italy is terrible.

2013: How a Dream Vacation Became a Nightmare

That headline is misleading; I only used the word nightmare to get your attention. The headline should be, "How Our Dream Vacation Became an Unexpected Adventure."

For many years, Shirley and I had talked about a tour of our great Western national parks. Over the 28 years we have been together (the best 28 years of my life), we traveled around the world and back and forth across our great country a dozen times. So last spring, as I was approaching my 75th birthday, we realized that any day sickness or accidents could curtail our travels. We decided to do the national parks tour.

We have learned over the years that working with a travel agent has big benefits and usually ends up saving money. During the summer, working with the travel agent, we researched many options and itineraries. We finally selected the one that best fit our needs.

We wanted to go in mid-September, after the kids are back in school, tourist season is almost over, and the oppressive heat of the West drops down a few degrees. However, mid-September was time for the Great Hamilton Chocolate Train Wreck Festival. I'm a member of the organizing committee and had committed to work the entire day. Hence, we signed up to leave town the end of September.

We flew to Denver and rented a car to drive up into the mountains for four days of sightseeing and visiting family who lived in Oak Creek, near Steamboat Springs. A few days before the tour's scheduled departure, the big news came of a possible government shut down. Our elected officials (yes, you and I put those jerks in office and, even worse, reelected most of them) would not be so stupid and incompetent to actually close down the government, I thought.

We had the travel agent contact the tour company to see if the tour was still on. Their answer was, "Yes, the last time this happened (1995) the entire staff of park employees was sent home, but each tour bus had a guide on board that knew all the parks well. There were no services, but you got to see 80-90 percent of everything."

On day one of the government shut down, we found this to be true. We were at Steamboat Springs, Colorado. It was beautiful, with snow covering the top third of the mountain. There was a nearby waterfall that we had visited on a previous trip. No park personnel were present. You could just drive up, park, walk a few hundred feet, and enjoy the falls. It was on government land. But after that day, the government spent tax money to haul up barricades, print signs, and block the road.

Back in Denver, when we had met the tour group, the tour director was wonderful. He also was an opera singer who sang popular and classical songs. His singing was great, and we looked forward to 14 days of his entertaining us along with the parks.

As we prepared to depart Denver, even though the government was down and all non-essential personnel were sent home, the most non-essential employees for the whole fiasco, Congress and the President, stayed on, got paid, and continued to do nothing.

It was snowing as we left Denver and headed north to our first stop in Deadwood, Wyoming. The snow got heavier, the wind came up, visibility got very poor, and the bus crept along at about 15 miles per hour.

The tour director got a call (cell phone). We were in the middle of an unexpected early season blizzard. Yes, a blizzard: 60 mile-per-hour winds and five feet of snow. Deadwood was closed, even if we could get there, and there was no power and no heat. The roads were blocked with downed trees and snow drifts were six feet deep. Then suddenly the road was blocked. A lot of southern people were ready to freak out. Many had never seen snow, much less a blizzard. To Shirley and me, it was no big deal. We're from Central New York.

The big bus had to turn around on a narrow country road in the snow, ice, and wind. We had a wonderful bus driver, and he handled it well.

Soon we came to a little convenience store. We stopped for restrooms and to buy snacks. We were thinking we might not get to eat for a long time. Our wonderful tour director Eugene was busy on the phone and found a nearby Holiday Inn that could take us, if we could get there. Ten minutes after leaving the convenience store, the roads were closed behind us. We almost spent the night on the bus. We found out later that another nearby tour bus had spent the night in a ditch. After 13 hours on the road, for a trip that should have taken four hours, we arrived at the Holiday Inn. The staff at the hotel did a wonderful job taking care of 51 unexpected guests. The tour director announced a meeting at 9 a.m. to assess the situation.

In the morning, the tour director announced that the administration had put out the word to make the shutdown as painful as possible to as many people as possible. The government had called back park employees, who were unpaid, and spent more tax money to haul in barricades and print up signs to physically block the entrance of every national park in the entire U.S., even open-air parks like the War Memorial in D.C. The tour now had to be cancelled. When the road was reopened, the bus would take us back to Denver.

The tour was scheduled to end in Las Vegas 13 days later. There were people on the tour from Australia, the UK, and all over the U.S. They all had plane tickets from Vegas to home. This was a huge mess for everyone.

The tour company was great. We received two free nights' hotel stay in Denver, free airfare to Vegas, a free night in Vegas, a full refund of the entire tour price, and a $250 voucher for a future tour. Also they worked with people to help change arrangements. Just that one little tour must have cost the tour company over $125,000.

Shirley and I had purchased tickets to six major shows in Las Vegas—all expensive and non-refundable—as we planned to stay in Vegas for a few days after the tour ended. Most of the big Vegas shows sell out, so getting tickets a couple of months in advance is important, especially for two non-gamblers.

In Las Vegas we saw Tommy Bridges (front), a Syracuse trumpeter who hit it big. Left to right: Joanne Scammel and Bob Luongo (Bob Barker, the hot dog king), Tommy Bridges, Art and Shirley. Bob and Joanne were very involved in the early years of the local Dancing with Our Stars program.

So what should we do? We did not want to spend three weeks in Vegas. Yes, it's a fabulous city, but a week is enough. Shirley and I are the type of people who, when most people look at a glass and say that it is half empty, we see it as two-thirds full. So when the government handed us a lemon, we made lemonade, opened a stand, and made some money. We decided to rent a car in Denver and go on a two-week adventure ending in Vegas in time to enjoy all our shows.

We asked the tour director if they would pay for the car rental. They said no! Shirley went back and pressed the director. I'm not sure if she just smiled at him or swore at him. They agreed to pay us the cost of two one-way air fares to Vegas. That would more than cover the car rental. So we made some money off the "lemonade."

We headed south and saw a sign for Pike's Peak. After four hours, we had experienced a fabulous and exciting tour, going up over 14,000 feet. The scenery and views were beyond description. Pike's Peak is run by the city of Colorado Springs and was open. So take that, Obama.

We went on to Santa Fe, New Mexico, where we visited old friends from Syracuse, Sam and Diane DeLuca. Sam and Diane built, with their own hands, a 10,000-square-foot mansion far out in the desert, high on a mesa. We had a great time listening to tales of all their wild experiences and seeing their beautiful home.

Shirley dragged me to the Georgia O'Keeffe Museum in Santa Fe. I must say, "Thank you, Shirley." I really did not know much about Georgia O'Keeffe. After viewing a couple of documentary films on O'Keeffe's life and seeing many of her original paintings, I was enlightened and enthused. I am now a Georgia O'Keeffe fan and admirer.

People from Central New York think our weather changes suddenly and often. Here Shirley and I were in the Southwest–New Mexico and Arizona. We were in 75-degree weather with sunshine. Suddenly, for a couple of hours, we found ourselves in a blinding sand and dust storm, quite common there. Then a couple of hours later we were driving in pouring rain, quite unusual there. Then we were suddenly in snow and freezing temps. The next morning, we woke up to lots of snow on all the hills. This was only early October down south.

We pushed on, arriving in Vegas a couple of days early. We got some last-minute tickets to a couple of the lesser shows and had a great week in Vegas. We saw about 10 shows, went to three Vegas buffets (what diet?), and explored the new City Center. City Center was built to the tune of 8.5 billion dollars. That is over the top, even for Vegas. We also saw the soon-to-open largest Ferris wheel in the world.

Yes, we had a great trip, but we were very disappointed. Our dream of seeing the national parks went down the toilet. Someone should remind the president that the parks belong to the people, not to him or Congress. As Harry Truman said, "The buck stops here." Even though our friends remind us that Congress had a hand in closing the parks, the guy in charge has to take the blame.

OUR LONG NATIONAL (PARK) NIGHTMARE ENDS

Not to be discouraged, we decided in spring of 2015 to try again. We signed up for the exact same tour with the same tour company and off we went. We could not have asked for a more perfect trip. All our airline departures and arrivals were on time. All our luggage showed up when we did. The tour was well-organized and well-run by our tour director, Bruce, and as an extra bonus no parks were closed!

We visited eight national parks. Each one was spectacular and different. We also visited several non-park locations. The most impressive was the Native American Crazy Horse monument, just 20 miles from Mount Rushmore. Crazy Horse is a monument carved into a mountain, like Rushmore, and dedicated to honor all Native Americans. It has been under construction since 1948 and will not be completed for another 10-15 years. They have refused all government funding, though millions have been offered. The U.S. government has "screwed" the Indians so badly so many times that they won't give them the opportunity to do it again here.

The Crazy Horse monument is the largest ever created by humans anywhere in the world, even bigger than the pyramids in Egypt. Ten Mount Rushmores would fit on just part of Crazy Horse's face.

I'm proud to be an American, and perhaps because I AM so proud, some things make me wonder. At the Crazy Horse monument there is a gift shop

Shirley and me at Bighorn National Forest in Wyoming.

that sells all kinds of souvenirs, all made in the USA. At Mount Rushmore there are similar souvenirs, all sold at higher prices, and most made in China. And of course, Mount Rushmore is run by the U.S. Government. When will the American public wake up and elect officials who will put the interest of America first? Especially hardworking, honest, middle-class Americans—a group Washington and Albany seem to be unfamiliar with.

As of summer 2015, Shirley and I together have visited 40 states, including Alaska and Hawaii, all the Canadian provinces except one, six European countries, four Central and South American countries, and seven Caribbean islands. Before we were married, we had each separately visited several other states and foreign countries

When we visited Jackson Hole, Wyoming, Shirley spotted a young woman wearing Syracuse University flip flops. She graduated from SU a few years ago and is now in medical school in Pennsylvania. She loved her time in Syracuse and, yes, remembered the Syracuse New Times well. She had a friend who went to Newhouse (SU's S.I. Newhouse School of Public Communications). Do you remember when President Johnson came to Syracuse to dedicate the Newhouse One building? I do. She thought her friend might have even interned at the New Times. Over the years, the New Times had many Newhouse interns. In fact, Tina Schwab-Grenis, who became editor-in-chief of the New Times and then editor-in-chief of Family Times magazine, started with us as an intern from Newhouse. Also Mike Greenstein, our long-time editor-in-chief, was a Newhouse adjunct professor, and Roland Sweet earned a master's degree there.

Sometimes it's OUR apparel that prompts a chance encounter. We were walking down the street in Jackson Hole, Wyoming. Actually it was a wooden sidewalk, as they try to fool the tourists into thinking it is still an Old-West town.

As we walked past a McDonald's (so much for Old West), we heard two young women exclaim, "Are you from Colgate?" Shirley had on her Colgate jacket. We stopped to chat and learned that one young woman grew up in Syracuse and had friends and family who went to Colgate. She had been away for about six years and was very excited to meet someone from her hometown.

She wanted to know if her two favorite places, Dinosaur BBQ and Pastabilities, are still in Syracuse. We assured her that both places are doing well. AND she had been an avid reader of the New Times, as everyone is. I was wearing my New Times jacket. The conversation expanded to skiing, which she also enjoyed. We talked about all the CNY ski areas. I had skied the Jackson Hole ski area over 35 years ago. She had skied a lot at the Cazenovia ski hill, where the Olympic skier Vicki Fleckenstein trained back in the1970s before the 1980 Winter Olympics in Lake Placid.

Before saying goodbye to us, she promised to buy a copy of this book.

In Las Vegas we spent a lot of time at Steve Wynn's hotel/casino. It is one of the most opulent and most beautiful hotels, not just in Vegas, but in the entire country. Steve went to school near Syracuse at the Manlius Military Academy, the descendant of which is the Manlius-Pebble Hill in DeWitt.

At one spot in Steve's hotel is a beautiful working carousel, but it is made of real flowers—a beautiful sight. I wondered if the carousel was a throwback to Steve's early days at Manlius, as across the street from his dorm room was Suburban Park, an amusement park with a beautiful carousel in the center. I imagine Steve spent many nights looking out his dorm window, watching the carousel across the street going round and round.

Unfortunately, both Manlius Military Academy and Suburban Park are long gone, replaced by a bunch of office buildings and condos. Is that progress?

As we spent time in Steve Wynn's hotel, we talked at length to several employees about this book, and quite possibly sold a half dozen copies or more.

Even at home, we are often amused at serendipitous encounters we seem to have. Recently, Shirley and I went to an Engelbert Humperdinck concert at Turning Stone. We had seen Engelbert several times in the past. He is almost 80 years old and still puts on a terrific show.

Before the show, we had dinner at Pino Bianco, the Italian restaurant at Turning Stone. Our waitress, Kathy, had moved to Syracuse in 1983 (I bought the New Times in 1984). Kathy had become an avid reader of the paper and still picks it up every week. Kathy had worked at the Hotel Syracuse with our friend, Van Sterio. Van and his wife share an anniversary date with us: same month and day, different year. Jim and Pat MacKillop also share our anniversary date. Van was in charge of arrangements for our wedding reception at Hotel Syracuse for over 600 guests. Even though it was his own anniversary, Van insisted on being present to make sure everything went smoothly.

During dinner at Pino Bianco, the supervisor, John Julian, came by. He remembered me and my bright-colored sports jackets and ascots I always wore around Syracuse. He was the former owner of Scratch Daniels restaurant which for years was a downtown destination meeting spot across the street from the Hotel Syracuse. Another friend of ours, John Sauro, the owner of Sauro's restaurant, also from many years ago, is the former manager of Pino Bianco. He has now moved across the hall and manages Turning Stone's Tin Rooster.

As we were seated for the show, the couple in the next booth said, "You are Art Zimmer, right?" They related that, for many years, they attended all the Cruizin' Thru the 50s shows and, more recently, had come to Hamilton for the shows I produced at the Palace Theater. They remembered many things about my past: the New Times, Zimmer cars, and colorful jackets and ascots. In further discussion, it turned out that Fred Verro, whom I mention elsewhere in the Minerva statue adventure, was his godfather. He knew Fred's family well, as did I.

Then his girlfriend said, "Art, you don't remember me, do you?" She proceeded to tell us about working in the office next door to the Rapid Graphics print shop John Jablonski and I owned and operated in the old railroad depot in Camillus in the late 1970s. We moved the print shop to the New Times building on West Genesee in 1985. She remembered all the wonderful free printing that we did for local nonprofits and the bright colored sports jackets I wore every day. I still have most of them and still wear them even though they are more than 30 years old now.

Just as the show was starting, Nick Mulpagano and his wife Lisa walked by. I had the pleasure of presenting Nick, the man of a 1,000 voices, on stage many times over the past 10 years in Syracuse and Hamilton.

THE BIRDS HAVE THE RIGHT IDEA

After returning home from the Army, for about 30 years the only time I left Central New York in the winter was to go someplace that was colder and with more snow, such as Canada, Europe, South America (in August), the American Rockies, and all over New England.

After Shirley and I were married, we spent a ski week in Canada. The temperature was about 20 degrees below zero every day. Then we spent a week at a newspaper conference on the Caribbean island of Barbados, where it was about 80 degrees every day.

I have not quit skiing, but I have not gotten around to hitting the slopes in over 25 years. After Barbados, we started to spend January and February in places like Hawaii, Acapulco, various Caribbean islands, Key West, the southwest states, and a couple of times Florida, and took six warm water ocean cruises. Now, Florida is not my favorite place to spend the winter, but it is by far the most convenient.

As we mature, we like to keep things simple. The past few years travel has become such a hassle, dealing with airports, airlines, security, passports, etc., etc., that we now find it much easier to just get in a car and drive to Florida and then drive home.

We have stayed in various parts of Florida and have decided we like the west coast best, north of Tampa and around the panhandle to Destin. However, we still like Central New York best and go away for only a couple of months.

Anyone who starts young and plans carefully can have the best of both worlds: 10 months in Central New York and two months a little further south. If you are one of those people who complain about upstate winters, do something about it.

You can if you really want to.

Home Again, Home Again

When we moved to Hamilton, our plan was to settle everything from our 13,000-square-foot Sentinel Heights home into our just-landed manufactured home and enjoy the five-minute walk to downtown. And we did. The first week.

But we also discovered and re-discovered the active and interesting community surrounding and including Colgate University. That adventure has kept us busy and happily involved ever since. Shirley and I find ourselves busier sometimes than we were when we were running multiple businesses. Hamilton has more going on than many much larger cities.

When I left Hamilton and moved to Syracuse, it was "home," the place to which virtually all my childhood and teen-aged memories were tethered.

Colgate University had an all-male student body; that changed in 1970 when it became co-ed. My sister Ruth was one of Colgate's early female graduates. Considering one of my continuing goals, physical recognition of Alexander Hamilton in the village that bears his name, you might think I'm disappointed that there already IS a Hamilton College down the road in Clinton. But I'm not. And I'm VERY glad that Colgate wasn't moved to Rochester in the 1800s. A group of trustees, faculty, and students were thwarted in that attempt. They left Colgate and founded the University of Rochester in that lovely city. And later Colgate's divinity department moved to Rochester as well, becoming Colgate Divinity School.

Colgate, which got its current name in 1890 after being Madison University for almost 45 years before that date, started as the Baptist Education Society of the State of New York and then the Hamilton Literary and Theological Institution. One of the early trustees was William Colgate. Yes, he was also a member of the founding family of a famous soap (and toothpaste) company.

Even more than not being recognized in the village that bears his name, I think Alexander Hamilton would be bothered if the venerable university at its center stirred thoughts of one of his political adversaries, James Madison. So I'm sure the name "Colgate" would suit him just fine.

Colgate's campus is referred to as "The Hill," as is Syracuse University's campus. Its lucky number is "13" to SU's "44." I mention some of these bits of lore because, as anyone who lives in a "college town" knows, the resources and foibles of academic institutions color the day-to-day lives of their neighbors, even those who have no official role in their operation.

We looked at every small town in Central New York before settling on Hamilton. I was actually a little surprised that we ended up back in my boyhood home. But people who know us didn't miss a beat.

Former Syracuse New Times Editor Mike Greenstein commented, "That Art and Shirley have moved to Hamilton, and that he still has media and theatrical endeavors going doesn't surprise me. Art is a born entrepreneur, and good at it. He makes things happen."

Harold B. Rollins, my high school classmate and long-time friend, says:

"In some ways he never left Hamilton. Since Art moved back, you might see him any day, his sidewalk-meandering punctuated frequently by one-on-one conversations, his arms filled with flyers or village maps: a one-person crusade against an affliction of modern urban society that Melvin Webber has called 'communities without propinquity'! We know much more about our Facebook friends than we know about our next-door neighbors.

"Art Zimmer has always displayed a behavioral idiosyncrasy: this passion for the more direct, the more personal side of human communication. In the early 1950s, I recall how my sleepy-eyed solitude, as I huddled in self-imposed isolation on the Hamilton school bus, would frequently be interrupted by a waving handful of comic books, ripe for barter for virtually any tangible possession. For Art, it was the act of barter, you see, not the object of barter.

"Consider Art's career, after he retired at age 33 from brief sequential positions as a sales rep: hotel owner, newspaper owner and publisher, owner of Zimmer Motor Car Company, mentor of small business entrepreneurs, producer of musicals, etc., etc. No behind-the-scenes invisibility here; no pushing buttons and pulling plugs from afar. Come on, a motor car company where each vehicle is custom-made for the individual buyer, and then only after a detailed conversation with Art?

"So, I challenge you to stroll on a summer Saturday along Hamilton's village green. I challenge you to find Art busily pushing his community with propinquity!"

Apparently Patti von Mechow has found my outlook to work for her, too.

" 'Go on up and introduce yourself to any person you don't know...'cause you never know.' That's some of the best advice (although I don't always follow it due to lack of nerve) ever given to me by Art Zimmer—the man.

"The man in the bright-colored suit jacket, always with a smile and a friendly 'how-do-you-do!' I have enjoyed hanging with Art and Shirley the past few years since they moved to Hamilton. They wear their true colors on the outside, always willing to support the arts and their friends. Art believes in his community and gives back as often as he can; through the Holiday Tree Lighting, Father's Day Fly-in Pancake Breakfast, Hamilton Business Alliance, live theater and concerts, he cares; it's that, plain and simple! He has great ideas and even though not everyone appreciates his vision, he respectfully moves forward, trying to make his dreams come true, always for the betterment of others and the community of Hamilton."

Hamilton's own Palace Theater

I met Patti von Mechow when she was executive director of the Palace Theater in Hamilton. In Syracuse for 10 years, I had presented musical shows at the New Times Theater on the New York State Fairgrounds. When we moved to Hamilton, I produced shows at their Palace Theater for several years, explaining to our friends from Syracuse that this was NOT the venerable Palace on James Street in Eastwood.

I produced three shows at Hamilton's Palace Theater and donated over $6,000 to local non-profits from the show proceeds. During 2013 I planned a negotiation with the theater and talent to bring two big family-friendly musical shows to Hamilton in 2014 and hopefully donate $8,000 to the area's non-profits from the shows.

I always planned my shows many months in advance to give adequate time for proper promotion. That was why all my shows completely sold out. As I had found in Syracuse, there was an opportunity to start a program in Hamilton by which I donated all profits from the shows to local non-profits. To many such small charitable groups in a small town, it was their biggest donation of the year. One day, Patti von Mechow called me with bad news. She had learned that there would be no more shows. The theater was owned by Colgate University, and they had decided that the theater would be used only for occasional student events. Patti retired.

The Palace was a significant economic engine for many village businesses. Each show others and I produced brought about 300 people into the village. We put on good shows and drew lots of people from Syracuse, Utica, Binghamton, and all the smaller towns near Hamilton. Over half of the shows' audiences would eat, drink, and even shop before and/or after the shows at the 16 restaurants and

A page from the Arts at the Palace Web site. *Photo by Alice Virden-Speer Photography.*

many specialty shops in the village, all a five-minute walk from the Palace. That would give village restaurants and retailers about $5,000 in extra income per show, with about 20 shows per year. That is about $100,000 in income, a large sum for a small village whose population is 1,700 people.

I talked to many residents about the demise of the Palace, and at a public forum asked Colgate President Jeffrey Herbst about plans for the facility. President Herbst would only say, "We are studying it." I think because of feedback from the village people and to Colgate officials I talked to, the University invited proposals for the Palace that they promised to consider.

I talked to Roger Bauman, the retired director of the Hamilton Initiative, a semi-affiliated group from Colgate that oversaw the Palace operation. We organized a little committee of area people interested in the arts. We decided to give Colgate a proposal that our group would take over operation of the Palace and make it a community center for the performing and visual arts.

Personally, I was not very optimistic that Colgate would accept our proposal. I was very surprised and pleased when they did. Much of the credit must go to Roger, as he was the spark-plug that made the whole deal work. Colgate is very supportive of the new Arts at the Palace. So now I am on the board of directors of Arts at the Palace (no, not named after me), and our group took over Palace operations on July 1, 2015.

I invite you: whenever you see a show or concert or art exhibit by Arts at the Palace in Hamilton, NY, please attend and spend lots of money in our village. Our Web sites are thisishamiltonny.com and artsatthepalace.org.

SWEET ON CHOCOLATE

One of my newer projects is the formation of a foundation to acquire, restore, and preserve the original site of the 1955 Great Hamilton Chocolate Train Wreck. A little about The Wreck. On Sept. 27, 1955, a 50-car freight train—the first two cars filled with chocolate from the Nestle plant in Fulton—crashed in the village of Hamilton after the front of the train jumped the tracks, spilling chocolate everywhere. Our farm was about half a mile away from the accident site. Along with most of the other kids and teenagers around at the time, I ran down to the site and stuffed my pockets with candy bars.

After Shirley and I moved back to Hamilton, I started volunteering on the long-standing organizational committee for planning an event—we had been meeting sporadically for about 10 years—to move ahead with celebrating The Wreck. The Great Hamilton Chocolate Train Wreck Festival is a completely separate function from the Chocolate Train Wreck Site Foundation. The festival is run by the Partnership for Community Development (PCD), a local organization that promotes local economic development.

The festival is presented annually in mid-September to celebrate the Great Hamilton Chocolate Train Wreck of 1955. It attracts 3-4,000 people into the village with various festival activities (music, kids programs, chocolate events, and trains). There is also an organized walk to the actual Chocolate Train Wreck site. I assume the festival will continue for many years, as it is a big success.

About 4,000 people attended the festival in 2013 and in 2014. Remember that Hamilton is a village of fewer than 1,800 residents, compared to more than 2,900 students at Colgate University.

The Chocolate Train Wreck Foundation is a private program that I am doing on my own. I formed the legal foundation. The foundation acquired the land where the chocolate train wreck actually took place. I am now in the process of cleaning up the site and doing some limited renovation to make it into an historic park for the village, whether they want it or not.

The original site of the Great Hamilton Chocolate Train Wreck has slowly deteriorated for 50 years. I'm developing a plan to create a Hamilton Historical site where the wreck took place. I spent 11 frustrating months working through the village bureaucracy to create an historic site for the village. I did this as a volunteer, paying expenses out of pocket. I have gotten the land legally transferred to the foundation's ownership. Restoration work began in the spring of 2014 and will take three or four years to complete.

COME ON BACK

In 2013 I created, organized, and promoted the first Hamilton Central School all-class reunion in many years. I have established it as an annual event and a promotional lead-in for the high school's Hall of Fame induction ceremony.

I'm the go-to guy for the class of 1956, which for the past two years has had a mini-reunion in Florida during the winter. I keep the class connected but sadly right now a lot of my job is sending out obituary notices.

Jean Galler Reynolds is a former classmate that I really didn't get to know until we moved back to Hamilton:

> "I was in school with Art from seventh to eleventh grade. I didn't know him well. He had to work on the family farm and missed quite a lot of school. Art is a success story about working hard, determination, and

My old friend, Dennis Calkins, worked his artistic magic again for this reunion poster.

not giving up on oneself. After many years in business he now devotes his time to promoting business, arts, music, and theater in Hamilton and the surrounding area.

"He plans our class reunions and makes sure everyone is contacted. Because of these contacts we (Larry Kinney and I) have become good friends with Art and his beautiful wife Shirley. We enjoy getting together for dinner, shows, Colgate football games, even dominoes once in a while."

The second annual July 3rd all-class reunions were a big success, drawing a few more people than in 2013. Over the next several years as the word spreads I see it getting bigger and bigger. People love the no commitment, just drop in. The knowledge that it is every year, July 3rd at the school, 11:30-1:30. An optional BBQ lunch is also very nice. For just one year, the 2016 reunions will be on July 2nd.

Another aspect that people really like is the chance to see friends who were a few years ahead or behind them in school. When each class has their own reunion every 5 years, you only see your actual classmates. Classes that are doing their own big 5 year reunion are adding the all-class reunion to their weekend plans.

The third annual all-class reunion in 2015 offered reunion t-shirts and golf shirts for sale.

As always, I'm open to ideas and suggestions to improve the reunion as long as it keeps things simple. My class, the class of 1956, has their big 60th reunion coming up. I'm looking for help and suggestions for that big one.

Shirley and I like to do most things together, but we also support each other's involvement in separate projects and endeavors. Just as she supports me, I support the events Shirley is involved with; she was president of the Earlville Opera House from 2012-14 and volunteers at the hospital, library, food cupboard, Second Chance thrift shop for animal rescue, Worn Again thrift shop, and Fortnightly Club.

A FEW OTHER THINGS WE'RE INVOLVED IN:

THE EARLVILLE OPERA HOUSE (EOH)

As Shirley was president of the Earlville Opera House board (a 125-year-old historic performing and visual arts center) and continues to be a member

The Earlville Opera House. Shirley was president of the EOH board of directors for two years, and we volunteer there frequently.

of the board, the Opera House is a constant and ongoing commitment. Every Saturday for seven months in the spring, summer, and fall, I operate an EOH booth at the Hamilton Farmers' Market.

We sold $2,800 worth of tickets of the $3600 raised in the EOH's first raffle. We helped organize and run two annual EOH silent auctions at the Colgate Inn, which raised at least $10,000.

COMMUNITY HOSPITAL AUXILIARY

We sell water on the Fourth of July, sell raffle tickets in the park, and promote raffle tickets at the Christmas sale in the Baptist Church. Shirley volunteers at the hospital's front desk.

ANIMAL RESCUE THRIFT SHOP

We volunteer about a dozen days a year working at the shop in Morrisville. I am in charge of promotion and marketing for the shop.

HAMILTON BUSINESS ALLIANCE (HBA)

As a member of the board of directors of the HBA, I developed, then co-chaired, the first Business of the Year awards program and annual meeting. Over 100 people attended the breakfast. I worked the Father's Day pancake breakfast at the airport. I also developed a Business-After-Hours Program, a quarterly "Show Hamilton" program, and a Hamilton Area Arts Council (pending).

HONORING OUR NAMESAKE

I am working on developing more recognition for Alexander Hamilton, the village's namesake. There is no physical tribute to Mr. Hamilton in the village, something I'm working to change.

SCORE

Even though my involvement with SCORE (Service Corps of Retired Executives) began while I lived and worked in Syracuse, I feel as if it followed me home to Hamilton, so I'll relate my experience with the national mentoring group here. More than 20 years ago, I had lunch with Dick Fountain in Syracuse. I know him from high school; he is a 1954 Hamilton Central High School graduate and a very successful business owner in Syracuse—now retired. Over the years we had kept in touch.

At lunch that day, Dick related that he was president of SCORE, a foundation which has chapters in most cities across the country. Dick was president of the Central New York chapter that covers four counties. SCORE used to be an acronym for Service Corp of Retired Executives. Today the organization has moved away from the initial acronym because many mentors are not retired, but rather are still active in their careers. SCORE felt it needed to come up with a tag line that truly showed what it is all about: SCORE FOR THE LIFE OF YOUR BUSINESS.

SCORE provides free, confidential, one-on-one counseling and advice to people who have a small business or seek to start up a new one. These people request some outside advice and help to become more successful.

The Syracuse SCORE chapter is very active, with about 50 successful business owners and executives. Some retired SCORE members continue to counsel and conduct workshops and seminars. Many banks require their clients to attend SCORE workshops and have a SCORE advisor before loaning them money for a business.

I told Dick that coincidentally I have been doing such advising on my own for years. As people discovered that I owned many successful businesses, they would seek me out and ask for advice. Sometimes it became a little parade of two or three people a week coming to my office several times each, seeking counsel about starting or running a business. I was always open and willing to help for free. Over the years, I helped several hundred people.

I consider many of my so-called failed counseling sessions to be my most rewarding. There is a fine line between helping and encouraging people to start a business and discouraging them from a dangerous venture. Unfortunately, many people with dreams decide to go into business for all the wrong reasons. Owning a business is difficult and complex. Many people are just not cut out for it. Frequently people's lives are ruined and bankrupt after trying to go into business. Many times after I explain, but try not to discourage, just what they are in for if they move forward with their business plan, they reconsider and don't do it. Perhaps I've saved a life or two?

Thanks to Dick Fountain's encouragement, I joined SCORE and channeled my business counseling through them. This made more resources and help available to people who came to me.

Eventually, SCORE colleagues wanted to establish a SCORE sub-chapter in Madison County to make its services more convenient to people in the area. Since I know Madison County well, they asked me to help set it up. I recruited a couple of people who lived in Cazenovia, and talked to the Cazenovia Chamber of Commerce. We set up a very helpful counseling group there that is still active today.

I remained very active in the Syracuse SCORE chapter until I moved to Hamilton. I am still on call to SCORE when they get a request for counseling out this way. If you live in the Hamilton area and want business advice, feel free to contact me. In other areas, call your local SCORE chapter.

IN ADDITION

I support every local non-profit fundraising effort that I hear about. I attend just about every event in town and encourage everyone to get up off the couch and get out and attend events in the community and at the school. Events can't be successful if people don't get out and support them. I try to lead by example.

I'm a volunteer business consultant to several new and existing businesses.

Shirley and I serve coffee at the indoor farmers' market. We meet new people, catch up with friends, and hear about interesting goings-on.

After creating the first-ever Hamilton and Colgate campus visitors guide and maps four years ago, I published the third edition in 2013 and the fourth in 2014, printing and distributing over 10,000 copies each year. The fifth edition came out in August 2015, with a new format and style. The Village and Campus Map and Visitor's Guide carries ads for local businesses to cover the cost of printing the map and to spread the word of their products and services at minimal cost. The maps have proved to be extremely popular and so far over 30,000 have been printed and distributed in a 30-mile radius around Hamilton to draw people into the village.

I assist Bruce Ward in promoting the "Local Music Project," Tuesday live music presentations at the Colgate Inn.

I travel to Utica frequently to serve on the Boy Scout Council Eagle Scout Review Board, working with candidates for the rank of Eagle. After the army, when I came back to Hamilton for a couple of years and then hitchhiked to Syracuse, one of the things that I did during that time was to become the scoutmaster of the Hamilton Boy Scout troop, where I had received my Eagle scout badge six years earlier. After moving back to Hamilton in 2010, I would meet people at various community events. The conversation would go like this:

"Hi. You're Art Zimmer, aren't you?"

"Yes."

"You don't remember me, but you were my Boy Scout leader 55 years ago."

And then we'd have fun chatting. This happened a lot. Also people remembered me from my years as a junior scout leader from 1954-56. One such encounter led to a second-generation interaction. Shirley and I were at the Poolville indoor farmers' market and met one of my former scouts, John Blackmore, from the class of 1964. John introduced me to his daughter Carrie and her fiancé, Matthew Whalen. The young couple told me that their dream was to open a beer brewing business in Hamilton. I offered to give them free advice, as I had operated 13 businesses.

Matt and Carrie are now married and owners of the very successful Good Nature Brewing in Hamilton. They brew really good beer. I cannot claim much credit for their success, but it was nice to be slightly helpful to them in the beginning.

Sad to say, John Blackmore died shortly after.

I'm an active member of the Hamilton Club. One project for them was my dinner program titled, "From the Randallsville Farm: The Life and Times of Art Zimmer."

I'm an active member of the Board of Directors of the Southern Madison Heritage Trust Foundation. Each summer I host (and cook for) a board meeting and BBQ dinner.

All those years of watching the New Times try to earn a Business of the Year designation in Syracuse may have somehow made me worthy of being named Economic Development Advocate of the Year for Hamilton in 2014.

We recently got a call from Linda Gorton, chairperson of the big annual Hamilton Fourth of July parade. Shirley and I have been selected to be the grand marshals of the 2016 parade. It is in recognition of the contributions we have made to the village over the years.

State of the... Art

People say to me, "Art, you are so lucky to be in your 78th year and in perfect health: no operations, no prescriptions, no medicine at all." I realize that tomorrow could be the day I have a heart attack or stroke, or get hit by a car. However, as long as I stay in Hamilton, I know I won't get hit by a train.

Luck is not the main reason I'm healthy. For most of my life I've made smart lifestyle choices, and each one increases my chances of living a longer healthy, happy life.

I don't mean to preach, but here are some of the choices I've made that I think could increase the odds of a better life for anyone.

I've never smoked and, for the past 25 years, have gone out of my way to avoid second-hand smoke.

Many years ago I did some light social drinking, but I have had no alcohol for 25 years.

I've always kept my weight below the medically recommended limit, except now I could afford to lose 8 to 10 pounds.

I've always been active and have exercised regularly. For 25 years we have had a gym set up in the house.

Shirley and I work on having a healthy diet: lots of organic foods, free-range and chemical-free eggs and meat, lots of fish and salads.

Even though I've owned 11 businesses, I never allowed all the things that most people stress about bother me.

I schedule regular doctor and dentist visits. I elect to have every medical test available, even when not covered by insurance. My theory is the government and insurance companies don't know what I need and they really don't care about me. But I do, so I'll pay for it.

I always use a seatbelt and replace the batteries in our smoke detectors (I know they work; when Shirley cooks, they go off!).

My fondest wish is that the last check I write will be to the funeral director, and that it bounces.

Sorry, Dave Tedesco.

More Stories and Memories

When this book debuted in September 2015, publisher Brian McDowell of Log Cabin Books ordered an adequate supply to last approximately two years, based on industry averages and his own experience in publishing.

In December 2015, just three months after the first printing, Brian informed us the books were selling so well we would soon be out of stock. We needed more copies soon. We decided to re-release the book with a new section following Chapter 12. This section contains additional stories of events from my life, and also events that resulted from the book. They are organized as much as possible to supplement the book's chapters. We also added eight more pages of color photos and enhanced some of the original 12 chapters and color photos with additional information and content.

We sincerely hope you enjoy it.

Art and Shirley Zimmer

I've been a publisher for 26 years of my life. And yet I was a bit unprepared for how I felt when I first saw the blue cover of my autobiography. In the weeks that followed, Shirley and I participated in book signings in Syracuse and Hamilton, and thoroughly enjoyed the book's official launch at the New Times offices, the book review in the New Times, and my interview on WSYR-TV 9's Bridge Street.

All along the way, people were supportive and complimentary (they were, after all, my colleagues and friends, for the most part). But even more gratifying to me, they offered comments on and additions to the anecdotes I related in the book.

This is why, when, as I related in the introduction, we needed a second printing, we decided to incorporate some of these memories into something of an afterword or epilogue.

Chapter 2
The ghostwriter finds a lively ghost, and a near-miss for the New Times
By Lois Gridley

There are two stories that I long to have had before this book's first printing, rather than mere weeks after: finding Art's high school girlfriend and hearing of something that had the potential to have ended the New Times before he had an opportunity to buy it.

One I knew about: my year-long search for Art's high school girlfriend. That came to an end when I decided to make one more phone call. The second I heard about at the book's launch hosted at New Times headquarters, where I encountered the charming Victor Ianno, long-time printer of the New Times when he was a partner at the Scotsman Press and later owner of Lakeside Printing.

First, here is what led to one of the highlights, for me, of writing Art Zimmer's story...

Mary Lou Willard. We had just finished a long and exuberant marathon through an outline of a life well-lived and enjoyed, when Art Zimmer referred back to one of the early chapters. He had mentioned his high school sweetheart as we roared through the 1950s. They met as counsellors at a Methodist camp in the Adirondacks, Aldersgate. They lived miles apart—he in Hamilton and she in Utica. Starting at only 13 years old, Art would hitchike from Hamilton to Utica regularly to see Mary Lou. They dated for four years, even becoming secretly engaged during their senior year of high school.

But it was more a farewell acknowledgement of their past together than an engagement for the future. They parted as good friends when she went to college—SUNY Potsdam—and he joined the Army. The last contact he had from her was a year later, when she wrote to let him know that she had gotten engaged.

He got engaged, too—31 years later, when he met the love of his life, Shirley Sherburne. He had girlfriends in between, people who remained in his circle of acquaintances—and always friends—after they each had moved on emotionally. Only Mary Lou was an unknown. Missing. It was perhaps his feelings for her that had prepared him, when he met Shirley, to know how to recognize the even deeper ones he felt when he met The One.

"Perhaps you'll come across Mary Lou in your research," he said to me. It was the one part of this biography we were planning that he hadn't shared with Shirley. Not yet. "I'll tell Shirley if we find Mary Lou," he mused.

As I prepared the timeline from which I would write the book, I joined ancestry.com and looked at Facebook. But there were many other details to attend to, and nothing came of the vague leads I found.

Until I saw "something" online, and at this point I can't remember exactly where it was, that included a web address for SUNY Potsdam's library.

On impulse, I sent an e-mail to the link. I wrote, in part:

> I am doing research for an autobiography and would like to find information on a Potsdam graduate....

Hours later, I received an answer from Linda Hansen, Potsdam's Senior Assistant Librarian, Interim Archives and Special Collections.

She confirmed the name, and asked for a little more information about my interest:

> Thank you for your e-mail request to the Archives.
> Can you be more specific as to the type of information you are seeking?
> I did find Mary Lou Willard listed in the 1960 year book, "the Pioneer."
> Her graduation picture, however, was under her married name of Mary Lou Gillespie. Please let me know if I can be of more assistance to you.

Her married name! New information! I wrote back immediately:

Thank you, Linda! I value your trust in sending me this
information, and I'd like to fill you in a bit. I am writing a biography--I
call it ghostwriting an autobiography because it is in his voice--of a well-
known Syracuse businessman. He and Mary Lou, in the vernacular of
the times, "went steady" all through high school, then lost touch when
she went to Potsdam and he joined the Army. He knew she got married,
and her parents moved away from Utica, but really nothing after 1957.

When we started working on the book, a project his wife started
as a gift to him on his 75th birthday, he gave me contact info for dozens
and dozens of friends and associates. But he said his one regret was that
he had no idea where Mary Lou is, or even if she is still living. He is
honoring her, along with his mother and his wife, in the dedication of
the book. In high school they both worked at a Methodist church camp
one summer and dated, with their parents' blessing, even though he
lived in Hamilton and she in Utica.

Let me assure you that there are no romantic motives in his
interest, but he credits Mary Lou with being the most important person
in his life as he struggled to complete high school and work on his
family's dairy farm. In retirement, he and his wife have moved back to
Hamilton (home of Colgate University) and continue their community
involvement there. In Syracuse he owned 13 businesses, including the
Syracuse New Times, for over 25 years. He used his status as a publisher
and revenue from the newspaper to support literally hundreds of nonprofit agencies, arts programs, and awards.

I am planning on using a quote from Garrison Keillor at the
beginning of the book that reads, in part: "....And one should not be
a person whose memoirs consist of notes from the classes you never
missed."
You made my day!

In turn, Linda responded:

What a lovely story!
I looked in the student newspaper, The Racquette, and found
out a few facts: April 12, 1957 page 2, mention of her engagement to

Floyd Gillespie, who attended Clarkson (attached) April 18, 1958
page 4, She pledges to Alpha Delta Sorority October 2, 1959 page .
She does her first of two practice teaching rounds in Massena public
school Feb 26, 1960 page 2. She is named to the President's Honor
list (all above under Willard). She graduates as a teacher with Honors
in 1960 under her married name. Good luck with the book!

Linda

I felt armed with complete information...until I discovered how MANY
Mary Lou Gillespies and Floyd Gillespies there are in the United States! I
had already found a Mary Lou on Facebook in Texas, 250 miles from a Floyd
Gillespie. Had they moved? Texans think nothing of 250 miles—to them
it might be like the distance between Hamilton and Utica! And this Mary
Lou LOOKED a bit like the black and white photo of Mary Lou in Art's
collection...

Then I thought of Dennis's nephew, Dorr Buckley Calkins Begnal. He
graduated summa cum laude in accounting from Clarkson. But even more
importantly, he was on that University's Board of Trustees for several years! I
texted him: I need help locating a Clarkson grad circa 1960....He texted back:
Stay tuned.

Hours later, he forwarded a message from a colleague who was conducting
a water purity conference at Clarkson that day. She had her laptop with her.
And Wifi access....Lester Floyd Gillespie, she reported. Graduated in 1960.
Worked for the government in Virginia, last known address.

LESTER. Floyd was his middle name, and apparently he didn't use it
once he graduated from college.

I turned to whitepages.com. And PeopleSmart, which offered me a trial
membership—one month for $19.95. But I had come so far for FREE. I
decided to think about this offer overnight.

Next day, there was a message from PeopleSmart in my e-mail. How
about a FREE WEEK of membership, they offered.

Sold!

Within minutes I found contact info —and some mystery. I have since
realized that looking for someone online involves using systems that are very

literal and often out of date, so the information I had found I now know to be inaccurate.

But it was intriguing: Until February 2014, it seemed that both Mary Lou and Lester F. Gillespie lived in Takoma Park MD, at the same address. Two other people were associated with the address: Thomas, age 45, who now lived in Great Falls, VA; and Martha Taylor, age 69. It looked as if Martha apparently lived across the street before moving to the same address as the others. In February, Lester and Martha moved to one address in Floyd, VA. Mary Lou remained in Takoma Park.

From their ages, it would seem that Thomas might be Mary Lou and Lester's son. Martha was a mystery, but circumstantially, it appears that she was a neighbor, then a tenant or guest, and now lived alone with Floyd. In another state. But this was all based on how PeopleSmart identified them as having some history with the same address.

A complete phone number was included for Lester; the same one was listed for Martha. But Mary Lou's number was incomplete. So I could write to her, but I could call only Lester. Which presented a problem: what if they were not on good terms?

I decided to lay out the story and give it to Art and Shirley to decide how to proceed! Who knows, I wrote to them, perhaps this will end up a sidebar in the book! The book went to press with just a few wistful lines in Chapter 1 about Mary Lou and her high school romance with Art. No mention of my so-far fruitless research.

Now I have the answers, and I like them so much more than my mystery theories. As I waited for publisher Brian McDowell to finish the daunting task of putting my words, Dennis' cartoons, and Art and Shirley's photos together and get them to press, I returned to the list of files associated with Mary Lou Willard Gillespie. I mused that there were actually *two* Thomas Gillespies, both living in Virginia. I called the one who lived nearest the addresses of Mary Lou and Lester. I left a message on a home phone. Within a day, he returned my call. He was not the Tom Gillespie I was looking for, but he loved the story and wished me luck in finding the "real" Tom. As we said goodbye, I found myself wishing that he HAD been Mary Lou's son.

Even with that positive feedback, it took me several days to be ready to call the "other" Tom Gillespie's number. I had a list of about ten numbers associated with his name over the years, likely former residences and businesses, cell phones and landlines. I called the first one, hoping it was still connected. It was. Within minutes I was talking to Mary Lou's son, and this Tom turned out to be as engaging as the "first" one I had called.

He quickly filled in some blanks in the scenario I had created. His parents divorced in the 80s and both remarried. Neither had lived at the Takoma address for over 30 years, explaining why my registered letter to that address early in my search languished and eventually came back to me.

Tom assured me that his mother would love to hear from Art and Shirley, and that the timing was particularly good as she was successfully recuperating from minor surgery, and would welcome hearing from an old friend.

Art sent Mary Lou a copy of the book. Later I sent her a copy of this new chapter. She wrote back immediately.

"I am excited to be seeing Art and meeting Shirley Zimmer in March when they stop in Roanoke on their way home from Florida. Thank you for sending these notes to me. You did amazing research finding my son Tom and finding Lester Gillespie who graduated from Clarkson in 1959. I have enjoyed the book and am amazed at all Art's business life. I am sure it will be an emotional meeting for us in March. Thank you for making it all happen."

Thank you too, Mary Lou!
After the March meeting, she wrote an update:
Last week, I had the pleasure of meeting Art Zimmer and his wife Shirley for lunch as they were driving home from Florida. I had not seen him for 60 years and had never met his wife. We had a lovely visit for over 3 hours sharing life experiences. There was such love among the 3 of us and I was thrilled to hear about all their adventures. I saw in Art's face the young man I had known so long ago, but also the man who had accomplished so much, and I felt so proud of him. Art's path to success is due to his God-given gifts that have propelled him to succeed in all of his business ventures. I saw how he and Shirley are a great team and I was thrilled to meet her and hear her stories too. She is an amazing woman.

Where, oh where, have 60 years gone? Art Zimmer, Shirley Zimmer and MaryLou Willard (right) met at a reunion lunch on March 18, 2016. It was the first time Art and MaryLou had been together since 1956. This book's editor Lois Gridley had tracked down MaryLou as part of her research for this book. Shirley arranged the reunion meeting. A 3-hour lunch was enjoyed by all.

This was an emotional meeting for all of us. My heart was so warmed with love for both of them, and I felt like crying and laughing the whole time we were together. I had never realized until this 60-year reunion what an impact that Art and I had made on each other's lives. I am grateful for the time we shared and hope this will be the first of many visits.

- Mary Lou

Shirley wrote back:

Hello MaryLou! What a blessing to meet someone who had such an impact on the love of my life, Art. When I saw the dedication Art wrote for this book, I wanted MaryLou to know the depth of impact their high school relationship had on Art. What I didn't know was that their relationship had the same impact on MaryLou. "We were two nobodies who became somebody through our relationship. It was the same for me." WOW – MaryLou and I were so on the same wavelength through our Christian faith. Our emails prior to our meeting in Roanoke and discussion at our meeting were open, honest and transcended any differences due to our sharing a love of Christ— and of Art.

- Shirley

Art added his thoughts as well:

I think it is a little strange when your high school sweetheart of four years becomes best friends with your wfe.

- Art

*****

Another momentous meeting in an upstairs downtown dining room

The other new story didn't have to be searched out; it found *me*. New Times owner and publisher Bill Brod graciously invited Log Cabin Books and Brian MacDowell to stage the book's launch at the New Times headquarters on West Genesee Street in Syracuse.

I met many of the people who are part of Art and Shirley's life and of their book. Many were people I know as well. Victor Ianno's name is familiar in Syracuse publishing and media circles. He introduced himself, and related his memories of a meeting with a New Times editor that HE had just days before the August 1984 meeting described on the book's back cover. His was with Peter Orville, long-time editor of the New Times in its early years, and Roger Scott, whose sometimes notorious adventures are well documented in Syracuse history.

Peter had asked Victor to meet with them to discuss a proposal Roger had made to him. At that point, the near-bankrupt paper owed Scotsman Press almost $18,000 for printing costs. Roger wanted to buy the paper...but only if Victor would forgive the debt AND give him a $20,000 line of credit for future printing services.

"I asked Peter to step into the other room," Victor relates. "I told him, 'Peter, you know I love you like a brother, but I'd rather see the New Times go out of business and you lose your job than give that man a line-of-credit he would probably never repay.' Peter wasn't surprised at my reaction. But he loved the New Times and was doing what he could to save it."

I was speechless, waiting for Victor's next words.

"We returned to the table and Peter told Roger the news. A few days later, I heard that Art Zimmer had bought the paper, and planned to pay off all of its past debts, including my sizeable invoice."

We smiled at each other. I wish I had known this a few weeks ago, I told him. If there is ever a sequel....and now there is.

EARLY YEARS IN SYRACUSE

Onondaga Ski Club

Chapter 3 is one of my favorites because I loved my years as a member and officer of Onondaga Ski Club. But I didn't include some of the details that my erstwhile fellow club members think I should have.

For many years starting in the early 1960s, I attended Syracuse University football games in Archbold Stadium, the venerable open-air stadium that formerly stood on the site of the current Carrier Dome. Usually I was with a group of ski club friends. It seemed like for most games it either snowed so hard you could hardly see the field, or it was very cold...or it rained. Of course, we were all young and somewhat crazy, and we would fortify ourselves with a "nip" or two. However, with the ski group, no one ever got drunk. We were all responsible drinkers.

As a sideline to this story, in all those party years, I got drunk only once. Now, I haven't had even one drink in 25 years. In those days I was on the ski club race team. I did it just for fun, and the after-race parties. Most races had about 100 entries, and I usually finished at around number 90. One year I was the club's bus trip committee chairperson. I ran trips all over New England and Canada. I organized a one-day bus trip to Snow Ridge ski area for the biggest race of the season, the Oneida Silver Cup Race sponsored by the Oneida/Griffiss ski club.

As usual, on the bus we had several kegs of beer. For no good reason, I started to "tip" a few more than usual on the two-hour drive to Snow Ridge. I rolled off the bus, feeling no pain. I could barely put my skis on. Nevertheless I entered the race...and placed 5th. Hmmm. My first thought was to get drunk every day and be on the Olympic team (and die young). My second thought was never to get drunk again for the rest of my life, so I never did.

50 Years with OSC

Art Zimmer celebrates 50th year as an active member in OSC

Art in 1969

December of 2012 marks the 50th year that Art Zimmer has been a member of Onondaga Ski Club. Art semi-retired two years ago and moved to nearby Hamilton, NY, so he is not seen around OSC activities as much much to our regret.

Some highlights of Art's service to OSC over the years are:

- 2 terms each as 2nd VP, 1st VP and President
- 22 years on the board of directors
- Club ski instructor back in the days that OSC had its own ski school
- Member race team 14 years
- Original founder of and director for 17 years of the Annual Ski Show and Ski Sale. The Ski Show and Sale financially funded the majority of OSC budget for 20 years
- Schuss Boomer editor 17 years
- Purchased the Vermont lodge and was Lodge Chairman for many years

Zimmermobile

Art and his wife Shirley hosted Road Rally parties over a period of 23 years. Art set up the Road Rally course for about 40 years. Art chaired European and western ski charters for many years, back in the days when OSC charted

Art hosting a Road Rally

entire airplanes to fly non-stop to ski destinations from Syracuse. Art also chaired the bus trip committee and social committee for many years as well as originating and chairing for many years the tennis programs.

Editors Comment: Art is a role model for members. Many of the activities and programs we now enjoy are due to his hard work and creative efforts. Next time you see Art and Shirley, express your gratitude.

Art and Shirley Zimmer

Back to the football games and all the bad weather. In the 80s, Syracuse University built the Dome, the only domed stadium in the country on a college campus. Of course, because it is on campus, there is no parking around the Dome. Our group had a nice parking area where we would tailgate, then walk 10 minutes to the Dome.

Now living in Hamilton, I can walk from my house to the Colgate stadium in just seven minutes. Now it seems as if it is warm and sunny at almost every game. In the Dome it is hot. Ironic since it is the Carrier Dome, named after the largest air conditioning company in the world. There is no AC; the Dome is frequently like a sauna.

In the winter the Dome is home to SU basketball. Yes, it's heated. Shirley and I had season tickets for years. Syracuse regularly sets basketball attendance records, even outdrawing NBA teams.

The Onondaga Ski Club's Vermont Lodge

Probably my best and longest lasting accomplishment for Onondaga Ski Club was the Vermont lodge. Today, after 45 years, the club still owns and operates its own private lodge, one of the very few ski clubs in the entire U.S. to do so.

In the late 1950s, the club leased a lodge for several seasons in Turin, NY, near Snow Ridge Ski Area, about 50 miles north of Rome, NY. Snow Ridge was one of the very first ski areas in Upstate New York. For several years after that, OSC leased a lodge at Whiteface Mountain, near Lake Placid. Then for one season OSC leased a lodge in Vermont, near Mad River Glenn. All the lodge operations lost money, but the fun, the parties, and the comradeship of having a private lodge for members made it all worthwhile.

Some members thought the club should buy its own lodge, a practice almost unheard of. Others said that if we lost money on leasing lodges, the club would have a "white elephant" and bankrupt the club. And anyway, they thought an all-volunteer club should not be in the real estate business.

In the mid-1960s, past-president Bob Baxter formed a committee to explore the possible purchase of a club lodge. Bob was a bank vice president and respected by everyone on both sides of the discussion. I was a member of the committee and 2nd vice president at the time. I learned a lot by watching how Bob operated. After over a year of hard work and a lot of research by the all-volunteer committee, the plan was presented to and voted down by to the board of directors. Everyone thought it was the end of the lodge question, forever.

I felt strongly the club should buy a lodge. I carefully analyzed the reasons I thought the Baxter plan failed. In 1967, I asked the board to appoint me as committee chairman of the now-defunct lodge committee. The board reluctantly agreed, but with no budget. They felt that would be the end of it. I was now the club's 1st vice president. I felt the major problem with the Baxter proposal was the absence of a specific location or property that would be recommended for purchase.

First I organized a small committee of like-minded people, none of whom had been on the Baxter committee. I wanted to start fresh. And I started the search for a specific property. I assigned one major ski area in New York or Vermont to each committee member. Each would go to their assigned area several times and scout out possible properties. They would drive around to find For Sale signs, read newspaper classified ads, and work with a local realtor, all at their own expense. Every three months or so, we would meet and discuss the various properties they had found.

We never made a report to the board. They thought the committee was inactive and probably out of business. I was assigned the Gore Mountain area. Gore is on the edge of the Adirondack Mountains, about 50 miles northwest of Albany. It was a fairly new ski area opened by and operated by New York State, as it still is today. I had drawn up a list of requirements that would be necessary for a property to be considered for the club to buy.

After more than a year's work, investigating over 50 properties near eight major ski areas, we decided the best one was in a little village called Lower Granville in Vermont, located halfway between Killington Ski Area (the largest ski area in the East) and Sugar Bush Ski Area (considered the ritziest ski area in the East). The building was a large farmhouse. The owner was an elderly farmer who was retiring and moving a half mile down the road to live at his son's farm.

Before reporting to the board, a financial plan had to be in place. Working quietly with club treasurer Dick Flaherty, we put together a plan to sell lodge bonds to members to raise the down payment and money to convert the farmhouse into a club lodge. One of my requirements was that the owner had to agree to hold the mortgage—with a substantial down payment—as no Vermont bank would give a bunch of skiers from New York a mortgage, and no New York bank would finance a bunch of skiers' crazy idea to buy a place in Vermont.

I was now president of the OSC. I presented the plan to the board of directors. All hell broke out. The board and the entire club membership were pretty evenly split on the topic. For the next three months it was hotly debated at board meetings, at committee meetings, at parties, and on ski lifts. Finally the board passed a motion that the lodge committee would need to sell enough bonds to raise the entire down payment and enough money for completely remodeling the farmhouse into a club lodge before the question to buy or not would be considered. They felt that would put an end to it.

Surprise: within three months, my committee sold all the necessary bonds and had the money in the bank. There were two more months of hot debate at board meetings that I now chaired as president. I then announced, "No more discussion. Everyone has their mind made up. At next month's board meeting a motion to purchase the lodge will be made. I'll allow no discussion, and the board will vote yes or no."

I pretty much knew where each board member stood on the subject. We had an 18- member board. I felt it would end up being decided by who was absent from the meeting. I called the meeting to order, had the motion to

purchase the lodge read, and asked for a show of hands in favor. I counted and was surprised no one else was counting. Now a show of hands opposed. Again, only I counted. I said, motion passed next order of business, and we moved on.

After the meeting, people asked me what the actual vote was. I said it was a tie and, in accordance with Robert's Rules of Order, the president votes in case of a tie and of course I voted yes. It was several weeks later before I began to tell a few close friends the motion was actually defeated by one vote. However it was not my fault as I failed 8th grade math and never did learn to count.

Now some more challenges came up. It took six months of working out a long list of problems to get to a final closing. Near the end, when it appeared the entire deal would collapse because the seller's lawyer did not want a bunch of New York skiers coming into their little village, I actually put up one of my apartment houses as collateral to make the purchase happen. A lot of credit must go to Bob Gang, a lawyer who was on the OSC board. Bob worked with me (for free) to overcome a lot of the legal challenges. In 2015, Bob Gang, now 97 years old, drove himself to an OSC old timers' reunion party that I helped organize. I am sorry to say Bob Baxter had passed away by then.

When I joined the OSC, there were 700 members. During the next 15 years, I created a series of marketing programs and several membership recruitment efforts. The programs I initiated – the trophy case, the Vermont Lodge, the ski show – all annually attracted many new members. When I semi-retired from actively running the club, the membership stood at 1,700, about the same as the entire population of the village of Hamilton.

Today, after 45 years, the OSC still operates that same lodge. Over the years, the lodge has been the glue that kept the OSC together and made it grow and prosper. Meanwhile, all the other ski clubs in the area (there were six) have folded and gone out of business.

I guess having never learned to count has its benefits.

Earl Alger

Earl Alger wrote to me after he read the book. Earl and I were ski buddies for several years. Earl became quite active in the Onondaga Ski Club, then

Earl Alger (right) at Disneyworld in 2004 with Art and Shirley (left) and Dona and Dick Flaherty.

he moved to Washington, D. C., where he has lived for the past 35 years. He joined the Washington, D.C. ski club and is a very successful realtor. If you decide to move to D. C., contact Earl. He can get you a home to buy or rent.

The Mark Teitelbaum he refers to was the general manager for many years of my Mount Snow, Vermont, ski lodge and hotel, the Austrian Haus.

Earl, Dick and Dona Flaherty, Shirley and I still get together each summer for a few days at the OSC's Vermont lodge. Every year as Shirley and I head south for the winter, we stop in D.C. for an evening and dinner with Earl.

***

AH, WHAT TO SAY ABOUT ART ZIMMER?
By Earl R. Alger, Art's Washington D.C. connection

I have known Art as a good long-time friend. We met on an Onondaga Ski Club weekend bus trip from Syracuse to Stowe, VT in the winter of 1968.

I had moved to Syracuse from Los Angeles and had a great good-paying job with numerous exciting challenges, but because of the cold weather, ice, and snow, I was having a hard time meeting people to socialize with. There was a dramatic change in lifestyles between Syracuse and Los Angeles; It seemed like most of the people in Syracuse were hibernating during the winter months How can you meet people if they don't go out?

I decided that if I did not meet at least 20 people in a month that I could meet for dinner and do things with, I was going back to California. A friend mentioned that a good way to meet people was to join a ski club and go on a ski bus trip. So I did. At the ski lodge I ended up with Art as a roommate.

He had some viewpoints that I found interesting and definitely not run-of-the-mill. He did not seem to be the type of person who would put up with life being boring and unenjoyable. He had a unique way of coming up with good ideas and interesting projects and following through on them. He was not easily discouraged and hard work did not seem to bother him. He had a steady pace and could take something simple and turn it into a lot of fun.

He also had a good sixth sense: a good sense of humor. These were my first impressions, and as we got to know each other better, they proved to be true.

Art said that if I got involved in helping running functions for the club, I would achieve my goal of meeting 20 or more good people. With his help, in less than a month I met way more than 20 people to enjoy life with.

An example of Art's sense of humor: one afternoon a bunch of us were at a clambake. We were about to leave and Art asked if anyone was interested in going to see his boat. It sounded like a good idea; five of us decided to go.

We drove to a boatyard at the south end of Oneida Lake and rented a small boat to go out and see his boat. We had motored out on the lake for about five minutes when Art said to cut the motor. We all looked around, and there was no boat insight. We asked where the boat was, and he informed us that it was at the bottom of the lake. It had sunk a while back. It was a beautiful day and we all got a good laugh out of our brief boating trip.

Over time Art has done a lot to add to other people's enjoyment. Not many people can make that statement. The amount of time, energy, expense, and effort he has put into running different functions, parties, fundraisers, etc., has been astronomical. I would definitely conclude that Art likes to see people have a good time and does more than his share to make it happen.

A friend indeed

If someone needs a helping hand, I have seen Art lending it gladly. Once we were at the Onondaga Ski Club lodge in Vermont for a ski weekend and it started raining. Skiing in the rain is not a lot of fun, so we were looking for something to do. I heard about a furniture auction in a small town nearby. I had been looking for some furniture for my apartment in Syracuse and thought it would be interesting to see what they had up for auction. Art asked me to see if I could get some folding chairs for the lodge.

Off I went to the auction. When I got there, I found out that three furniture stores were going out of business and had consolidated some very expensive furniture for the auction. I was talking with a man who had come to buy some furnishings for his rental units and he said that the furniture that they had was way too nice for rental units.

The auction began. Things were selling for about a tenth or less of what their normal value would have been. I bought a headboard for my bed and, since I did not have a way to get it back to Syracuse, I also bought a nice living room chair and a ten-foot crushed velvet couch. The terms of the auction were that the furniture had to be removed within 24 hours. I went back to the lodge and Art asked me if I was able to buy some folding chairs. I told him no, but told him what I had bought. He asked me how I was going to get it all back to Syracuse. I told him that I didn't have a clue. At that time Art had a Volkswagen van. He said we could move the furniture back in his van. I said that I didn't think that the furniture would fit in the van. The next morning, we drove to the auction site. We put the bed frame and the couch in the back of the van with the rear door open and about four feet of the couch sticking out. We tied the chair on top of the van.

I wish that we had taken a picture. It was quite a sight. All the furniture arrived back in Syracuse safely.

Art, the practical joker!

One weekend Art, Mark Teitelbaum, and I were roommates on another ski trip. I was at a restaurant that had a good band; Art and Mark had gone back to the lodge earlier. Something about getting a good night's sleep for the next hard day's skiing. When I came back around 2 a.m., Art and Mark had set a paper cup of water above the door. I opened the door and the cup of water fell on my head. I yelped and the two of them started laughing hysterically.

Art was sleeping in the upper part of a two-level bed. I went over and lifted up the upper part of the bed that he was in and when I let it go the two pins at each end dropped out and Art and the upper bed dropped to the floor. I could not immediately figure out why it had dropped. There was Art, lying on the floor laughing. Mark was laughing even harder. He was sleeping in a single bed. I picked up the end of his bed and was lifting it up and down with his head hitting the wall.

The three of us were laughing so hard that we woke up the people in the next room. All of the people we woke were on the ski trip with us. There was a knock on the door. I thought to myself, I wonder who would be knocking on our door at 2:30 a.m.? I opened the door and there stood the owner of the lodge and about 15 people in the hall. When he looked into the room, it looked like we had destroyed the place. He mentioned that he had just spent $150,000 renovating the lodge. At that point I figured Art, Mark, and I had a chance of getting free room and board at the local police station. I told the owner to come back in the morning and if there was any damage we would either pay for the damage or buy the lodge. I then asked him how much he wanted for the lodge. The owner looked at us for about a minute and then said he would be back in the morning to check to see if there was damage. We were able to put the bed back together. When the owner came back in the morning he found no damage. All in all, he took it good naturedly and he asked if we had been serious about possibly buying his lodge. A couple of years later, he sold the lodge. Later on Art bought two ski lodges. And Mark was one of his lodge managers. I wonder if Art came up with the idea of buying lodges from that night.

***

Pico Bavarian Haus ski lodge

I touched on my Pico-Killington Bavarian Haus property in Chapter 4, but didn't explain how I lost it to a spectacular fire.

The Bavarian Haus was 30 miles south of the Onondaga Ski Club's lodge. It had about six acres of vacant land around it that was directly adjacent to the

Pico Ski Area parking lot. The Killington Ski Area was on the other side of the same mountain. There had been rumors that the larger Killington would buy Pico.

Frank Heald was the general manager of Pico Mountain. I knew Frank well, as for several years he had been the marketing director of Pico. As marketing director, Frank came to the Syracuse Ski Show/Ski Sale that I founded and ran for 18 years. Each night after the ski show closed, a group of ski club workers and exhibitors would go out and party. Frank was a fun party person who always joined us.

One day I got a call from Frank. He said, "Art, stop in to see me the next time you are at your Pico hotel." I went up there twice a week. When I visited Frank, he told me that Pico Mountain was expanding and needed more parking spaces. Frank said, "Last week the Pico Mountain board of directors authorized me to purchase your hotel for $650,000." That was 35 years ago. Today, that would be about 1.5 million. I said, "First of all, I'm not interested in selling, and if I were, the price would be $750,000. Thirty-five years ago inflation was almost 10 percent a year. Banks paid 8 to 10 percent on savings accounts and money was borrowed at almost 20-percent interest. Property values were going up 8 to 10 percent every year.

A year later, Frank called for another meeting. Frank told me the board authorized him to buy my hotel for $750,000. Frank, I said, "I don't want to sell, but if I did, the place is now worth $850,000." A year later the same thing happened; now my price was $950,000.

Two months later the hotel burned to the ground. Days later Frank called me to say he was sorry about the fire, and to assure me that Pico had not torched it. Then he made an offer: "We'll buy the land and the smoldering remains, clean it up (an expensive job) and pay you $200,000." I said, "No thanks, Frank. (All through this we remained good friends.) I'm going to build a new hotel."

I wasn't interested in selling the vacant land, as I had a vision to construct a large condominium project on it. I made plans for the new construction and went to the town for the building permit. I worked with a contractor on the redevelopment. The contractor had done work for me on the ski club lodge 30 miles away. The town refused to issue a permit, but had no legal grounds for the rejection. My plan was to build a new hotel in the same place and same size as the old one. I realized that Pico Mountain is the largest and primary land owner, taxpayer, and employer in the town. The town was controlled by Pico. Most town officials were Pico employees. In spite of that we, the contractor and I, went to court.

The first court was town court and we lost. I told Frank, and we were still friends, "I am going to state court. You don't have any influence up there." All of this had taken over a year. A few days before our state court appearance, Frank called. "Okay, how much?" "$400,000 as-is." He said okay.

Two days later, Shirley and I went to Vermont for the closing. When the check came across the table, I was surprised, as it was not from Pico but from Killington Ski Resort. Almost 10 years later, Killington did buy Pico Mountain. Selling my land turned out to be the best course of action, as a year later the country went into a recession right when I would have been opening a new hotel at the beginning of an economic downturn in which the Vermont ski industry suffered badly.

Surprisingly, to me at least, almost 30 years later all that land still sits vacant, unused, and now overgrown with trees and brush.

Chapter 5

I got a call on February 19, 2016 from Charles McChesney. Charles is a former Post Standard editor and former editor-in-chief of the Business Journal. Charles said, "Congratulations, Art, you have been selected for induction into the Syracuse Press Club Wall of Honor on April 30." The press club Wall of Honor is to recognize the long term positive accomplishments of a few in Central New York media (radio, TV, newspaper). I think this honor is more for the Syracuse New Times newspaper than it is for me. But, hey, I accepted it with humility. (My acceptance speech is found at the end of this chapter.)

As I said in Chapter 5, I consider Walt Shepperd the best political reporter I've ever read, and we were fortunate to have had him on board during his 35-year tenure at the New Times. He is quoted in the book, and recently he wrote to me about the years we worked together.

"There was one encounter (with me) early on that for me defined our relationship as one of trust and respect. A first-time Common Council candidate came storming into the Franklin Street facility yelling that I was in cahoots with her opponent on coverage of their contest. You, showing the zenith of your penchant for calming things down, told her to come sit in your office for as long as she needed to talk things out, but that, no matter what transpired, you would be supporting me. Another element of that relationship was evident when, several times, you made significant financial contributions to my youth program, the Media Unit, thus aiding us in avoiding extreme fiscal crises, without ever taking or asking for public mention or credit."

Bill DeLapp wrote a review of the book in the New Times (SNT) shortly after its launch.

ALL ABOUT ART
A Review by Bill DeLap

Published in the Syracuse New Times Nov. 25, 2015

When Art Zimmer was publisher of the Syracuse New Times, he would occasionally travel down memory lane at the office and resurrect some amusing tales from his past.

One story from his days during the swingin' 1960s as a dashing man about town concerned his cohabitation practices. Young ladies would ask Art if he was living with anyone at the time. "Why, yes," he replied. The ladies seemed upset by that response, but then he added, "And she's black." Next came the topper: "And she's a bunny."

The ladies, of course, understandably jumped to the conclusion that available bachelor Art was indeed living it up a la Hugh Hefner with a Playboy playmate. Art never let on that he indeed was the owner of a female black bunny named Smokey that was scampering about his pad.

Art eventually thought it was time to break off the relationship with Smokey, but the local zoo officials nixed his idea of donating the bunny to them. So one night Art donned an oversized overcoat so he could smuggle

Smokey into the zoo, and dropped her off at the bunny patch, where she presumably lived up to her mistaken Playboy pedigree.

The Smokey story won't be found amid the 200-plus pages of Making It Count: From A to Z, The Life and Times of Art Zimmer, but there are plenty of other nuggets to be mined from this autobiography. The softcover [first] edition from Hamilton's Log Cabin Books retails for $19.95, with Zimmer hitting the book-tour trail to heighten awareness of its yuletide stocking-stuffer potential. Given Art's penchant for entrepreneurial promotion, he'll likely be pushing his book for weeks to come.

To bring A to Z to the printed page, Zimmer, 78, wrote down many historical chunks in longhand. The material was then typed into a computer by Shirley and then turned over to editor Lois Gridley for refinements, an ongoing process that took a year to complete.

The book works best during its chronicles of Art's adolescence, which provides a welcome reference point for his later years. Indeed, who woulda thunk that the tenacious teen who somehow managed to avoid flunking out of high school would morph into the ascot-wearing publisher of an award-winning alternative newsweekly?

Along the way readers will also discover Mary Lou Willard, Art's first sweetheart; learn how Art's typing skills kept him out of the rigors of 20-mile hikes in the Army; and laugh at Art's attempts at embarking on a two-year sailing adventure without having any previous nautical experience.

Zimmer isn't afraid to name names, either. During his long reign with the Onondaga Ski Club, Art booked 1960s-era super-skier Jean Claude Killy for a Syracuse appearance. But the sports star could not speak English, forcing Art to hire an interpreter. And things got worse when Killy didn't arrive at the press conference on time because he was allegedly dallying with an airline stewardess in his hotel room.

Perhaps the biggest surprise for readers is that the Syracuse New Times does not command a considerable chunk of print from A to Z's recollections, although there are some contributions from previous editors-in-chief Mike Greenstein and the late Roland Sweet which cite that Zimmer's 1984 purchase of the bankrupt newspaper saved it from certain extinction. Instead, the Syracuse New Times is just one component of Zimmer's long journey, which includes efforts as a playwright (specifically his annual Cruizin' musical salutes), as a mover-and-shaker for the Syracuse Area Live Theater (SALT) awards, and as an auto magnate of neo-classic models that bear his surname.

There are several constant themes at work throughout A to Z, such as the notion that long hours, hard work and being a persistent self-promoter really will pay off in the long run. And it also helps that you marry the right girl: In Art's case, she's the former Shirley Sherburne, and they've been happily-ever-aftering since 1987.

So maybe there is a sequel to Making It Count: From A to Z, The Life and Times of Art Zimmer, if only because Art still has many other stories. There's another tale that he revealed in the office about his days as a handyman for an apartment complex, especially when he attempted to work on the room of an extremely rude and uncooperative tenant. The first thing that Art did when he bought the property was to give that tenant an eviction notice!

Art Zimmer will conduct a book signing on Tuesday, Dec. 1, 6 to 8 p.m., at the DeWitt Public Library, located on the lower level of Shoppingtown Mall in DeWitt.

****

In the review, Bill referred to an anecdote I told him 25 years ago. I felt that I had to explain a bit when I wrote to thank him for the article:

"Thank you very much for the nice article in this week's Syracuse New Times. As per your story on Smokey the rabbit [my house-broken pet] : It was probably 25 years ago I told you that story and details fade over time. I still tell the story to people today, and it probably should have been in the book.

However, after 25 years, you left out some important details that make an even better story...so here are the full details. First of all, I always start with a history lesson before I tell the story. As it took place in the early 1960s, most people don't know or remember what the culture was like.

First, in those days, young men and women—any age, actually--did not live together until after marriage. It just wasn't done. A few did, but usually in secret. If they were found out, they were often looked down upon.

Second, interracial dating was still taboo. It was considered by both black and white communities as unacceptable.

Third, the Playboy Bunny Club had popular venues in big cities, but Syracuse was a small city with no playboy club. However, one bar owner opened a sleazy knock-off bunny club on James Street in Eastwood. It eventually was exposed as a thinly disguised cover for a prostitution ring, and many of the women hired to work there as servers were actually prostitutes. The place was a dump and no decent man would admit going there or associating with a "bunny."

Now, the story. I never told it to girls. It was barroom talk reserved for groups of guys, usually the majority of whom I did not know. I would drop the comment that I was living with a female. That would raise a few eyebrows. Then I'd drop the fact that my roomie was black...and she was a bunny. I could feel the surprised hostility around me. Sometimes I would tell them the rest of the story, à la Paul Harvey, the famous national radio newscaster whose last comment always contained, "page two, the rest of the story," as he was famous for saying. And sometimes I did not tell the rest of the story. So even now there are some senior citizens around Syracuse who, if you say you are a friend of Art Zimmer, will look at you in disgust and say, Did you know he used to shack up with a black whore???

With my sick sense of humor, I think it is all very funny. What happened to my roomie, Smokey? I decided to end the relationship with Smokey because my various jobs frequently took me out of town for a week at a time. I would have friends come in to check on her, but I thought it was unfair for her to be alone so much of the time, as she was very much a 'people' bunny.

I donated her to the bunny park at the Burnett Park Zoo, where she lived happily ever after.

Chapter 6

The car that keeps on giving: three more Zimmer-related anecdotes

In Chapter 6 I had lots of anecdotes about the Zimmer Motor Car Company. And I missed more. Three examples:

- Many of my transactions for the company started with a phone call that included an unusual request such as this: "I want to buy a new four-door Zimmer Golden Spirit Motor Car. And I want to come to Syracuse to meet you and make the deal in person. "OK, I'll pick you up at the airport, but remember I don't 'deal' on the price. Everyone pays the same list price."

The caller agreed, but later called back: "Don't pick me up at the airport. The airline ticket is too expensive. I'll drive. It's only 900 miles." I began to wonder if this deal would take place. He was buying a $150,000 car and didn't want to pay for an airline ticket.

But the potential buyer and his wife did arrive. I put them up in one of the best hotels in town: Norm Swanson's Genesee Grande. I had purchased property from Norm 30 years before and we had become friends. That night Shirley and I had dinner with the couple. He turned out to be a very interesting self-made entrepreneur millionaire. Someone should write a book about him.

When the car was done, I called him to arrange shipping of the car in an enclosed van, as I did with all the Zimmers. He said the $700 shipping charge was too high. He would rather rent a car, drive to Syracuse, and drive the Zimmer home. And he did.

-Another deal that began with a phone call was from a man who wanted to buy a four- door Zimmer. But first he wanted to know how long it was. I told him, and he hung up. A week later, he called and asked how long a two-door Zimmer would be. I told him, and again he hung up.

The next week, another call. The man explained that he lived in a condo. The garage was too short for a Zimmer. He had planned to have a nice looking finished-off extension added to the garage, but the condo association said no.

He said, "I'm still going to buy a Zimmer. I'll just cut a hole in the wall in the front of the garage into the kitchen. The condo association won't know it." His next statement floored me: "I can have the front of the Zimmer in the kitchen because my wife died last year."

I guess he liked having company while he cooked.

Why New York's economy is in the toilet...

-Almost from the beginning, I wanted to move the Zimmer manufacturing process to Central New York. I did not want any government assistance. The fact is I would refuse any corporate welfare offered to me. I pay more than my share of taxes, but I won't take any of it back in government programs. Several were offered to the New Times, and I always politely refused.

However, I did decide to run a little experiment. I wrote a letter explaining what the Zimmer Car Company was, its potential in job creation and economic impact to any area where it was located. I explained I was going to move the company to a new location and wondered what assistance would be available in their area. I then mailed copies of the letter to the economic development office of the city of Syracuse, Onondaga County, and New York State, as well as the states of Virginia and North Carolina. In about four days, I started to get phone calls and letters from Virginia and North Carolina. How can we help? What can we do? Here are some great incentive programs if you bring your company to our area.

I have not yet heard from Syracuse or New York State. However, at a party, Nick Pirro, when he was Onondaga County Executive, told me if there was anything he could do to help me bring Zimmer manufacturing to Onondaga County, to just ask him.

All I can say is shame, shame on you, Syracuse and New York State.

Chapter 9 - Shirley

The Art of being a smart husband?

Chapter 9 may be my favorite, because I got to talk about Shirley. I never mentioned one of her best talents: she is a wonderful cook and meal planner. Most husbands, if they're smart, never tell their wife that their mother's cooking was in any way better than hers. After Shirley and I were married for about two years, I got up enough nerve to say something. I thought that with the very close, loving relationship between Shirley and my mother, it would be okay.

Shirley is a very good cook, and I help in the kitchen a lot. For our first Thanksgiving together, we had 23 family members and friends over for dinner. Shirley prepared everything from scratch. It was a delicious meal. Even for everyday meals, Shirley would  prepare stuffing or dressing for a turkey or chicken from scratch and it was very good.

But eventually I said, "Your stuffing is good, but my mother's is better." So Shirley asked my mother for the recipe. My mother laughed and said, "I just use Stove Top..." For the next year, Shirley bought Stove Top. Then one day we read the ingredients on the package. It is full of chemicals and additives we don't want to put in our bodies...back to scratch. Shirley's recipe is very good and much more nutritious.

After that, I got really brave. I ventured, "Your potato salad is good, but Mom's is better." Shirley asked my mother for the recipe. My mom laughed and revealed that with a family of six, rather than using diced-up boiled potatoes, she used leftover mashed potatoes. Try it...you'll like it.

Last year, there were just the two of us for Thanksgiving. Everyone else had passed away or moved far away. So we walked up to the Colgate Inn and enjoyed a great holiday dinner.

Kiwi the killer dolphin

Shirley loves dolphins. In her office at the New Times, she had dolphin statues on her desk. Over the years, we rented several beachfront condos around the Gulf of Mexico and in the Caribbean. As often as possible, Shirley would sit on the balcony and watch dolphins swim by.

One year in Hawaii, we were on a whale watch in a small rubber boat and were suddenly surrounded by about a dozen whales, leaping in and out of the water all around us. We were concerned one would come up under our little boat. This went on for about an hour. Our guide called it a true National

Geographic moment and a true Kodak moment. He had never seen so many whales, so nearby, before. Shortly after that, we were surrounded by about 20 dolphins that wanted to play with us. They would come right up to the side of the boat. This went on for over a half hour. We certainly got our money's worth and more on that trip.

One year, when we were spending the winter on the Florida panhandle, I saw a newspaper ad: swim with a dolphin named Kiwi. I told Shirley to pack her swimsuit for a day trip, and surprised her with a swim date with Kiwi.

Soon, Shirley was having the time of her life swimming and playing with Kiwi. It was just Shirley, Kiwi, and the dolphin trainer in a giant pool. I was standing at the edge of the pool taking pictures. Another Kodak day for Shirley.

Suddenly Kiwi swam over to me, and on impulse before the trainer could warn me, I reached out to pet her. The back of my hand slid across one of her sharp jagged  teeth. Suddenly blood was spurting all over the place (like the tuna can on the TV show). When I tell the story, much to Shirley's embarrassment, I say I was attacked by a killer dolphin, with blood all over the place, claiming it was lucky I was not killed. The trainer saw the blood and swam over, extremely upset. He was new on the job, afraid I would sue and he would lose his job. I told him if he got me a Band-Aid, I would not tell anyone....

Chapter 10
Trading for fun and profit

In the book, when I talked about 50 years living and working in Syracuse in Chapter 10, I mentioned Bernie Bregman as my mentor and friend, but not this vehicle he introduced me to (in this case not a car!) that had an important impact on my life and businesses.

My first experiences with barter and trading were on the school bus in Hamilton. It was around 1952 and my most frequent trading partner was Bud Rollins, my good friend who rode the bus with me.

After more than 63 years, I still see Bud frequently, and we sometimes discuss who owes what to whom from our last trade that probably involved comic books and arrowheads.

Fast forward to the early 1980s. I had moved to Syracuse and owned several businesses. I had done some minor trading or barter, all on an ad hoc basis. Then I heard about the Syracuse Trading Exchange (TX), a group of businesses that traded among themselves. I walked into Bernie Bregman's TX office in the University Building, probably without an appointment if I remember correctly. That was when we met. Bernie introduced me to Sandy Giannuzzi, his colleague in promoting and managing TX. We quickly became friends and associates; I consider our interactions as some of my best in Syracuse.

The Trading Exchange made perfect sense to me. Instead of direct trade, members did one-way trades and earned trade dollars, which the TX office documented and reported in monthly statements. Members could spend their trade balances with any other member. Bernie and Sandy also facilitated interesting and profitable social events for trade members, all paid for on trade between members.

I put all of my businesses in the Exchange. This was a great marketing opportunity, as it gave me exposure to many Syracuse area businesses and their owners. Soon I had Trade Exchange tenants renting some of my apartments, new advertisers in the New Times, and people paying for visits at my Vermont hotels and ski resort with trade dollars. In turn, Shirley and I and the New Times and the hotels benefitted from goods and services provided by fellow TX members.

Bernie was a master at putting plans together for Exchange members, and recruiting new participants when members consulted with him about finding something they needed.

In one instance, he organized a weekend trip to my Pico hotel in Vermont, all on trade. But at the last minute there was a glitch: only 14 people had signed up. I said, I guess we will have to cancel it. Bernie said, Oh, no; I rented a 15-passenger van on trade. I said, "Great! Who will drive it?"

Bernie said, "YOU!"

There I was, the owner of the hotel, offering a great weekend on trade and serving as the van driver for the trip. THAT is personalized service! The good news: it was a great summer trip, and we all had a lot of fun. For years after, people told me it was one of the best vacation trips they had ever taken.

My biggest single trade? A 100-percent-trade sale of a new Zimmer motor car. The New Times ad sales on trade accumulated, too. I decided to reserve Mid-Lakes Navigation's entire Skaneateles Lake dinner cruise boat for one memorable evening. The entire newspaper staff and their families enjoyed the evening with Shirley and me. And Mid-Lakes enjoyed the Trading Dollars, I'm sure!

Soon after I met Bernie, I began to realize he was a master promoter and marketing guru far beyond TX. Bernie had more original ideas for marketing programs than anyone else, and he was a doer. Many people with great ideas never accomplish much. But Bernie did, and constantly amazed people. I began to spend as much time with him as my mentor as I could. If people compliment my marketing expertise, I tell them I learned it all from Bernie.

Chapter 11

Shirley #2

In Chapter 11, I referred to one of Shirley's best friends, also named Shirley (Ronkowski), Shirley #2 as they both like to refer to her. She has lived in California since 1980. We sent her a copy of the book, and she called to reminisce about some of our adventures  with her in California and Las Vegas, and also about her time in Syracuse as my Shirley's colleague, friend, and roommate. Shirley #2 relates:

"Shirley has been my best friend since we met in the teacher's room in 1971 when I came to teach at Gillette Road Middle School in North Syracuse. She remembers my calling out to her to get her attention, "Hey, lady in the headband." I kidded her about the hair accessory choice, and we've been fast friends ever since. We had many interesting experiences from having the

Left to Right: Shirley Ronkowski, Debbie Reynolds, Shirley Zimmer

At the Debbie Reynolds Hotel in Las Vegas, NV
December 31, 1996

same first name. When we shared a house in Liverpool, people would call and ask to speak with Shirley. Our response was always, 'Which one?'

"Even though I moved to Santa Barbara, California in 1980, Shirley and I kept in close contact and still do today. I remember when Shirley's phone calls became filled with talk of a man she had met who didn't fit any of the categories of her former boyfriends. She sent me a picture of her standing in front of a black chauffeured limousine and next to a man dressed in a suit complete with ascot. Really? An ascot? This was definitely a man of a different sort, and as it turns out, a man of distinction. The picture she had sent was of the evening Art asked her to marry him. I was so happy to serve as bridesmaid in their wedding. It has been such a joy to witness their happiness as they create their interesting life together and demonstrate an ever-deepening love for one another.

"Art loves to surprise Shirley with gifts, trips, and even people. In 1996 he called me and asked if I wanted to surprise Shirley by meeting them in Las Vegas for New Year's Eve. I had a small Dolphin motor home at the time and Las Vegas is only a six-hour drive from Santa Barbara. So on the morning of New Year's Eve, I pulled into the parking lot of their hotel. Coincidentally, Shirley was looking out the window as I parked in plain view of their hotel room and she saw me exit the RV.

"We celebrated that New Year's Eve at the Debbie Reynolds Dinner Show. With Art's encouragement, Shirley and I had a lovely chat with Debbie (one of Shirley's favorite actresses) and had our picture taken with her."

Shirley is a lifelong, avid fan of Debbie Reynolds. When I learned Debbie was doing a special New Year's show at her hotel in Las Vegas, I decided to surprise Shirley with a trip to see her. A few years earlier, Debbie's husband, Harry Karl, was revealed to be an addicted gambler who had gambled away his 25 million and her 15 million.

Debbie declared bankruptcy and lived in her car for a while. A few years later, she had rebuilt her finances and purchased a hotel in Las Vegas and renamed it the Debbie Reynolds hotel. She then turned her finances over to her son, who squandered all her money once again. Debbie lost the hotel and was bankrupt for a second time.

In recent years we have seen Debbie perform several times. She does a great comic routine, managing to make light of those painful days and also the Liz Taylor and Eddie Fisher saga.

I called Shirley #2 to add to the surprise and join us in Las Vegas. I was talking about my plans to Bob Luongo (a.k.a. the late Bob Barker, the hot dog king of Central New York). Bob told me he owned a time share of a luxury suite in the Debbie Reynolds Hotel. Debbie and he were personal friends. Bob invited me to be his guest and use his suite at Debbie's hotel.

There were other highlights on that trip. During Debbie's performance she said that there was a special presentation for the audience. A giant movie screen descended on the stage and we witnessed live the imploding of the Hacienda Hotel, about four miles away. As it blew up, we could actually feel the ground tremble under the showroom. Several years earlier I had spent a week in the Hacienda Hotel as the guest of Dr. Albert Lowery, the real estate bestselling book author. While there I attended a concert by Liberace, who I found out years later had owned a Zimmer Golden Spirit motor car. Shirley and I got to see Liberace's Zimmer on another trip to Las Vegas.

Shirley #2 continued:

"Art is a quiet guy with a unique sense of humor. While we were in Las Vegas we went to a magic show at Caesar's Palace. As part of his act, the magician enjoyed talking to the audience. He asked me my name and then asked Shirley hers. We told him and assured him we weren't kidding. We were both Shirley.

Then he asked Art his name. Straight-faced, Art proudly announced his name as "Shirley." We all laughed heartily, including the magician.

Another time the three of us were window shopping in Santa Barbara. We stopped at a travel office window advertising San Francisco. Spontaneously, Art and I quietly broke into the song, "I Left my Heart ..." Given that Art has never been known to sing, I felt very honored."

Shirley #2 also related something about the Zimmer Motor Car Company story in Chapter 6.

"A year after the Las Vegas trip, I met Art and Shirley in Palm Springs, where they had been attending a newspaper conference. Shirley and I took my RV out into the Arizona desert for an overnight. We spent the day at the Quartzite Gem and Mineral Club while Art stayed in Palm Springs. He met us the next day in Quartzite to celebrate my 50th birthday at the Club's pancake breakfast. He told us about a car showroom he found with a genuine Zimmer motorcar for sale. In fact, I think there were two. What a find.

"Sensing Art's delight, Shirley encouraged him to go back to Palm Springs to take another look. They bought one of the Zimmers and had it shipped to Syracuse. What I want to point out is Shirley's unconditional support for Art. Not just for his ideas but for the person he is. Art offers the same loving support for Shirley. To me that is a perfect definition of love"

Chapter 11

In Chapter 11 I related examples of my "small world" perspective. And we already have more. When you talk with people you've just met, you never know what will happen or what you will learn.

In January 2016, Shirley and I attended a concert in Destin, Florida, at AJ's Banjorama, a restaurant that sponsors a rousing music event we had attended several times in the past. The band played all kinds of music. I requested some Hank Williams, Sr. songs. I have always thought Hank was one of the greatest singer/songwriters and entertainers ever. I remember the day I heard of his passing, January 1, 1953, as vividly as I remember the days Kennedy and Elvis died.

Rusty, the banjo player, said that Jabbo, the keyboard player, had an uncle who was in Hank Williams' band. On their next break and after the show, I talked at length with Jabbo about Hank. Jabbo showed me the photo below and pointed out his uncle, Paul Dennis, second from left. The photo was taken in the early days of Hank's career, before he became world-famous.

Uncle Paul was a farm boy who worked the farm with his father. He was the only boy, with three sisters. When Hank went to Nashville and became famous, he asked Paul to go with him, but Paul's father would not let him leave the farm. As a parting gift, Hank gave Paul his guitar, the one he is holding in the photo. Years later Paul gave the guitar to Jabbo, who still has it at home. It is probably very valuable, but he won't sell it.

Jabbo told me several stories about Hank's early years that Uncle Paul had told him. One that I found most interesting: One night the band was coming home from a one-night gig at a smoky honky tonk bar a few miles from Montgomery, Alabama. They were all drunk, as usual, when they passed Lake

WCOV Radio – Montgomery, Alabama - Hank Williams Sr. and band in the early years. Photo taken at WCOV Radio, Montgomery, Alabama. Uncle Paul is 2nd from left; Hank is third from right.

Martin, where there was a community called Kawliga. They got a flat tire in front of the town's general store, which had a wooden Indian out front. As the band changed the tire, Hank sat there writing a song as he frequently did. As they finished, Hank tossed the paper on the ground, saying that it was no good. One of the band members picked the paper up, and sometime later when Hank was sober showed it to him and said that it might make a good song.

The band recorded the song. It became one of the biggest hits ever, not only for Hank, but for dozens of other artists over the years. Ray Charles had a big hit with it in 1962. The song, of course, was Kaw-Liga, that poor old wooden Indian. I still hear it played quite often, now on satellite radio, Sirius XM on channel 5 (1950s music) and channel 59 (Willie's Roadhouse, classic country).

On February 9, 2016 we returned to AJ's restaurant for another Banjorama concert. The concert was over at 6 p.m. and we left for home at about 6:10. On the way home Shirley got a call from our friend, Judy Clark of Hamilton. Judy and her husband Dave had attended a Banjorama at AJ's with us a few weeks before. Her sister lives across the street from AJ's; she had called Judy to say that at 6:15 a fire had started at AJ's and that the entire place was engulfed. It turned out to be a major fire, but not burned to the ground.

Out and about

Banjorama is the latest example of something Shirley and I have always done: gone out of our way to get up off the couch, turn off the boob tube (there is almost nothing on TV worth watching, anyway), and get out and do things. One of our favorite activities is going out to live shows and concerts. We do this at home and in all our travels around the world. We both like old-time country music (and most other kinds of music) and have made several trips to Nashville and the Grand Ole Opry.

On our second date, we went to see Mel Tillis at the Three Rivers Inn. On our third date we went to a Johnny Mathis concert at the Landmark Theater in Syracuse. We would attend almost every national act and touring musical show that came to Syracuse and Turning Stone. We would take overnight trips to Rochester, Buffalo, Hartford, CT, Binghamton, Watertown, and many other northeastern cities to see shows and attend concerts. It has really enriched our lives and has been a lot of fun.

Las Vegas is one of my favorite cities, and I don't even gamble. We go there frequently for the shows. It is the entertainment capital of the world. Last year, I counted 132 shows and concerts playing in one week in Vegas. The Cirque du Soleil shows are the epitome of entertainment. The shows are almost beyond belief, and yet you are sitting there actually watching. So far we have seen 14 Cirque shows, a couple of them several times.

One Caribbean cruise we took was with a group of Grand Ole Opry stars, a wonderful up-close and exciting time.

In Syracuse and Hamilton, we regularly go out to local and regional theater productions and local music concerts. My six years on the Syracuse Stage Board of Directors were most rewarding. Shirley's time on the Syracuse Symphony Association board and her two terms as president of the board of the Earlville Opera House (an historic performing and visual arts venue) were also very exciting.

To list what entertainers and what shows were our favorites would take another book. Perhaps that could be our next project. In the meantime, we will continue to be entertained in this manner as long as we can. Perhaps we will see you at a show or concert.... If so, please stop and say hello.

Chapter 12 - Life in Hamilton

Hollywood, here I come!

Right after the first edition of this book came out in early fall 2015, I got a call from Eric Vinal. He is the movie film commissioner for New York State for this area. Mr. Vinal's message was that he and some representatives of a major Hollywood movie production company were meeting the next day with New York governor Andrew Cuomo to finalize details for the filming of a major motion picture in Upstate New York. Mr. Vinal said they would do the filming in one of three villages: Cazenovia, Skaneateles, or Hamilton.

They had been given my name to be the Hamilton "point" person. That was defined as being an influential and knowledgeable person from each village to help them decide which to choose for the filming. The "point" person was to be a volunteer. They wanted to meet with me the next day, after their meeting with the governor. The next day I met with them in the lobby of the Colgate Inn.

I drove them around the village and Colgate's campus and questioned them at length about what they would need to choose Hamilton as the filming location. They told me whatever village they chose, that would be the site for exterior scenes for the movie to be called "Pottersville." The interior shots would take place at a new $15 million sound stage that had been constructed in East Syracuse.

They would bring a crew and cast of about 60 people to the chosen village for the first two weeks in January. The movie story was set at Christmas, so the snow and weather in early January would be ideal. I was extra enthusiastic, as this would make a positive economic impact to the village in a very slow month for area businesses. In January, all the Colgate students are away. Many professors leave town for vacation or study programs. Many members of the large senior citizen population head south. Many village businesses just close down for some or all of January. And now this: a major movie filming in Hamilton. What fun and excitement for all! Better yet, it would be a family-friendly comedy.

The advance crew had a lot of work to do that would take time and cost money. So I decided to volunteer to do as much of their detail work as possible to smooth their way into Hamilton. I could write an entire chapter here with all the details of what I did over the next three weeks, but I won't bore you with all that. To sum up, the crew said they never had anyone do so much for them to get the myriad details set and to get everyone in town, especially the elected officials and business owners, enthusiastically behind the project. Needless to say, they chose Hamilton.

Three e-mails that I am proud of from this process:

Hi Shirley – please tell Art I said hi. We are all thinking about how much he did for our movie and your community. Hamilton has been one of the greatest location experiences of my career and I believe the town has been happy we've been here. None of this would have happened without Art's diligence, kindness, intelligence, and experience. Thank you very much for everything!

Brian Papworth
Unit Production Manager
Pottersville

Hi Art,

I just wanted to extend another thank you for all of your help and assistance with Pottersville. You have been, and continue to be, a huge asset to the film.

Best,

ERIC VINAL
ONONDAGA COUNTY
OFFICE OF ECONOMIC DEVELOPMENT
FILM COMMISSIONER

First day was awesome. Could not have done it without you.

Thanks,

Don
Donald Titus, Assistant Location Manager

Now that Hamilton had been chosen, the fun started and the projects grew in size. I got a call from Eric Vinal: "Tomorrow Ron Perlman is coming to Hamilton. Ron is a Hollywood actor and producer. His production company is one of the principal producers of Pottersville. Ron played the part of Vincent on TV in "Beauty and the Beast" with Linda Hamilton (maybe that influenced their choice of our village?). We want you to take charge of Mr. Perlman for the day.

The next day I hosted Ron Perlman for six hours. I must say he was the nicest, most down-to-earth guy you could meet. I drove him around town, showed him the sites we had chosen for filming, and briefed him on the arrangements that had been made. Over lunch at the Hamilton Whole Foods store, Ron told me two interesting things. He said, "Art, I have a couple of filming projects in the pipeline, and from what you have shown me today, I can see doing some more filming here in the future." Then he said, "With what you have shown me today, I can see us doing some interior filming in Hamilton, rather than a sound stage." He paid for my lunch, a $4.95 veggie burger, and asked for a signed copy of my book (First Edition). Perhaps he will make it into a movie.

The film crew had told me they would use about 200 local people as extras in the film, adding to the fun and excitement for the village people (no, not the music group by that name). The first week of filming, a casting call for extras. Over 1,300 people showed up. This is in a village of only 1,700 residents. As it turned out, more than a dozen actually got speaking parts. The whole village was going "Hollywood."

Shortly after my day with Ron, the film company told me that instead of 60 people in town for two weeks for exterior shots, they would do some indoor filming and bring in almost 100 people for four weeks, an even bigger economic boom for the village!

A couple of weeks before filming was to begin, they said, "Art, we really appreciate all your help. So we are going to write a nice part in the film for you." I had made previous commitments, before the movie project came up, to be out of town all of January. I quickly started to fantasize how this could launch my Hollywood career. I would become rich and famous. I would move to Hollywood, live in a big mansion, and have a chauffeur to drive me around in my Zimmer Golden Spirit motor car. Then I came back to earth... trade Central New York for California? No way; that would be a bummer. Trade all my wonderful Central New York friends for the "plastic" people of the West Coast? No way. And don't forget that I am at heart an undereducated farm boy from Randallsville. No, no. I said. Thanks, but no thanks.

On Christmas Day, Shirley and I departed for the South. One of the leading business women in the village, who co-owns a business that was getting involved with the movie, told Shirley that the movie people asked her to talk to Shirley to try to have her talk me into staying in town for the filming.

As filming time was approaching, the entire Northeast was having an unusually mild Fall. On December 24, it was 75 degrees in Hamilton and not a flake of snow was falling. The movie people were getting very nervous about that Christmas snow they envisioned. I made a suggestion that they thought was brilliant: if we get no snow, I'll ask local ski area owners to lend us some snow-making equipment. You could just hook them up to some fire hydrants and lay down a few inches of fresh snow for the scene. As it turned out, the snow started just before filming was to start.

So now, the filming of Pottersville is done. Studio and post-production will continue for about a year. Look for its release at the end of 2016 or early 2017.

In about the third week in January, I sent the following e-mail out to about 60 people in the village, including elected officials, business owners, and residents.

Now that the dust (or snow) is about to settle on the Hamilton filming, I would appreciate it if you would send your opinion and reflections on the entire filming project. You know that I worked with the advance film crew for several months as their official "point" person and was instrumental in their decision to come to Hamilton and not go to Cazenovia or Skaneateles.

Due to prior commitments, I had to leave town on Christmas day. So I would appreciate feedback from you. Please reply soon, as I might use your comments in my next book. I have a book deadline of January 29. Please send your overall opinion and answer these questions:

Was the movie experience a fun, exciting and worthwhile experience, or just a big inconvenience pain in the butt to you and to the village?

Was the filming a big economic plus to the local businesses or a big "bust" moneywise?

When the movie comes out, do you think Hamilton will get extra visitors and added economic benefit or not?

If they want to film another movie in Hamilton, would you be in favor of it or tell them to go to Cazenovia?

Any comments on specific dealings you had with the movie – positive or negative.

As official point person, is there more I should have done in advance? What?

Thanks for any feedback you may have.

-Art

Art Zimmer, Official movie point person

P.S. If you don't have a copy of my book yet, they are at the Colgate Bookstore.

Some of the return comments were:

- There were long lines to sign up to be extras; that showed great interest to be in a movie and earn $110.
- Fun and exciting all around the village, especially at the Inn.
- Definitely an economic plus, despite some short term inconvenience. More business for me, especially during a very slow time.
- There should have been signs to say "pardon our appearance, movie filming, all businesses open.
- I hope they will premiere the movie here; Hamilton should make a big deal of it.
- I met a number of tech stars; they were down to earth, gracious and lovely people.
- It was fun to have something exciting and current to talk about, especially at a slow time.

- Considering it was January, there was definitely a big economic plus. Another time of year, we could have taken a financial hit on their shoe string budget.
- The filming was the biggest thing to hit Hamilton since the big 1895 fire.
- I heard some complaints from long time residents who hate any change at all. (I, Art Zimmer, moved here in 1948, change can be good.)
- I saw crew and cast out eating and drinking all month.
- We found Pottersville a new world of things to learn. For us it kept our people working in January when they would otherwise have been on unemployment. Those of us who stepped up to the plate and positioned ourselves to participate certainly made money. The ones who sat back and waited for it to come to them are still waiting.
- It brought so much energy and excitement to Hamilton, especially in a challenging month for all. We saw more traffic in the village with lots of people visiting stores and restaurants. It was exciting to watch the movie crews.

My Electric Tractor

Here I am over 35 years ago on my electric tractor. Yes, electric. This photo shows a snow blower on it. I also had a 60-inch lawn mower attachment. I still don't understand what was wrong with Americans, why they weren't more green-minded about electric tractors. With very little demand, manufacturing

was stopped after a few years. I continued to use the tractor summer and winter for 10 years.

I still believe that all small tractors, riding mowers, and push mowers should be cordless electric. Most people don't realize small engines actually create more air pollution than a car. As a side note, I did things to try to be "green" long before "green" meant anything to most people except grass and trees. When I bought the New Times building, a 125-year-old 24,000-square-foot structure, I did an extreme insulating project during the first two years. When I was getting bank financing for the new Quadex typesetting machine, the bank would not believe how low the utility expenses were on my financial report. The three homes Shirley and I had were "green" ahead of their time. The 125-year-old Otisco farm house was insulated and sealed up in every way possible. The big house (13,000 square feet) in Sentinel Heights was extra insulated and used far less power than a comparable home.

The home we had constructed in Hamilton went super "green." I think it is the most energy-efficient home in the area. It has triple-pane thermal windows, insulated doors, eight zone heating controls, insulated basement walls and ceiling, 46-inch attic insulation, and walls built with two-by-eights with 8-inch insulation in every wall. Most new homes are wrapped with one-quarter-inch foam insulation board; we used one-inch insulation. Now back to the "green" tractor...

The tractor was manufactured by General Electric. It had a 48-volt system. The batteries produced today last longer than those made 35 years ago. I bought the tractor from the International Tractor Farm Equipment company in Syracuse, owned by Hank Fischer. Years later his daughter Kathy Fischer worked as our office manager for years at the New Times.

I could mow about 10 acres of lawn on one charge. On the Otisco farm, we had about 12 acres of lawn. The tractor was fast and powerful and, with a 60-inch cut I mowed a lot of grass in a short time. After a half-hour partial recharge, just enough time for a couple of cold beers, I could complete the 12 acres. I especially liked to use it around my apartment complexes, as it ran silently. I could get up at the crack of dawn, mow all the lawns before work, and not disturb the tenants.

Established 1951

SYRACUSE PRESS CLUB

PO Box 5424   Syracuse, New York 13220-5424

Mr. Art Zimmer
51 Eaton Street
Hamilton, NY 13346

Dear Art,

It is with great pleasure that I inform you the Board of Directors of the Syracuse Press Club has chosen you be placed on the **Syracuse Press Club Wall of Distinction, Class of 2016.** This is the highest honor the Club can bestow upon a member of the Syracuse media. Your plaque will be placed at the Civic Center, joining the likes of Ron Curtis, Bill Carey, J. Leonard Gorman, Dick Case, E.R. Vadeboncoeur and more.

Your work as the long-time publisher of the Syracuse New Times has earned you the admiration of Syracuse area reporters and editors, who nominated you for this honor. The award will be bestowed at the club's annual scholarship dinner and awards banquet April 30th at Drumlin's Country Club on Nottingham Road, DeWitt. Cocktails are at 6 p.m., dinner and the awards program at 7 p.m.

As an award recipient, the Press Club will cover the cost of you and one guest to attend the banquet. You are free to invite additional family or friends to the event. *The cost for additional guests is $45 per person.* Reservations for any extra guests can be placed on www.syracusepressclub.org.

There are two important things that we need from you. Please e-mail a clear photo of you in .jpg format to josh.cradduck@twcnews.com. This will be used in the program and also for the plaque. We'll need that sooner rather than later.

You'll also have the option of having a special introduction by a close relative, friend or colleague. Please advise us if you choose this route and let us know who'll be making that special introduction.

We look forward to presenting you with this award. If you have any questions please feel free to contact me at my office. Congratulations!

Sincerely,

Josh Cradduck
President
Syracuse Press Club, Inc.
Office: 315-234-1010 Extension 2
Mobile: 315-657-3956

Syracuse Press Club

Wall of Distinction, Class of 2016

ART ZIMMER, 2016 Honoree

Art's acceptance speech – April 30, 2016

ART ZIMMER
Syracuse New Times

I thank the Syracuse Press Club for this prestigious honor. However, I must make it very clear from the beginning that this honor is not for Art Zimmer. It is in recognition of the journalistic excellence demonstrated over the 26 years that I was the owner/publisher of the Syracuse New Times. A journalistic and overall general excellence created by a hard working, very dedicated and highly talented staff. The staff deserves most all of the credit for this award tonight.

It is always dangerous to name names as some deserving people are inadvertently left out. However, I will name some names as they deserve the credit for this award.

First of all at any newspaper the editor-in-chief is the key editorial person. I've had the pleasure of working with five of the very best. My first editor-in-chief was the late Roland Sweet. Roland set the tone for excellence when I first purchased the paper (1984) out of bankruptcy. After Roland left Syracuse for bigger things in New Orleans, he continued to create the popular column "News & Blues" that the New Times published for 30 years.

My next Syracuse New Times editor-in-chief was Mike Greenstein. I'm sure many of you remember Mike. Mike was at the New Times as editor-in-chief from 1986 to 1998, 12 years, and received the Syracuse Press Club Lifetime Achievement Award in 1996. Mike loved the New Times and did not want to leave. His wife was offered a super job in Seattle, Washington...Mike told me that it was either the New Times or a divorce...so off he went to Seattle.

We then conducted a national search and found the most qualified to be the amazing Tina Schwab. Tina was a Newhouse graduate and worked as an unpaid intern at the New Times. After graduation, Tina had grown to love the New Times and wanted to stay, but at that time, we had no full time openings. Unlike most communications companies, we had very little turnover. Tina continued as a part time free lance writer, then full time when an opening occurred, and then succeeded Mike as editor-in-chief.

During this time Tina married and became Tina Schwab Grenis. Then Tina became a mother, and after a while, wanted more time with family. As she loved the New Times, Tina asked to step down as the very time consuming editor-in-chief but stay on as a writer. I said yes, of course.

Then the New Times created a new publication, Family Times, a monthly parenting magazine. As a monthly publication, the editor-in-chief's job would be much less time consuming than the weekly newspaper. Tina became editor-in-chief of Family Times, still the only parenting magazine in Central New

York. Family Times quickly became famous for its overall excellence and won
dozens of national, regional and local awards. As Tina's family grew from one
to three children, Tina stepped down as editor-in-chief but remains with the
company for many years as a writer.

Now – back to the New Times, Molly English replaced Tina as editor-in-
chief and continued Tina's excellent work for many years. Bill DeLapp went to
work for Shirley and me over 34 years ago. Over the years Bill covered every
job in the editorial department, all with dedication and excellence, even with a
messy desk. Sorry Bill – but I need to tell the truth. Now Bill is editor-in-chief.

Yes, those five editors-in-chief – Roland, Mike, Tina, Molly and Bill –
deserve a tremendous amount of the credit for this award.

The next group includes long time full time staffers who remain with the
paper to this day. First and foremost is Michael Davis, the dean of all New
Times employees. Michael, the New Times chief photographer has been
with the paper over 35 years. WOW!!! Michael's photos have won dozens
of awards, both nationally and locally. Michael taught several of the Post
Standard photographers all they know about photography and one of his
protégés became chief photographer at the Post.

We all know that selling advertising is essential to any media's success.
The advertising department is equally important to the success of a paper as
the editorial department. Both must be excellent to achieve success. The best
sales rep ever is Lesli Mitchell, still with the New Times today after 22 years.

The administrative management of any business requires excellence for
success. A young lady who started with the New Times over 15 years ago. She
worked up through several departments and is now the General Manager and
Comptroller of both the New Times and Family Times. Yes, Deana Vigliotti
has been a wonderful inspiration to us all.

Reid Sullivan a New Times writer and long time editor-in-chief of Family
Times works both publications with excellence.

And Maggie Lamond Simone started with Family Times in the very
beginning and remains a top writer today.

Most publications have a group of part time, freelance staff. The New
Times because of its overall excellence over the years has attracted some of

the best in the industry. Many have gone on to full time prestigious jobs after getting their start at the New Times. Walt Shepperd, what can I say about Walt??? We all know Walt very well – a past president of the Press Club, over 35 year staff member at the New Times who remains a free lance writer today. Walt was for many years the dean of all Central New York political editors, respected and trusted by more politicians than any other journalist in all of Central New York. Walt is also on the Syracuse Press Club Wall of Distinction.

Jim MacKillop, the most prolific live theater critic and writer who remains with the New Times today after more than 42 years. Every theater producer, director and actor respected Jim's honest reports on their work. Hundreds, perhaps thousands, of people over the years would wait for Jim's review in the New Times before deciding whether to attend a certain play or not. Over the years Jim has probably had more work printed than any other Central New York journalist.

Other excellent long time free lancers who remain on staff today are Carl Mellor, Jessica Novak and J. T. Hall.

Yes all these excellent staffers who remain on staff today are the ones this honor this evening goes to.

There is one additional person who must get much credit for this honor. She started part time almost 30 years ago. She ran several major departments; she for years became the glue that held the entire staff together, the go to person for everything, the problem solver for every department. She was even accused of sleeping with the publisher - the number one person at the New Times and in my life, Shirley Sherburne Zimmer. Stand up Shirley.

In closing, I would be remiss if I did not say many detailed stories of the New Times and 13 other major corporations I owned and the many famous people from all over the world I dealt with are outlined in the book on my life that Shirley inspired. The book is titled, "Making It Count: From A to Z, the Life and Times of Art Zimmer. It is available from www.logcabinbooks.com and is the number one best-seller at the Colgate University bookstore in Hamilton.

And so on behalf of all the wonderful, talented staff I had the pleasure of working with for 26 years, I say thank you. This award is for you.

Making it Count
Introduction

The attached poem you are about to read may not make too much sense to you until you read the book it is based on. The book is **Making It Count: From A to Z, The Life and Times of Art Zimmer.** After reading the book, then the references in the poem will be crystal clear to you.

The poem is written in the same style as Robert Logan Rogers' book, Rungle in the Jungle, a fun style for children and adults.

Yes, two great books. You should buy several copies of each for yourself and gifts. Please see the last 4 pages for the books' info and ordering details.

Illustrations & Cover
Design by Dennis Calkins

Art Zimmer was a fellow
Who often told a tale
He never knew impossible
The wind was in his "sale"

Born in a hurricane
Ready to run
Cows would kick him
Just having fun

Up every day
Just before dawn

School for Art
Just made him yawn

He was no student
His grades not great

So working real hard
would open his gate

High school diploma:
They gave him a choice

Move on from here

And find your
own voice

2

So choosing the Army
He started to go

Got on his scooter
And started his show

After his time
of digging those ditches
Art would pursue
A bowl full of riches

3

Florida bound
On a boat

Plans were spoiled
It didn't float

He then would gather
A group to ski

A club of
Folks

while
drinking
tea

4

Here he learned
To take the lead
Instruction given
They would heed

Corruption once tried
To close his show

But loyal friends Kept
His ducks in a row

Nothing stopped
His driving force

Obstacles got him

5

Back on his horse

One day he left
Debris on his street

The cops hauled
Him off

To Jail
was his
Treat

6

The judge threw out
The bogus charge

He cleared up the mess
His heart was that large

He then became
A real estate trader

Buying apartments
A landlord
Crusader

Bribes were
Common
To keep a false
Code

Art would tell them
To hit the road

7

He refused to pay
A political bribe
To an honest deal
He would subscribe

A promoter at heart
In public relations
Becoming a publisher
To pursue his creations

A Syracuse newspaper
with a small circulation
He made it well known
All over the nation

Wearing an ascot
A bright jacket too

Ideas would just flow
He never was blue

He lectured a cop
talking on his cell
while driving his car

8

The cop sure could yell
Art almost got taken
To the station
Lecture being an obnoxious
Sensation

A tenant would cut his hair
For free raising the rent
He just could not see

At the end of the day
He saved no money
But friends he would have
Like bowls full of honey

Driving his newspaper
To success every year
Awards to be won while
Competition shed a tear

One day a movie was filmed on his lot
But he got cut from the plot

9

A picket tried to stop
His paper Art gave him Coffee
To end his caper

STOP
THE PRESS

Up steam he went
Just like a Swimmer
A car he found was called
A Zimmer

He had to own more than one
Buying the Company
Gave him some

Many celebrities
Wanted his cars
Powerful Princes and Hollywood stars

George Forman he drove
In a parade All of the Georges
Made up the Cascade

Selling his cars
With expensive wheels
Art loved the business
of making good deals

10

- 263 -

THEN... Art had met Shirley
He was almost fifty
Living with him became
Oh so nifty

They actually grew up
In the same little town

NOW... they would marry
In a Tux and a gown

Their romance full
Of many surprises

Years of living in an apartment
Shirley needed a better compartment

He bought her some acres
With plenty of land

A house they would built
Cost more than a grand

11

They took time to build
Each connecting addition
Carpenters and plumbers
With plugs by electricians

No sooner finished then time
To retire

One more house
And a contractor to hire

Moving once more
Where it all began
Bringing their stuff
And renting a van

Hamilton it was with no farm or hay
This time for them
It was time to play

They wanted a plot for
Eternity's rest
A graveyard spot

So finding a place

12

On a hill they would save
Plenty of space
To have a nice grave

This being settled
With gravestones to match
Beautiful flowers
On a wonderful patch

Walking to town
Kept them in shape
Life was so simple
Without the red tape

Art would meet Rudy
South America they met
Rudy loved to gamble and bet
In Las Vegas with Shirley too
The three musketeers
Stuck together like glue

13

Rudy Spoke Spanish
Which Shirley knew
So Art would wonder while
Tying his shoe

So missing the thing
Art was out of the loop
Just smiled not knowing the scoop

Rudy passed away - their sky was gray

Yet Art and Shirley had each other
Closer than skin like on a brother
Life is exciting hard times can be
Just Something not to labor

So paint a dream
Smile at your neighbor
And eat Some ice cream

Art and Shirley
Want you to know
that every present
Is your special bow

14

Lois Gridley

is a writer and editor who lives in DeWitt, NY. She earned a master's degree in magazine journalism at the S.I. Newhouse School of Public Communications and a bachelor's degree in creative writing and French from Houghton College. She expanded her education and worldview as a restaurant server while establishing her career, working first at the Wellsville Daily Reporter, then the Catholic Sun, WCNY-TV/FM, and ultimately Syracuse University.

Writing is her first love and was indispensable to her when she branched into marketing and advertising. As assistant director of marketing/media coordinator at SU's University College, she produced and placed radio, television, print, and electronic ad campaigns to recruit part-time students. She also wrote brochures for and marketed Minnowbrook Conference Center, SU Independent Study Degree Programs, the English Language Institute, and other SU schools and colleges.

Now she has returned to what got her career started: writing and editing for periodicals and publishers. But this time without the restaurant work.

Dennis Calkins

is a commercial and graphic artist who lives in DeWitt, NY. He started his career as a sign painter when he was a teen in Fulton, NY. He worked as a layout artist at the SealRight®, a national paper packaging company then based in Fulton, immediately after high school.

He came to Syracuse to be the art director at the city's then-largest advertising agency, Barlow/Johnson. When WNYS-TV was launched as Syracuse's ABC affiliate in 1962, he became its first creative services/art director, a position he held until 2003, when he retired. His projects included logo designs, courtroom sketching, copywriting, promotional and sales events, technical illustration, cartooning and caricatures, video and print projects, and design and construction of television and theater or stage sets. At one time or another, he produced projects for just about every ad agency, radio, and television station in Syracuse. He designed and illustrated Channel 9 meteorologist Dave Eichorn's children's book.

Since he retired, he has continued his freelance art services business and has returned to now-WSYR-TV9 to design and build sets. He also designed and built the news set for East Syracuse-Minoa High School and multiple-use sets for the Media Unit.